World Wisdom
The Library of Perennial Philosophy

The Library of Perennial Philosophy is dedicated to the exposition of the timeless Truth underlying the diverse religions. This Truth, often referred to as the *Sophia Perennis*—or Perennial Wisdom—finds its expression in the revealed Scriptures as well as in the writings of the great sages and the artistic creations of the traditional worlds.

The Power of the Sacred Name: Indian Spirituality Inspired by Mantras appears as one of our selections in the Perennial Philosophy series.

The Perennial Philosophy Series

In the beginning of the twentieth century, a school of thought arose which has focused on the enunciation and explanation of the Perennial Philosophy. Deeply rooted in the sense of the sacred, the writings of its leading exponents establish an indispensable foundation for understanding the timeless Truth and spiritual practices which live in the heart of all religions. Some of these titles are companion volumes to the Treasures of the World's Religions series, which allows a comparison of the writings of the great sages of the past with the perennialist authors of our time.

Cover: Detail of woman with *japamāla* (rosary of 108 beads), Bombay.

The Power of the Sacred Name

Indian Spirituality Inspired by Mantras

V. Raghavan

Edited by
William J. Jackson

Foreword by
M. Narasimhachary

World Wisdom

The Power of the Sacred Name: Indian Spirituality Inspired by Mantras

Library of Congress Cataloging-in-Publication Data

Raghavan, V. (Venkatarama), 1908-1979.
The power of the sacred name : Indian spirituality inspired by mantras / V. Raghavan ; edited by William J. Jackson ; foreword by M. Narasimhachary. -- [Rev. ed.].
p. cm. -- (The perennial philosophy series)
Includes bibliographical references and index.
ISBN 978-1-935493-96-9 (pbk. : alk. paper) 1. Names, Personal--Religious aspects--Hinduism. 2. India, South--Religion. I. Jackson, William J. (William Joseph), 1943- II. Title.
BL1215.N3R35 2011
294.5'4--dc23

2011031404

Printed on acid-free paper in the United States of America

For information address World Wisdom, Inc.
P.O. Box 2682, Bloomington, Indiana 47402-2682
www.worldwisdom.com

To the three rose windows
in my life:
Roselle, my mother,
whose faith includes the rosary;
Rose, my daughter,
singer of love in many names;
Marcia Plant, my wife,
beautiful bright woman

CONTENTS

Part IV: Concluding Essay

V. Raghavan

Acknowledgments

The publisher gratefully acknowledges Mr. R. Kalidas (Trustee), Dr. R. Charudattan (Patron Member), Mrs. Priyamvada Sankar (Patron Member), Mrs. Nandini Ramani (Managing Trustee), and the Dr. V. Raghavan Center for Performing Arts (Regd.), Chennai-20 for granting permission to use the original manuscripts of Dr. V. Raghavan.

I am grateful to V. Raghavan's daughter, Nandini Ramani, for helping me locate rare publications and translating Tamil pieces; to Professor Charudattan, V. Raghavan's son, and to V. Raghavan's wife for information and encouragement. Thanks to my colleagues in the Department of Religious Studies, Indiana University-Purdue University at Indianapolis: Jim Smurl, Jan Shipps, Tony Sherrill, and Ted Mullen. Thanks as well to Professors Purushottama Bilimoria, Klaus Witz, and Raymond Williams, and to Charles Hallisey, an idea-suggester if not a friend. Thanks to Evelyn Oliver, Kathryn Engstrom and Kimberly Long, for typing and other manuscript preparation assistance in the original 1994 edition. Thanks as well to Ruth Barker at IUPUI for interlibrary loan help, and to Indiana University for a summer faculty fellowship, and manuscript preparation funding. I also owe a debt of gratitude to those at World Wisdom publishing who helped me prepare this revised edition. Thanks to R. Krishnamurthy for permission to use his photographs as illustrations. Finally, thanks to *Sruti* magazine in Chennai, for permission to use the artwork depicting Sadāśiva Brahmendra, courtesy of the Sruti archives.

Foreword

Immense is my delight in writing this foreword to the book *The Power of the Sacred Name* (*Nāmasiddhānta*) of my revered late-lamented Professor, V. Raghavan, which is being published for the first time outside of India in a revised edition by Professor William J. Jackson. I deem this as the indirect command of my guru to write it. Nothing can be more gratifying, nothing more edifying, and nothing more enthralling than writing this foreword to the book which brings out another dimension of Prof. Raghavan, as a devotee and devout admirer of the Name of the Lord. His mastery in the entire gamut of Indian literature in general and in the *Alankāra Śāstra* in particular, a work on Indian aesthetics which was very dear to his heart, is quite well known to the world of scholars. His inborn interest in and rich contributions to Indian culture in its varied expressions as music and dance, are at once significant and stupefying. He was the adviser to many leading artists of the day like M.S. Subbulakshmi and M.L. Vasanta Kumari among musicians and Balasarasvati among dancers, who held him in high admiration. He was also interested and well-versed in technical subjects such as "fountains," "air-conditioning systems," and flying machines, as revealed from his studies on works like the *Yuktikalpataru* (a work on ship-building) and *Samarānganasūtradhāra* (a text on temple design and construction).

Professor Raghavan was a man of many parts. A polymath and polyglot, he had in him a happy and rare blend of scholarship (*panditya*) and poesy (*kavitva*). He bore significant titles like *Kavikokila* (poet-nightingale) and *Vidvatkavindra* (poet-laureate of wisdom). Several national laurels such as *Padmavibhushan* (the second highest honor awarded by the government of India) and *Vachaspati* (Doctor of Literature degree) came to him unsought. He believed that Sanskrit can be popularized not only by writing and speaking in Sanskrit, but also more successfully through dramatic performances. He used to advise students of Sanskrit, "Speak Sanskrit; do not speak about Sanskrit." It is with the view of popularizing Sanskrit among the common people that he started the *Samskrita Ranga*, which prepared productions for the stage for several old and modern Sanskrit dramas. The "Dr. V. Raghavan Center for Performing Arts," founded by his talented daughter Smt. Nandini Ramani, is trying to realize the dream of the Professor by bringing to light many of his pending works.

One learned scholar rightly observed that none can really gauge the mind of Dr. Raghavan—the range of his scholarship and the plans he had in mind to unfold the variety of his scholarship. With his demise, the world has lost the chance of seeing many more works of his, which he had on the anvil of his intensely active and creative mind. The present publication speaks volumes about the merits of the gifted encyclopedic writer.

Let me, as one of the humble students and ardent admirers of his, present in this foreword some of his extraordinary qualities which are perhaps not known to many who did not have the fortune of either seeing him in person or studying at this feet. I had the good fortune of being the student of Professor Raghavan during 1959-61 while I was doing my Masters degree in Sanskrit in the Vivekananda College, Chennai, affiliated to the University of Madras and later, from 1963-67 when I did my Ph.D. in Sanskrit under his unique guidance. During my Masters course, I had the blessed opportunity of listening to his lectures on the *Dhvanyaloka*. The thrill and bliss which I enjoyed then, are still fresh in my mind. Not a single word or a single minute was wasted by the great teacher. With his wide, in-depth scholarship in *Alankāra Śāstra* starting from the hymns of poetic charm found in the *Vedas*, covering rhetoricians like Bhamaha, Dandin, Udbhata, Anandavardhana, Abhinavagupta, Mammata, Rudrata, Kuntaka, and Bhoja, coming down to the later writers like Vidyanatha, Appaya Dikshita, and Jagannatha, the versatile Professor vividly presented before our mental eye a rainbow-like picture of the *Alankāra Śāstra*. He told us with a beaming smile emerging from personal conviction: "Friends, so far you have been enjoying the beauty of the works of Mahakavis like Kalidasa and Bharavi, without exactly knowing where the charm lies. After reading the *Dhvanyaloka*, you will be able to know where the charm lies. Thanks to Anandavardhana, your admiration and appreciation of Sanskrit *Kavyas* [poems] will be redoubled, thereafter." This he demonstrated by his superb exposition of the *Dhvanyaloka*. The time I spent as his student, I am proud to state, constitutes the golden period of my studentship and my life as an academic.

Another unique characteristic of Professor Raghavan was his eye on perfection. He was the most uncompromising and fastidious critic and research guide I ever came across in my life. He did not brook any lethargy on the part of the research scholar. "Hard work is the key to success and there is no short-cut method for it," he used to exhort. He was hard working, without allowing even a minute's rest to his tired body, even when he was not keeping good health. Once he was admitted to the Ranga Nursing Home, Chennai, for the removal of a gall-bladder. I went to see him and wish him a successful operation and speedy recovery. Even a few minutes before being taken to the operation theater, he was correcting some proof. I submitted: "Sir, why do you strain yourself like this even when you are not well?" He smiled and said "No, boy! We do not know the value of time. Time and tide wait for no man. Better keep working till the last moment." I was amazed at his deep sense of the value of time and stoic indifference to physical comforts.

While he encouraged with fatherly love and affection students who were sincere, hardworking, and committed to studies, he came down heavily upon those who used to fritter away time in unnecessary pursuits and who did not stick to the timetable he gave them. He was a strict disciplinarian and he did not mince words when it came to scholarly work. As a result many fell short of his expectations.

He used to encourage students to go to the libraries, pore over the large number of manuscripts, and bring out unknown works to light. He used to say that many ancient works of our land which are believed to have been lost are not really lost; they are hidden and lie buried in the codices of manuscripts bearing wrong labels and titles. He was absolutely right. For instance, a large tract of the first Śrīvaishanava Āchārya Nāthamuni's *Nyayatattva*, which was believed to be lost and which remains in the form of fragments, was identified and retrieved by the present writer from a codex which bears the general name, *Advaita-khandanam.*

Dr. Raghavan's works are invariably thorough and scholastic to the minutest point of detail. The world of scholars is ever beholden to him for his monumental and mammoth work, *Bhoja's Śringāra Prakāśa*, which is a "massive thesis on the massive mind and work of King Bhoja," in the words of his professor and mentor, S. Kuppuswami Sastri. There is no exaggeration whatsoever if one says that future generations, impressed by the range and depth of the all round scholarship of Professor Raghavan will wonder if such a scholar ever trod this earth.

* * *

In the present work, the learned author focuses his attention on the writers of the Kāverī delta who flourished between 1650 A.D. and 1850 A.D. It encompasses in its vast scope the individual and inspiring approaches of great saint-singers like Tyāgarāja, Bodhendra, Sadguruswāmi, Srīdhara Venkateśa Āyyavāl, and Nārāyana Tīrtha to chanting the divine *Nāma* (Name). The most popular names of the Lord which have strung the entire humanity on one thread are those of Śrī Rāma and Śrī Krishna. Dr. Raghavan was an ardent devotee of Lord Rāma and one can see flashes of his special attachment to Rāma in the lines of this book. Agreeing with what Saint Tyāgarāja said in his memorable song, *Telisi Rāma*, my Professor says that the recitation of the *Nāma* should not be a mere mechanical muttering. It should be based on a full realization of the significance of that Name. The *Nāma* and *Nāmin*, the Name and the Named, being identical, the chanting should be rooted in real love (*bhakti*) for the Lord.

With his usual thoroughness, the Professor has, in the present work, studied the lives and accounts of the great saint singers with an eye on the history of religions. The learned author traces the origin of the *Nāmasiddhānta* tradition to the earliest document of human wisdom, viz., the *Ṛigveda*, which comprises hymns on various deities like Agni, Rudra, and Vishnu. These hymns are praises of the names and qualities of the deities. Stressing the unity of the *nirguna-saguna* aspects of the Lord, the Professor rightly observes that even in the *Upanishads*, the supreme *Brahman*, which is really without (or rather, beyond) attributes (*nirguna*), is characterized by expressions like *satya* (truth), *jnāna* (knowledge), and *ananta* (infinity), which facilitate its conception, description, and meditation as possessing attributes (*saguna*).

The merits of the present publication are more than one to recount: one can see the blending of scholarship and devotion in these pages. Religion without scholarship is a tree without fruits; scholarship without religion is a tree without roots. Man attains perfection through love for God, his creator. God will be happy with man who is His own creation, when he loves Him. Thus the import of the names of the Lord, *stavyah* (One who deserves praise) and *stavaprīyah* (One who is fond of praise) mentioned in the *Śrī Vishnusahasranāma Stotra* becomes clear and relevant.

I now wish to convey my thanks and best wishes to the learned editor, Professor Jackson, and the publishers World Wisdom, for their love and commitment to bringing out a revised edition of the *Nāmasiddhānta* for the benefit of scholars and laymen alike. I am sure all lovers of the sacred names of the Divine will welcome this work, which has long been out of print.

M. Narasimhachary
Chennai, India

Preface

Devotion via the Name

This study is about devotion to holy names—names such as Rāma, Krishna, or Devī—in India, especially in the Kāverī delta[1] from 1650 to 1850 A.D. During that time leaders such as Veṅkaṭeṣa Āyyāvāl, Bodhendra, Sadāśiva Brahmendra, Nārāyaṇa Tīrtha, and Sadgurusvāmī sang, repeated, and taught about the holy names as a Hindu way of religious life leading ultimately to *mokṣa* (deliverance). These *Nāmasiddhānta* (path of attainment through the name) leaders practiced revolving the name in their minds and singing holy names aloud as ways to keep a hold on the ultimate amid an ever changing world of disturbance and confusion. They saw the name as a simple direct way to taste *bhakti* (devotional love), to plunge the individual into contact with the holy through evocative utterance.

Sitting in a temple holding a *japamāla* (rosary of 108 beads) or engaged in their daily labor, devotees practiced the repetition of holy names as their constant companion; it offered stability in this world and hope of transcendence beyond. For years they would repeat such mantras centered on names as "*Om namo Nārāyaṇāya*" or "*Om namaḥ Śivāya*" or "*Rām Rāmāya namaḥ.*" Singing songs composed of divine names along with others in public places or meditating on the beloved form of the deity alone at home in the quiet predawn hours, devotees of the name dwelt on this focal point which was intimately individual yet in long continuity with ancient Hindu traditions. Its simplicity gave humble people access to holy presence, and its depth gave philosophers and yogis a wealth of lore and metaphysics to consider. To musicians and enjoyers of the beauty of art it gave an entry to the ancient metaphors of supreme harmony as the base of the universe, and the sweetness of *ānanda*, spiritual bliss, which can be tasted through discerning the changeless amidst the always-changing world.

The *bhakti* saints of the era under scrutiny and those of the few centuries preceding it (Jñānadev, Caitanya, Ānnamācārya, Rāmadās, Kabīr, Tukārām, Nānak, for example) were like bees returning to the hive: after discovering a great store of sweetness they had to communicate to the rest of their communities how all could reach that source of *ānanda*. Bees

[1] The Kāverī river originates in southwest Karṇāṭaka state, and flows southeastward through Tamil Nadu to the sea.

perform a waggle dance which encodes directions to the honey; the saints composed songs, guided listeners by suggesting practices, of which repeating and singing the name were central ones. In the Kāverī delta, saints such as Bodhendra, Sadāśiva Brahmendra, Tyāgarāja, and Upaniṣad Brahmayogin are typically pictured as *sādhakas* (spiritual aspirants) devoted to the name, seekers who after years of striving tasted realization or had *darśan* (vision of the divine), before they began singing songs and guiding others through their spoken words and poetry.

It has been said that poetry measures being.[2] Divine names, called on over a lifetime can be said to be markers in consciousness which also "measure being." The *sādhana* (spiritual practice) of name repetition measures obstacles and resistances to one's effort, offering a standard in the face of moods and the unknowns of change in the life-experiences of name devotees. Practicing repetition of a holy name over long years the devotee can be said to measure the power of fate and transcendence, and to measure human weaknesses and limits as well as human potential for perseverance. Repeating the name over periods of time helps measure more of human life in spiritual terms than most other events and repeated practices which are of briefer duration. The name is said to be a companion which helps the devotee measure the meaning and rewards of self-sacrifice. In other words by reciting the name for so many millions of times, it is not just the number of names that is measured. Though it is a measure of one's spiritual striving and commitment, recitation of the name millions of times, such as was done by the south Indian singer-saint Tyāgarāja, it is also a measure of being—a fathoming of human being in time; it indicates vast being beyond the human and beyond time; it is an instrument for winning a vision of the holy in one form or another.

To call upon one's favorite form of the sacred by repeating the deity's name, seeking spiritual help in uncertain times, and to practice this form of devotion regularly to fend off mishaps and to rivet attention to the sacred is a central practice of *bhakti. Bhakti* has been called the "sweet path" (*mādhurya*) because it employs beauty, including attractive images, flowers, and enchanting music in worship, and because it is a heart-centered mode of spiritual practice. The taste of love between the devotee and the divine is experienced as an inner nectar. Repeating and singing

[2] William V. Spanos, *Heidegger and the Question of Literature* (Bloomington: Indiana University, 1979), p. xiv. See also introduction and Chapter 7 of Martin Heidegger, *Poetry, Language, Thought*, trans. A. Hofstadter (New York: HarperCollins, 2001), p. 209, ff.

holy names are ways to engender in the psyche the beauty and glory of the holy. The *Nāmasiddhānta* path enthusiastically promotes these practices, offering a way of concentration and refinement for the simple as well as for the sophisticated. *Nāmasiddhānta*'s goal is to saturate the whole brain, the whole psyche, the whole memory, the whole life with what the name connotes. *Nāmasiddhānta* is a method directed toward an experience. The primacy of experience in Indian religions, from the earliest yoga schools onward is of significance here. Like Zen masters and Sufis, like the iconoclastic North Indian poet Kabīr and other mystics, *Nāmasiddhāntins* were often skeptical toward book learning, which is no substitute for spiritual practices and religious experience.

Name and Sound

For millennia there has been continual widespread use of holy names and invocations not only in South Asia but in Egypt, Rome, Africa, Arabia and many other parts of the world as well. Historically, whether for "conjuring the gods by magic formula" (the probable original meaning of the ancient term for Tibetan indigenous shamanic religion—Bön[3]), or used in pious monotheistic prayer to cultivate remembrance and longing, the Name has long been a preferred mode to reach inspiration, dream, trance, and mystical vision, among seekers worldwide. In India repeating the name is one form of mantra, a "mind tool" for breaking down conditioned perceptual structures of time, and the built up patterns of language and mental concepts in human consciousness, measuring the limits of the realms of the unconscious. Rhythmic repetition affects the human organism when performed mentally; and acoustic vibrations make an impact on the nervous system. Rhythm potentially can re-empattern a person's thoughts, feelings, and perceptions.

Indian musician-yogis developed further in mystical directions the theory and practice of the sacredness of sound and its effects on the human nervous system. For example, in a traditional Hindu music treatise it is said that "In the center of the body is the *prāṇa* (life-force or vital breath); in the center of the *prāṇa* is the *dhvāni* (sound); in the center of the *dhvāni* is *nāda* (musical sound, harmonious primordial vibration); and in the center of the *nāda* is Sadāśiva—the Supreme Lord."[4] Thus, in *nāda-yoga* the

[3] Helmut Hoffman, *Religions of Tibet* (New York: Macmillan, 1961), p. 14.

[4] Śloka 6, *Svarārṇava* manuscript found among Tyāgarāja's books. *Journal of the Music Academy of Madras. Rāmārahasyopaniṣad*, cited by V. Raghavan, *Spiritual*

vibration of chanting the name ultimately participates in the nature of that which is named. The mantra sound which tunes one in to the mystery of the ultimate *nāda*—the cosmic "music of the spheres," the sound of the name ringing in one's heart and voice—harmonizes one with the infinite eternal hum of Being. (In keeping with this concept, chants and songs are called the deity's clothing in a Tyāgarāja lyric.) The idea of the extraordinary power inherent in the recited name and in the mantric vibrational force of sound was developed and culminated in masterpieces of devotional music created by *Nāmasiddhānta* and *bhajana sampradāya* saints of the Kāverī delta. *Bhajana sampradāya* was a devotional movement of groups who gathered regularly to sing in this region, organized to follow set programs of devotional songs (*bhajans*) written by venerated composers. In India we find that ritual, yogic, musical, and *bhakti* beliefs all have tended to impel Indians of various persuasions to repeat sacred names and powerful sounds as means to spiritual realization.[5]

Nāmasiddhānta

The word *siddhānta*, which forms part of the term *Nāmasiddhānta* (used by V. Raghavan to denote the movement of devotees of the name in the Kāverī delta, giving the followers a unity which might otherwise be elusive), is intriguingly ambiguous. *Siddha*, meaning "accomplished," is the past passive participle of the root *sidh*, which means to succeed or to attain, and *anta* means "end." Thus, *siddhānta* means "final result," or "established supreme attainment," or "settled opinion or doctrine; accepted truth." Thus, *Śaivasiddhānta* means *Śaiva* orthopraxy, expounding final liberation through devotion to Śiva, and *Advaitasiddhānta* is a term used to designate Śaṅkara's path, "the way of non-dualism." *Nāmasiddhānta* is used in this way by Raghavan to mean "the way of salvation by means of the name." Or, because "salvation" is so associated with Christianity, "the

Heritage of Tyāgarāja, eds. C. Ramanujachari and V. Raghavan (Madras: Ramakrishna Mission, 1966, 2nd edition). See Śarṅgadeva's *Saṅgīta Ratnākara* I.iii.

[5] Charlotte Vaudeville asserts belief in the name and in its infinite potency as a means of salvation is common to the *Sant* and medieval *Vaiṣṇava* tradition: "it is evidently a Tantric conception inherited by both" (*Kabīr* [London: Oxford University Press, 1974]), p. 141. A.K. Coomaraswamy in his book entitled *Yakshas*, describes *bhakti* practices, including the repetition of the name, as originating with *Yakṣa* worship.

way to perfection or complete spiritual attainment through the power of the name."[6]

V. Raghavan has interpreted it both as the practice of "recital of God's name as the most potent means of salvation" (the ultimate attainment of *mokṣa*), and also as the means to *siddhi*, full spiritual attainment or empowerment.[7] Possibly because it has such a range of meanings and associations, and hence is a word with powerful overtones, it appealed to Raghavan, who popularized it by identifying mystic exponents of the name in the Kāverī delta as *Nāmasiddhānta* saints.[8] In the tales of their lives the leaders of *Nāmasiddhānta* are depicted as having attained wondrous powers. Sadāśiva Brahmendra, the mysterious naked *sādhu* (renunciate), especially seems to be associated with *siddha* characteristics, as we shall see.

Nāmasiddhānta is not exactly a sect, though one aspect of the multilingual *bhajana sampradāya* was oriented to particular congregations of villagers along the banks of the Kāverī river. Sadgurusvāmī (1776-1817), for example, after years of traveling in an "itinerant ministry" established the Rāmakrishna *Bhajana* Math at Marudanallūr, near Kumbakonam, and initiated followers into the practice of Rāma-*nāma*. He was a householder, and he named as his successor someone in the family which first welcomed him to settle in that village. That *matha* and others established in Tāñjāvūr by Sadgurusvāmī and by Bodhendra generations before him, have been institutional centers for the promulgation of *Nāmasiddhānta*. But these halls largely serve as meeting places for local nonsectarian *bhajan* singing. In general, *Nāmasiddhānta* practices tend to de-emphasize sectarian

[6] Some scholars have taken *siddhānta* in the term *Nāmasiddhānta* in the more conventional meaning of philosophical "doctrine"; for example T.K. Venkateswaran translates *Nāmasiddhānta* as "the philosophy of the Divine Name and its singing" (*Krishna: Myths, Rites and Attitudes*, ed. Milton Singer [Chicago: University of Chicago, 1966]), p. 164.

[7] V. Raghavan in *Cultural Heritage of India*, vol. IV, p. 512, and in *Spiritual Heritage of Tyāgarāja*, p. 122.

[8] It would seem that Raghavan popularized the term *Nāmasiddhānta*. *Nāmasiddhānta* is used by Dr. Seetha in *Tanjore as a Seat of Music* (Madras: Madras University, 1981), R. Krishnamurthy in *Saints of the Cauvery Delta* (Delhi, Concept Publishing, 1979), and T.K Venkateswaran's essay in *Krishna: Myths, Rites, and Attitudes*, ed. M. Singer, pp. 139 ff. N. Raghunathan also used it in "Bodhendra and Sadguru Swami," in *Seminar on Saints*, ed. Mahadevan (Madras: USGR, 1960), pp. 133 ff.

differences. This tendency is found in other movements of *bhakti* in India as well. The obliteration of differences and even motives is stressed in a passage by Bodhendra, in his Sanskrit work *Nāmāmṛitarasāyana*:

> In whatever way, under any circumstances, by the performance of the chanting and singing of the Name, all sins get destroyed and release does happen, whether the Name is recited by woman or man. It may be by any man [of any caste or position], or by one insane, by one having faith or without faith.[9]

While this is the professed doctrine, Bodhendra himself repeated his mantra 108,000 times per day—a strict and strenuous discipline following a specific rule. Bodhendra also fostered the musical expression of loving devotion to the name. But the cited passage hyperbolically stresses the merciful offer of maximum openness and laxness, saying any repetition of the name has saving power. The intention is to encourage hope of free access. Any person is free to recite the name, just as many kinds of people can be *bhajan* singers.

In actual practice some groups singing *bhajans* may be composed of members of certain castes more than others. In India the professed ideal of free access has often not materialized as a homogenized or random composition of communities of worship. *Nāmasiddhānta* in its most extended sense would seem to mean the faith of any and all who are involved in the repetition of a holy name, whether they sing or say it, and more specifically the forms it took in the Kāverī delta under the promotion of the five leaders. *Nāmasiddhānta* is probably best thought of as a *bhakti* discipline which many different kinds of people have enthusiastically followed. It was one of the ways in which *bhakti* has tended to offer experiences which cut across or include *varṇāśrama dharma* (caste and life-stage obligation) differences. In the Tāñjāvūr District villages, and in Madras and other cities today, *Nāmasiddhānta* does not denote a well-organized community with hard and fast rules, the members of which assert an identity in contradistinction to, or alongside of, other sects. To what extent *Nāmasiddhānta* enthusiasts aspired to reorder the existing Hindu communities by harmonizing antagonistic forces, or by offering new group

[9] Raghavan's translation quoted by T.K. Venkateswaran in Singer's *Krishna: Myths, Rites, and Attitudes.* In that book Singer discusses the social background of Madras *bhajan* groups. See R. Rangaramanuja Ayyangar's *History of South Indian (Carnatic) Music* (Madras, n.d.), pp. 213-214.

activities, is difficult to say. Spokesmen I met when I traveled to several traditional centers in 1989 researching this topic said *Nāmasiddhānta* sought to spread fervency of interior practice and personal sincerity in *bhakti*, not to build a new sect or push for external change.[10]

The leaders of Kāverī delta *Nāmasiddhānta*, in part because they lived in Tamil Nadu, often wrote not in their mother tongue, Telugu, or in the regional language, Tamil, but in Sanskrit, like the *smārta* (orthodox Brahman scholars who preserved Hindu traditions) writers of the *Purāṇa*s, and unlike many sectarian *bhakti* leaders who used their mother tongues for religious writing. In their spoken teachings the leaders employed the regional languages. Being conservative innovators they also sought, as earlier *smārtas* had, to carry forward essential traditions, yet to adapt the message to meet the chaos of changing times, the turbulence in society.

These leaders seemed to take seriously the idea expressed as early as the *Maitri Upaniṣad*, written between 800 and 600 BC: "Some contemplate one Name, and some another. Which of these is the best? All are eminent clues to the transcendent, immortal, unembodied *Brahman*: these Names are to be contemplated, lauded, and at last denied. For by them one rises higher and higher in these worlds; but where all comes to its end, there he attains to the Unity of the Person."[11] But they believed not only in the transparency of all names and forms; they also had a faith in the miraculous power of the name to bring protection and salvation.

The Delta Region in Tamil Nadu

The Kāverī delta is a "nodal region" which for centuries has attracted cultivators and radiated culture. V. Raghavan wrote affectionately of the Kāverī river as "the silver anklet at the feet of Mother India," a golden stream enriching the soil "with juicy crops, and the natives of that soil with superior qualities of intellect and speech." The Kāverī delta is an important generative core of South Indian regional culture and economy.

[10] Madras Hindus whom I interviewed said most people who take part in *bhajanas* and name-recitation do not identify themselves as *nāmasiddhāntins* per se, but identify themselves as *Vaiṣṇava* or more generally, as *bhaktas* devoted to the names and forms of their favorite way of picturing God (*iṣṭadevatā*), whether as Viṣṇu, Śiva, the Goddess or otherwise.

[11] Translation by A.K. Coomaraswamy, *The Bugbear of Literacy* (London: Dennis Dobson, 1949), p. 57. Full text available online at: http://www.archive.org/stream/bugbearofliterac035352mbp/bugbearofliterac035352mbp_djvu.txt

The singing and saying of the name which became important there was declared by the *Purāṇas* to be the primary mode of access to the holy for Hindus in this "fallen age," the *Kali Yuga.* The *bhakti* path, which features devotion to the name as a central practice, is thought of as a gift of grace, a pleasant, easy way and "special offer" extended in difficult times to troubled people in need of a path to God. As such it is still immensely popular in South India, while other paths—of meditation, Vedic ritual, and *haṭha-yoga*—have fewer followers. The roots of name-devotion may offer a key to understanding Vedic kathenotheism ("one-God-at-a-time-ism") and to reconciling bewildering strands of Hinduism—polytheism and monotheism, *advaita*, *bhakti*, and *tantra.* V. Raghavan's work helps us focus on the role of name-devotion in Hinduism's diverse past. While translators and scholars such as Ram Mohan Roy, Vivekananda, and S. Radhakrishnan have presented the philosophical *advaita vedānta* side of Hinduism to the West, which served as a corrective to prevailing one-sided opinions (e.g., that Hinduism is only polytheistic with no unifying concepts), V. Raghavan brought out the full range of rich religious life expressed organically in cultural creativity. His studies have helped bring out the rich treasury of Kāverī delta culture: aesthetics, *bhakti* poetry and music, narratives and philosophies, dance dramas, hagiography and musical discourse (*Harikathā*). *Nāmasiddhānta*'s social impact has been significant in Tamil Nadu. As a rather broad-minded path it seems well-suited to the new democratic era; fostering a sense of equality and harmony, it has sanctioned greater interaction among previously separated communities.

Tāñjāvūr, as a thriving playground for the enactment of these concepts, has been a region known for producing literature in several languages. It is thought of as a hospitable cradle for development in *bhakti* music because of unique historical conditions. The Chola dynasty used Tāñjāvūr as capital until 1320 when Muslims from the North invaded. They ruled South India for nearly fifty years, until defeated by forces of the Vijayanagara empire. During that half century many Urdu words were added to the Tamil vocabulary. During the succeeding Vijayanagara reign, the Nāyak chieftains, viceroys acting as provincial regents representing the Vijayanagara emperor, ruled from Tāñjāvūr and Madurai, and they brought into those provinces Telugu and Kannada scholars, musicians, dancers and artists. After the Vijayanagara empire fell, the Nāyaks who continued ruling in Tāñjāvūr and Madurai became independent rulers, and they continued to support culturally creative Telugu and Kannada speakers and scholars. When the Nāyak kingdoms were overrun by Marātha forces the Marāthi language was added to the forms of expression used there. The Marātha regime began in Tāñjāvūr in 1676 and ended in 1855. During the Marātha rule scholars, dancers, musicians, and *Harikathā* performers from Mahārāṣtra added to the layers of Tāñjāvūr culture. The Marātha descendants of Śivajī inherited his mission of arousing a sense of Hindu identity by encouraging popular *bhakti* and the arts. The Marātha kings introduced some Hindustani music to Tāñjāvūr, and patronized musicians speaking Marāthi, Telugu, and Tamil and sponsored other regional artists and scholars.[12] Thus, in Tāñjāvūr a rich mixture of regional cultures and languages thrived under the patronage of Hindu rulers who themselves were connoisseurs, *bhaktas*, and sometimes poets and composers.

V. Raghavan's Contribution

V. Raghavan (1908-1979) was a Sanskrit scholar and musicologist who specialized in Karnātaka music and was world-renowned during his own lifetime. He served as the secretary of the Madras Music Academy for 35 years, from 1944 to 1979. He devoted many years to translating texts and helping reconstruct and understand aspects of Indian culture which were lost in colonial and earlier times. He conducted in-depth research into the lives, documents, Sanskrit texts, history, and cultural vitality of the fertile Kāverī delta region, focusing on the *Nāmasiddhānta* saints and their background as one of his favorite areas of exploration. His studies on *Nāmasiddhānta*, scattered over the decades in various journals, music society publications, and scholarly booklets, have not been very accessible to Western scholars. Though these articles have a thematic unity, V. Raghavan did not unite them or place them systematically in the context of world religions. It was as if he prepared the materials and information to make a lens with which to focus on the topic of *Nāmasiddhānta*, but he did not live to grind and polish the lens as a completed instrument. He also wrote comprehensive overviews on Indian religious culture, but did not bring those together with his *Nāmasiddhānta* studies, perhaps because he died rather suddenly. (He died of a massive heart attack in the middle of the night on April 5, 1979—auspicious Rāmanavami day. In fact he had just a few hours earlier delivered a lecture on the greatness of Rāma at the Kuppuswami Sastri Research Institute in Madras.) Raghavan was a world-renowned Sanskritist who conducted many important Indological research projects, especially concerned with religious aesthetics and Sanskrit literature. He published

[12] This background on Tāñjāvūr is based largely on an explanation received from T.S. Parthasarathy, Madras, July 21, 1981, and with help of V. Raghavan's daughter, Nandini.

over 120 books and 1,100 papers. His work, like that of other devoted scholars, retrieved neglected aspects of culture, and organized, preserved, and kept alive reflections of useful and beautiful accomplishments which have evolved in the course of Indian civilization.

By bringing together some of his studies published in hard-to-find journals on this particular topic and arranging them and discussing them in larger historical and comparative contexts, my goal has been to complete what he began, but also to update it, to take an important subject a step further and bring it to the attention of today's students of world religions. In the following introduction to religious veneration to sacred names and to the history of *Nāmasiddhānta*, as well as in footnotes, I have tried to bring out the relevance of name traditions and related religious phenomena, rather than leave them as disconnected and isolated topics of academic curiosity. As the American Sanskritist Daniel H.H. Ingalls said, Raghavan "earned by his discoveries the admiration of all Sanskritists and has won their deep gratitude for his making possible by his researches still further discoveries that may be their own." He successfully combined precision and breadth of knowledge, and thus as Ingalls said, became "a living example of those different abilities, the exact and the broad, or call them the traditional and the modern, which when combined form the only adequate basis for interpreting the complexity of Sanskrit literature,"[13] and the diverse and complex life of India.

The articles about *Nāmasiddhānta* which V. Raghavan wrote for various journals and books I have brought together and organized in this single volume. Some of the pieces assembled here were written for a popular audience—for example the essay on Sadāśiva Brahmendra. Others are more technical and detailed—for example the essay on Upaniṣad Brahmayogin. All of them are careful assessments of significant topics which should prove valuable to students of Indian religions and comparative studies. The "lens" which V. Raghavan prepared to make but left unfinished has determined in large part the "optics" under consideration in this volume. I have supplied translations of words to clarify the text, omitted passages when constraints of space demanded it, and placed some matter in footnotes, and augmented some footnotes. In some places I have changed phraseology to current American forms of English to make for an easier reading. I have tried in all of these editorial tasks to preserve what I took to be V. Raghavan's original

[13] Daniel H. H. Ingalls, introduction to *Bibliography of the Books, Papers and other Contributions of Dr. V. Raghavan*, ed. A.L. Mudaliar (Ahmedabad: New Order Book Co., 1968), p. x.

intentions and presentation of information, and to make his work more accessible to the interested reader of today.

Personally speaking, my own childhood has no doubt been a factor which led to my interest in this topic. I grew up as a member of the Roman Catholic church, learning traditions from priests and nuns at a time when the Latin liturgy was still current. I grew up hearing and repeating Gregorian chants, like "Kyrie Eleison," and with the repeated sound of rosary prayers ("Our Father" and "Hail Mary") going round and round. I can understand how short repeated prayers can be considered a central form of devotion, and how mantras can calm the mind. In 1989 I traveled to Madras, Kumbakonam, Tiruvidaimarudur, Puttaparthi, and other devotional centers, meeting exponents of devotion to the name, videotaping interviews with them. I'm glad the world has grown smaller in the years since I was a child, and that people enjoy the freedom of religion, and can share their experiences with others. I think in our age people can use a spiritual practice like repeating a mantra to help them through life's topsy-turvy changes, and also to navigate through times of ease.

Before turning to V. Raghavan's studies, let us consider the historical and religious context of the *Nāmasiddhānta* saints' lives and works, and some archetypal images and patterns in the stories told about them.

William J. Jackson,
Professor Emeritus
Department of Religious Studies
Indiana University-Purdue University at Indianapolis

Introduction:
Reading the Signs of the Times and Beyond: Kāverī Delta *Nāmasiddhānta* Saints' Lives

Traditions of Transcendence

Naitāvad enā paro anyad asti ("Beyond this world there is a transcendent reality") (*Ṛig Veda* X.31.8)

In the earliest surviving literature of India, the *Vedas*, there are many symbolic indications of vision and mystical experiences "transcending the human condition."[1] *Ṛig Veda* hymn X.136 pictures long-haired sages (*munis*): "When gods get in them, they ride with the rush of the wind. 'Crazy with wisdom we have lifted ourselves to the wind. Our bodies are all you who are merely mortal can see.' He [the sage] sails through the air, seeing appearances spread out below."[2] In the *Ṛig Veda* there are also many references to an orientation in which transcendent reality gives proportion to life on earth. Three-fourths of the cosmic Puruṣa is beyond this world (RV X.90), and Viṣṇu's third step is beyond the mortal realm and the flight of birds (RV I.154-5; VII.99-100). The *Bṛihadaraṇyaka Upaniṣad* (II.3.6; III.9.26; IV.2.4; IV.4.22) employs remotion ("*Neti neti*"—"Not this") to suggest that the ultimately real is not to be confused with this perishable world. This shows an ancient focus of religious experience in India: the consciousness of eternal being beyond time and change. The issue of access to the transcendent has been an ongoing soteriological concern for Hindus, and a number of approaches have developed to answer it.

In classical Hinduism, humans are thought of as being born in the noise of *saṃsāra*, with an inborn restlessness for the peace of the eternal. Amid

[1] Jan Gonda, *The Vision of the Vedic Poets* (The Hague: Mouton and Co., 1963). Mircea Eliade, in *The Sacred and the Profane* (New York: Harvest, 1959), p. 175, writes that in India "the fundamental mystical experience—transcending the human condition—is expressed in a two-fold image, breaking the roof, and flight."

[2] This translated passage is based on one found in J. Frits Staal, *Exploring Mysticism* (London: Univ. of California, 1975), p. 197. See also Mircea Eliade, *Yoga: Immortality and Freedom* (Princeton: Princeton University Press, 1958), p. 102, and Ralph T.H. Griffith, tr. *The Hymns of the Ṛig Veda* (Delhi: Motilal Banarsidass, 1973 reprint), pp. 636-637.

fluctuating cycles of rebirth, Hindus seek "the other shore." They follow a trajectory beyond this life's desires and joys, aiming at release from the wheel of rebirth and re-death. To attain *mokṣa* or *nirvāṇa* is the goal of yoga. Paths of ritual, dedicated action and philosophy, aim at finding the timeless. The *tāraka mantra* invoking Rāma's name with devotion (*bhakti*) is an "enabler of crossing:" These are a few indications of an extensive strand of Hindu faith concerned with the hope of transcending this world. "Asceticism, not only as a way of salvation, but as a general orientation, the tendency towards a negation of the world—ultramundaneity—has deeply imbued Hinduism," as Louis Dumont wrote.[3]

In Hindu culture there are also many life-affirming symbols, images of *rasa*, for example, the divine essence or "juice," like a vegetal sap bespeaking the holy's immanence in the organic life of this world. To be sure, there are religious actions performed in the hopes of enjoying this world's offerings. Yet, there is also much mention of "burning the seeds" of karma, and cutting the roots of thralldom to this world. The *Bhagavad Gītā* mentions the unmanifest (*avyakta*) as man's true self and goal.[4] In India, in each system which has two or three manifest parts, there is also a third or fourth part which is transcendent: the Ganges and Jumnā are visible rivers; the Sarasvatī river is the unseen third. The legitimate ends of human life: *kāma* (pleasure), *artha* (success), and *dharma* (duty), are followed by *mokṣa* (release), the transcendent fourth. The *varṇāśrama* system is crowned with *sannyāsa*, in which the first three stages are left behind. The tripartite *mantra prāṇava*, A-U-M, has *turīya*, a fourth dimension which is infinite, dissolving in silence. *Sattva*, *rajas*, and *tamas* are the finite strands of nature; *Brahman* is the changeless eternal consciousness on which they are superimposed.

Śaṅkara, the *smārta* Brahman *advaita* philosopher and reformer of Hindu traditions, who lived in the ninth century, distinguished between two levels: *vyāvahārika*, the relatively real "this-shore" world, and *paramārtha*, the Absolute beyond, "the other shore." "I am not mind, ego, senses, elements, I am Śiva, *Sat-cit-ānanda*, changeless, all-pervading," he wrote in his verses on *Nirvāṇa*.[5]

[3] Louis Dumont, tr. M. Sainsbury, *Homo Hierarchicus* (Chicago: Univ. of Chicago, 1970), pp. 184-187; in 1980 edition see Appendix B, "World Renunciation and Indian Religions," p. 273.

[4] *Bhagavad Gītā* II.25; VIII.18.

[5] Śankara, *Thus Spoke Śrī Śankara* (Madras: Rāmakrishna Mission, 1969), pp. 47-50.

Śaṅkara took one of India's ideals to its logical and mystical conclusion, and popular Hinduism did not disown him, but held him all the closer, attributing to him hymns of praise as well as philosophical treatises, humanizing him but not ignoring the extreme of transcendence-realization associated with his life. Śaṅkara is a classic example of a Brahman of cultural initiative, a renunciate who was also an active worker in this world, drawing on popular *bhāgavata* traditions in culturally creative ways. Sanskritist Daniel H.H. Ingalls warns: "Do not jump to conclusions about Indian philosophy and religion" from the work of such individuals as Śaṅkara.[6] Yet without the world-renouncer and the transcendent *Brahman* for which he lived, one would have a much reduced and faulty picture of the Hindu religious worldview. Faith in such subjective religious experiences as *samādhi*'s super-consciousness has given India some essential aspects of her character.

Furthermore, there are many other examples of yogis like Śaṅkara who did not merely sit on the periphery absorbed in *samādhi*, but who were "great integrators" who sought to convey access to the transcendent through a thousand names of the divine, setting them to music and leading the dance. In India there is a mutual interaction of inward and outward realms of religion, a blurring of distinctions between *advaita* and *bhakti*. That such blurring makes the Western mind uncomfortable may say as much about the limits of the modern Western mind, as it does about the Hindu synthesis.

In any case, illiterate sense-bound villagers have been much taken by saints in whose lives the Absolute, *paramātma*, was said to have been experienced, and the saints themselves often willingly served as "rafts" to help others, including simple villagers, cross *saṃsāra*'s inevitable flux of pains and change. In India the saint whose authority and inspiration came from *samādhi* or vision was often at the center generating the ideals, values, religious, and cultural life of society. The authors of scriptures, leaders of sects, keepers of traditional mores, tenders of the sacred fires of Hindu faith are often pictured as inspired by vision and *samādhi* in the minds of the masses: their charisma comes from signs of their experience of the transcendent. The logic being: who but one who has seen the farthest and known the deepest is fit to guide?

Religion as Reaching Beyond

Though historical conditions vary, the saintly life can be considered in

[6] Daniel H.H. Ingalls, "Dharma and *Mokṣa*," *Philosophy East and West*, Vol. VII, nos. 1 and 2, April-July 1957, p. 48.

terms of a striving beyond, a yearning toward the reality which saves from the unsatisfactory conditions of mortal life. The urge toward one or another kind of solution which saves or offers access to the transcendent seems to be at the heart of many of the intense lives of those who are remembered as saints. The saint is *homo religiosus* par excellence, and J.L. Mehta has suggested that

> Going beyond, the movement of self-surpassing, is as much constitutive of the human state as defining and setting up boundaries. It is this self-transcending movement, this reaching out and reaching down within, inherent in man, which defines him as *homo religiosus*, a bridge thrown across, from the realm of the visible to another shore. It is part of this movement to give itself a symbol or concept of that toward which it strains, its mode of being, its nature, its nearness or remoteness.[7]

For *Nāmasiddhānta bhaktas* the "symbol or concept" of the holy was the *Name*—of Rāma, Śiva, Krishna, or the Goddess—the Name was a *means* to the transcendent, and also a way that shared the very nature of the goal—divine being. Through the Name its sayers and singers are linked to the Supreme which is named. By purifying practices, by cultivating devotional longing, and dwelling on divine reality through repetition of the Name, the *Nāmasiddhānta* leaders of the 17th and 18th centuries demonstrated that the devotee could experience the divine—in dream, trance, or vision. Thus rather than being merely a representational sign, the Name is thought of as a symbol through which the holy is made present; the sayer and singer participate in holiness, through the calling of the beloved's Name.

Bodhendra, the renowned *Nāmasiddhānta* leader of the 17th century, describes the unconditional power of the Name: "In whatever way, under any circumstances, by the performance of the chanting and singing of the Name, all sins are destroyed and release is effected, whether the Name is recited by woman or man."[8] An entrance to a new mode of being is pictured here: a purifying transformation and release—*mokṣa.*

The spiritually liberating release associated with *mokṣa* is one example,

[7] J.L. Mehta, *India and the West: The Problem of Understanding* (Chicago: Scholars Press, 1985), p. 203.

[8] V. Raghavan, ed. tr. *Nāmāmṛtarasāyana*, quoted in the introduction to *Ākhyāṣaṣṭi* (Kumbakoūam and Madras: Kāmakoṭi Kośaṣṭhānam, 1944).

but there are also other experiences of self-forgetfulness in *Nāmasiddhānta bhakti*, which would qualify as forms of transcendence. Participating in and attaining awareness of realities greater than one's solitary self, can take many forms. There are various ways in which individuals are subsumed in something greater or have their egos eclipsed. "He who loses himself shall find himself," is a principle found in non-Hindu piety as well.[9]

[9] The human capacity to experience life as a threshold, or to travel a path from the seen and known here to an unknown sphere or "shore" beyond, may explain why in China the human has been called the "middle creature," and in traditional Western thought is the pivotal hinge-like being between the animal world and the realm of angels—the link between matter and spirit. What does it say about the human being's condition that he or she has the capacity for trance and ecstasy? Such experiences as love, nostalgia for roots, obsession with power, the need to escape pressures, the attraction of fantasies promising temporary freedom, the impulses of humor and heroism, the addiction to drink and drugs—all of these can be interpreted as unconscious forms of the impulse to reach beyond, to seek further. Transcendence may be an active motive point in people's lives without being consciously recognized as such. The ultimate meaning of human actions seems more intelligible in light of this. In *The Meaning of Transcendence: A Heideggerian Reflection* (Chicago: Scholars Press, 1981), Robert P. Orr points out, "Transcendence, from the Indo-European root *skand*, names passing beyond with respect to what is fixed, determinate, delimited" (p. 6). The isolated individual can experience interconnectedness, growth, depth. "The demise of the experienced meaningfulness of any transcendental reality is due precisely to the current cultural sovereignty of the task of world-appropriation" (p. 12). The mastery of surfaces, purposiveness, the calculative mode of thought, utilitarian materialism, technology, I/it attitudes—all diminish the sense of transcendence. Purposive rationality forgets the systemic nature of reality—cosmos with realms of nature, the network of human culture, and the life of individual man—mental, physical, emotional, and their interrelationships. The interrelated levels of the whole, the "interconnectivities" demand a profound depth detector to do justice to the realities. Crude determinisms ignore the depths and explain motives in caricature.

Humans still have the capacity to surpass, to reach out, to become more than yesterday's definition. This non-static view can include the awareness of some power or mystery beyond the individual's calculative brain and limiting skin. What Ken Wilber calls "the Atman Project" is the yearning which man naturally feels for wholeness, the need to realize the nature of being infinite and eternal. In the face of death, and with no means to reach the infinite, people use symbolic substitutes: sex, food, money, fame, power, drugs, and knowledge as substitute gratifications for the true release possible in wholeness.

Robert Bellah's essay "Transcendence in Contemporary Piety" is an example of his thought on this topic, *Beyond Belief: Essays on Religion in a Post-Traditional*

There are various kinds of experiences noted in the history of religions which may be considered as relating to transcendence, from spiritual love and transpersonal socializing which widens horizons and multiplies capacities, to the solitary Taoist sage described by Chuang Tzu as "returning to the origin" in stillness. There is the *satori* of a Zen monk. And, a study by Francis X. Clooney points out, there is also the Hindu example of transcendence involved in Jaimini's *mīmāṁsā* interpretation of sacrifice in which the individual view is surpassed in relation to the sum total of values and viewpoints in a religious ritual which precludes the supernatural.[10] There is the "crossing over" of Jain *tīrthaṅkaras*, and the prophetic encounter with God as radically Other, and many other modes of reaching beyond as well.

Though experiences of transcendence would seem to be a universal human capacity it would seem that the forms the experiences take depend in part on cultural conditioning by tradition, and on the historical times of the world in which one lives. I believe that an examination of the signs of transcendence in the *Nāmasiddhānta* leaders' lives will firstly illuminate continuities with earlier Indian religious traditions, and secondly reveal aspects of the new situation to which their lives are an answer. But before considering specific signs of a reach beyond, and images of a reality not reducible to mind, senses, words, which is pictured as reaching into the lives of *Nāmasiddhānta* leaders, let us look at the general social and political conditions in which they lived. A better grasp of the background, the historical conditions in which the leaders lived, helps us understand better the responses they developed and the experiences for which they are remembered.

World (New York: Harper & Row, 1970). Dietrich Bonhoeffer (*Letters and Papers from Prison* [New York: MacMillan, 1971]) and Paul Tillich ("Religion and Secular Culture" in *The Protestant Ethic* [Chicago: Chicago Univ., 1957]) are cited by Orr as opening new discussions on transcendence. See also W.C. Smith's "Transcendence" Ingersoll Lecture in *Harvard Divinity Bulletin*, Fall 1988, Vol. XVIII, no. 3, pp. 10-15.

[10] See N.J. Girardot, *Myth and Meaning in Early Taoism* (Berkeley: University of California, 1983) and Francis X. Clooney, "Jaimini's Contribution to the Theory of Sacrifice," *History of Religions*, vol. 25, no. 3, Feb, 1986. See also Carman on Rāmānuja's concept of Viṣṇu's *paratva* (transcendence) and *saulabhya* (accessibility), *Ānvikṣiki* (Research Bulletin of the Center of Advanced Study in Philosophy), Banaras Hindu University, Vol. I, nos. 1-2, Aug.-Dec. 1968, pp. 77-78; and Coomaraswamy, *Selected Papers*, Vol. I (Princeton: Princeton Univ., 1977), p. 75.

Historical Conditions at the Time of *Nāmasiddhānta*'s Origins

Nāmasiddhānta leaders Āyyāvāl, Bodhendra, Sadāśiva Brahmendra, Nārāyaṇa Tīrtha, and Sadguru Svāmī lived during the 17th, 18th, and early 19th centuries in the Kāverī delta kingdom of Tāñjavūr. This was a time when Europeans were already present in the region where these leaders lived. The Dutch were active in establishing settlements on the Coromandel Coast from 1612 onward, the Danes from 1618, the English from 1639, and the Portuguese settled and then lost their footholds during the first half of the 17th century. The French occupied Puducheri (which also became known as Pondicherry) before the end of the century. European rivalry for coastal trade advantages led to deeper foreign involvement in the region.

During this period the Mughal empire expanded southward into Karṇāṭaka and the Coromandel coast, becoming a destabilizing element, upsetting the economic relationships and trade patterns already in place, undermining political and administrative systems and preparing the way for deeper and wider European entrenchment. In the North the Mughals brought unity to the monetary system. They standardized customs duties, and communications, and integrated regional economic growth. In the South, the Mughal presence was a different story. The Mughals could not draw the region together under one rule, but their aggressive presence helped rip it apart.[11]

The Tāñjavūr rulers during this time—first Nāyaks (regional governors) of the period toward the end of the Vijayanagara empire, and then after 1675, Marāṭha kings—faced political threats to their authority from all sides, as well as natural destabilizing forces. For example, famine—there was a major famine in 1659. The Nāyaks of Madurai and Tāñjavūr were unsteady allies—to each other and to the other powers around them, both Hindu and European. The Tāñjavūr Nāyaks soon developed a "healthy respect" for the Dutch, granting them concessions and accepting their naval dominance, leasing ports and villages after staging an ineffective siege against the Dutch in the 1660s.

In the 1670s Tāñjavūr suffered from the war between the Nāyak of Madurai and the Nāyak of Tāñjavūr, and the Dutch profited from the situation by extending their own rights and privileges during that time. When the Marāṭha rāja Ekojī drove out the Madurai Nāyak and established his rulership in Tāñjavūr in 1675, he canceled previous concessions granted

[11] For more on this see the excellent study by Sinnappah Arasaratnam, *Merchants, Companies and Commerce on the Coromandel Coast, 1650-1740* (Delhi: Oxford Univ. Press, 1986), p. 91.

to the Dutch. After strife with the Dutch he learned to respect their strength. He returned their previous concessions in exchange for annual revenue of gold and elephants, but he at least recovered two important ports. Ekojī also made a costly peace with Sivājī, his half-brother. It was during this time and in these historical circumstances that two *Nāmasiddhānta* leaders, Bodhendra and Āyyāvāl, were born.

In 1677 and 1680 Kāverī floods played havoc with the region. Despite Ekojī's war efforts he seems to have found the resources to promote Hindu culture also. The royal family of which he was a part was Śaivite, especially devoted to Śiva as Tyāgeśa in the Tiruvārūr temple, not too far from the Tāñjavūr city capital.

In 1689 when the Mughal emperor Aurangzeb's forces overran the area, the Dutch renegotiated their rights with the Muslims. Tāñjavūr Marāṭha rulers after the reign Ekojī experienced serious financial difficulties and relied heavily on Dutch funds, for which they willingly exchanged concessions. Marāṭha King Śāhajī (1684-1710 or 1712) attacked Nagapatnam villages in 1691 when Dutch gifts were deemed inadequate. Śāhajī laid siege to the city and harassed Dutch trade. The Dutch attacked and broke the siege in August 1691. Śāhajī sued for peace and signed a treaty returning old privileges. In 1698 Mughal authority was established up to the frontiers of Tāñjavūr state, and the rāja had to pay an annual tribute of 30 *lakh* rupees. (A *lakh* is 100,000.) In the 18th century Tāñjavūr rulers were weakened militarily and financially, paying large tributes to the Mughals to keep them at bay. They were also kept busy fighting Madurai and Ramnad forces, while the Dutch presence gradually grew stronger during these years.[12]

Āyyāvāl, one of the *Nāmasiddhānta* leaders, wrote a long work in Sanskrit about the Marāṭha royal family, especially Śāhajī II, who was his patron when he was a young man. During the rule of Śāhajī II in the latter 17th century, there was recurrent, almost constant, fear of Muslim invasion. Śāhajī II sent troops to aid Rājarām, son of Sivājī and the ruler of Ginjee in the fight against Kulfikar Khan, Aurangzeb's commander. V. Raghavan has interpreted Śāhajī II's attacks on Christians and Muslims as a heroic defense of *dharma.* Not surprisingly, Śāhajī appears far more successful in this venture in Sanskrit literature than in Muslim, Dutch, or English records. Raghavan writes in his introduction to Āyyāvāl's *Sāhendra Vilāsa* that the way Śāhajī fought against "the new menace of the Christian missionaries masquerading as Roman Brahmans, weaning away the masses and reviling Hindu faith and worship . . . [shows] that our hero's zeal for

[12] Ibid., pp. 77-79, 45.

the safeguarding of the country's religion was really comprehensive in its sweep. No wonder that Nallā, alias Bhūminātha, takes Śāhajī's biography as a holy chronicle and record of *dharma* in his *Dharmavijaya Campū*."[13]

To help buttress Hindu culture, Śāhajī II in 1693 gifted Tiruviśanallūr village on the banks of the Kāverī to Brahman scholars, authors, and *bhaktas*. *Nāmasiddhānta* leaders Āyyāvāl and Bodhendra were associated with this village.

According to historians David Ludden and Kathleen Gough, slave labor played a part in South Indian economy during this period. A major famine in 1729 made the slave trade brisker, with European companies buying slaves for work in their ports and settlements. Both Mughal and Marāṭha rulers alike frowned on the growth of a large scale slave trade in the Coromandel, but they were unable to halt it altogether. It was during this time of famine and distress that Sadāśiva Brahmendra and Nārāyaṇa Tīrtha, two of the major *Nāmasiddhānta* leaders, were active. But historical references do not show up in their works—they were poets, not historians.[14]

After 1740 Tāñjavūr seemed to teeter on the brink of financial collapse year after year. The rulers had to make repeated indemnity payments to the Mughal rulers in 1741 and 1750. During this time the rājas mortgaged large areas of coastal territory to the Dutch for cash. The Dutch were not strong enough to fully exploit the situation by deepening their involvement with Hindu allies. The Dutch had commitments in Java and Ceylon which

[13] V. Raghavan, ed. *Śāhendra Vilāsa* (Tiruchi: Kalyan Press, 1952), p. 74. Manucci, *Storia do Mogor or Mogul India 1653-1708*, Vol. III (London: J. Murray, 1907-8), pp. 327-332.

[14] In *The Religions of Man*, Huston Smith states "India never sank to slavery" (New York: Harper and Row, 1958), p. 67. Srinivasa Ayyangar, in *Tamil Studies, Second Series* (Delhi: Abhinav/South Asia Books, 1986), on p. 66 writes: "Slavery as an institution of the type that existed in ancient Greece and Rome has never prevailed in Tamil Nadu. But kings, chieftains, and landed magnates here had such complete power over the people, that for the bulk of them feudal subjection was a common lot." I cannot claim to be an expert on this topic, just as social scientists cannot claim expertise in the study of religion. For a discussion arguing there were slaves (*adimai alukal*) in Tamil Nadu see Kathleen Gough, *Rural Society in Southeast India* (Cambridge: Cambridge Univ., 1981), pp. 105-106. Gough notes that though slavery was legally abolished in 1843, the conditions of many Harijan laborers' lives changed little during the British rule (p. 131). See also Sinnappah Arasaratnam, *Merchants and Companies on the Coromandel Coast* (Delhi: Oxford University Press, 1986), p. 211, and David Ludden, *A Peasant History of South India* (Princeton: Princeton Univ. Press, 1985).

prevented them from giving hinterland rulers the military aid they desired.

During the period of the earlier *Nāmasiddhānta* leaders—Āyyāvāl and Bodhendra—the British rivaled the Dutch for trade privileges, sometimes siding with the Muslims against the Nāyaks. Gradually the English response to challenges became bolder. The British had gained a foothold in Chennapatnam (1639), and they strengthened their stand by building Fort Saint George (1641) which became a planning center and staging area for landward ventures. Then the British expanded their holdings, acquiring Devanampatnam in 1690, and in the early 1700s they began negotiating agreements with Mughal rulers.[15]

Thus, political change, social instability, and economic distress, as well as increasingly disruptive foreign encroachment, mark the time of the *Nāmasiddhānta* leaders. The rice production statistics from that time show how fertile and abundant the Kāverī delta was, but also how the crops could diminish in times of turmoil. From Ekojī's reign to the end of Śāhajī's reign, 1675-1711, over 824,000 tons of rice were produced annually in Tāñjavūr, some of which was exported. From Śarabhojī's reign to the end of Tukojī's reign, 1711-1735, over 617,000 tons of rice were produced annually. In Tulajī's reign, beginning in 1735, the usual rice production was 514,285 tons. In 1744 only 96,000 tons were produced and famine ensued. There were other catastrophic low points, such as the period around 1781, when the Muslim leader Haidar Ali, father of Tippu Sultan, invaded and there was famine. In 1781 the gross yield dropped to one seventh of the previous year's yield, causing extreme distress. A Christian missionary, F. Schwartz, active in Tāñjavūr at this time, described healthy persons as rarities and said most people looked like "wandering skeletons." It was during and following this time that Tyāgarāja, the culminative *Nāmasiddhānta* composer grew to manhood, and Sadgurusvāmī, the last "ācārya" of the movement, appeared on the scene. They must have felt the impact of the catastrophic famine in their formative years. From 1771 to 1860 the British conquest of South India re-shaped the production mode and Tāñjavūr became an agricultural hinterland of the British empire, and Tāñjavūr traditional crafts died as exports dwindled under British policies. Villagers were in distress in the region off and on from 1812 to 1850, with severe famines in 1811-12 and 1823-26.[16]

[15] Sinnappah Arasaratnam, *Merchants and Companies on the Coromandel Coast*, pp. 90-91.

[16] Kathleen Gough, *Rural Society in Southeast India*, pp. 120 and 410-411. Pearson, ed. *Memoirs of Schwartz*, Vol. I, pp. 348, ff. C.K. Srinivasan, *Marāṭha Rule in*

Responses to these historical conditions varied, and it is no simple task to summarize what the time meant for all the Hindu communities trying to survive or keep their way of life afloat as the tides of fortune changed. Invasions, famines, demands for exorbitant tribute were but some of the destabilizing sources of insecurity. During the initial phase of the European companies setting up business on the Coromandel coast new co-operative ventures were organized and launched. New groups of Indian merchants entered into trade partnerships among diverse social and religious groups. Strategic reorganizing went on at various levels of Hindu society; at the level of poor peasants, subsistence and survival were still the perennial concerns. In mid-17th century, European companies found Coromandel trade "a major growth area." Dutch intrusion and aggressiveness made a strong impact along the Coromandel coast in the 18th century, as in Tāñjavūr and other "hinterland" capitols Hindu administrations weakened and faltered.[17] The *Nāmasiddhānta* movement, in part, may be seen as a response to these conditions—a way offered to Hindus amidst the waves of change.

Telugu Brahman Patterns of Response: *Niyogi* and *Vaidiki*

A pattern of response to the increasing presence of powerful alien forces is evident among Telugu Brahmans in South India: two models of adaptation and response seem to have existed in association with two types of Brahmans: *Niyogi* and *Vaidiki*.[18]

The *Niyogis* (literally, "functionaries or commissioned officials"), who often worked as village accountants, adapted to fit new administrative positions which were opened up by the Muslim and European powers. During the 17th and 18th centuries they worked as clerks, administrators, and translators for Muslim rulers and zamindars and for European companies, and often found the professional bureaucratic lifestyle agreeable. They incorporated some new ideas from the Westerners, and this gradually had a modernizing impact on Hindu society. The *Niyogi* survival strategy appears to have been "You can't beat them, so join them." Political psychologist and social theorist Ashis Nandy has pointed out that by co-operating and

the Carnatic (Annamalainagar: Annamalai Univ., 1945), pp. 308-310.

[17] Sinnappah Arasaratnam, *Merchants and Companies on the Coromandel Coast*, pp. 354-5.

[18] V. Nārāyaṇa Rao, "Telugu Intellectuals," *South Asian Intellectuals and Social Change*, ed. Y.K. Malik (New Delhi: Heritage Pub., 1982), p. 315.

serving the Muslims and the companies, these Brahmans at least survived (unlike the Aztec priests uncompromisingly facing Spanish invaders).[19] This strategy could include humoring and acting agreeable to the new masters, even when the situations were not humorous, and inwardly the servant disagreed with the colonizers.

The second group of Telugu Brahmans, *Vaidikis*, were traditionalists who learned and preserved the scriptures. They chanted the Sanskrit texts and studied the *śāstras*—the books of knowledge and rules of conduct. The *Vaidikis* had a different response. We might say that they imitated Satyavrata (the "Hindu Noah" who nurtured a fish which grew to save him and others during dissolution, *pralaya*; the fish saved Satyavrata by advising him to build an ark stocked with seeds for new life).[20] The *Vaidikis* were concerned with preserving essentials of tradition, sometimes with the help of creative adaptiveness. Some of these knowers of the orthodox code chose elements from resources of the past, fashioning a creative answer in response to the changing times brought about by the presence of Muslim and European powers. While traders, kings and the wealthy, as well as the *Niyogi* Brahmans progressively learned to co-operate with Europeans

[19] Ashis Nandy, *The Intimate Enemy: Loss and Recovery of Self Under Colonialism* (Delhi: Oxford University Press, 1983), p. 113.

[20] *Bhāgavata Purāṇa* VIII 24, 32-37. According to legend, Satyavrata was a royal sage who lived on nothing but water. He ruled over the Dravida territory. One day a strange fish appeared in his hands while he offered handfuls of water to his ancestors at the river; the helpless fish was fearful and Satyavrata resolved to protect it. The fish expanded rapidly, outgrowing each container—coconut shell, jar, lake, ocean. When the fish was 800 miles long Satyavrata could no longer contain himself. "Who are you?" he asked, guessing Lord Hari had come himself in this form to help. What was the huge whale's mission? "At the *kalpa*'s end the dissolution of the universe comes," the fish told the sage. "Seven days from now the three worlds will be submerged in the ocean. I will send a mysterious boat to you. Take herbs, plants, seeds, animals and the seven seers, and sail, guided by the seers' light. Tie the boat to my horn with Vāsukī the cosmic serpent. I will roam in the water throughout the night of Brahmā, and you will realize my glory as Para Brahmā." The king did so, and in the ark preserved a way of life. In *Śatapatha Brāhmaṇa* I, 8.1.1-6, Manu is the "Noah" who saves the fish and builds an ark. A more modern analogy of the endeavor of preservers and revivers is that of the hologram. The creative conservator seizes means which produce a kind of hologram image, which memory researchers use to explain how information is distributed in the brain. The interrelations are such that if "part" is lost the whole is still available in other parts, e.g., a song of Tyāgarāja holds essentials of *sanātana dharma*, the ancient tradition.

and Muslims in order to survive, the *Vaidiki smārta* Brahmans were more conservative. They tended to be less assimilationist and more communal. They avoided much contact with the "others" and remained protective of the cultural religious heritage being endangered by historical change and interaction with colonialist civilizations.

In this category are the five *Nāmasiddhānta* leaders, most of whom were Telugu *Vaidiki smārta* Brahmans. Also in this category was the "culmination" of the tradition, Tyāgarāja. These men's lives tell us something about their ideals and hopes, their thrust toward the transcendent, their holding on to what seemed to them most valuable and essential. For them, the Name was the "*tāraka mantra*," enabling the crossing. Like Satyavrata's boat, it carried the condensed minimum cargo necessary for the survival of Hindu faith. The Name was simple enough for all to use, holy enough to uplift and save, able to link this world and the person in it to the ultimate security of a transcendent reality beyond change. The designation "*smārta*" deserves more attention than many historians have given it. J.N. Farquhar, in *Outlines of Religious Literature in India*, traces the term *smārta* to Gupta times, when it was used to distinguish followers of the *Gṛihya śāstras* who kept up household rites from those Brahmans who kept up all the elaborate vedic (*śrauta*) rites. As I mentioned earlier, *smārtas* were creative re-shapers of the *Purāṇas*, incorporating folk devotion into Sanskrit texts, and were known for *pañcāyatana* worship, a ritual in which five deities are represented with emblems, with the worshiper's favorite form in the center. *Smārtas* possessed of a more universalist vision synthesized regional rites and practices into a larger pan-Indian system. *Smārta* in South India is also a term associated with Ayyars or Aiyars, distinguishing them from Ayyangārs (Vaiṣṇavas), and hence has sometimes been oversimplified to mean Śaiva, though in actuality there seems to be a strong non-sectarian side to the community.[21]

[21] J.N. Farquhar, *An Outline of Religious Literature in India* (London: Oxford, 1920), p. 141, which places the term *smārta* in Gupta times. Yoshitsugu Sawai, "Faith of Ascetics and Lay *Smārtas*," 1984 Harvard Ph.D. thesis on *Smārta* traditions and the Śringiri Maṭh. See also V.S. Pathak, *Smārta Religious Tradition* (Meerut: Kusumanjali Prakashan, 1987). Milton Singer makes very helpful observations about *smārtas* in *Krishna: Myths, Rites and Attitudes* (Chicago: Univ. of Chicago Press, 1966, 1971). See also my "Questions About the Rememberers: *Smārta* Brahmans as Renewers of Tradition," in William J. Jackson, *Tyagaraja and the Renewal of Tradition: Translations and Reflections* (Motilal Banarsidass, New Delhi, 1994).

The Five *Nāmasiddhānta/ Bhajana Sampradāya* Leaders: Stories Reflecting Signs of Transcendence in Their Lives

The term "signs of transcendence" is meant to indicate incidents or symbolic occurrences which point to faith in, or experience of, a reality beyond mere individual physical existence. These signs in hagiography often stand for some extraordinary moments of inspiration in the saints' lives, or reflect some unusual power which later generations find inspiring to recall. The sources for these stories are oral traditions and written literature about Kāverī delta *bhakti.*

In terms of modern scholarship, the Kāverī *Nāmasiddhānta* movement has been researched most influentially by V. Raghavan, who based his publications on Sanskrit texts as well as written and oral Tamil hagiography available during the first seven decades of the twentieth century. Raghavan gathered these traditions and wrote articles for journals, book introductions, newspapers, music society and *maṭh* publications, and he prepared talks for seminars, conferences, and festivals, placing the *Nāmasiddhānta* leaders on the map of modern scholarship, and keeping them in public awareness as a viable part of the 20th century Hindu cultural self-image. Raghavan's studies of *Nāmasiddhānta* saints' lives and works represent the "standard" traditions about the saints' current during the first half of the twentieth century. His accounts add musicological information to the popular accounts, as do the works of South Indian musicologists P. Sambamoorthy and R. Rangaramanuja Iyengar.[22]

None of these scholars' accounts seem very concerned with contextualizing the lives historically, as I have found it necessary to do in the foregoing section. It is the exception rather than the rule to find specific "historical" references in the saints' stories; in part this may be due to an attempt to calm and not disturb memories of communal conflict between Muslims and Hindus, as well as a reflection of Hindu ahistoricism. I have sought out and highlighted episodes reflecting both historical conditions and signs of the transcendent. A concern with the transcendent constitutes a rich dimension in religion even if it is not of much interest to sociology, anthropology, linguistics, and economics.

[22] V. Raghavan, "Sadāśiva Brahmendra," *The Hindu*, Feb. 18, 1970. "Tīrtha Nārāyaṇa," *The Hindu*, Jan. 4, 1970; "Introductory Thesis" to *The Spiritual Heritage of Tyāgarāja*, C. Ramanujacari (Madras: Ramakrishna Math, 1981); P. Sambamoorthy, *Great Composers*, Book I (Madras: Indian Music Publishing House, 1978); and R. Rangaramanuja Ayyangar, *History of South Indian (Carnatic) Music* (Madras: Author, 1978).

1. Bodhendra, who was named Puruṣottaman at birth, was born in Kāñcīpuram, west of Madras in the early 17th century to a *smārta* Brahman couple who had hoped for a child for a long time. The boy's birth was interpreted as a reward for the parents' faithful service to the 58th Jagadguru ("Pontiff" or "religious authority") of the Kāñcīpuram monastery. An early sign associated with transcendence concerns a vow he took while still a boy.

After studying *śruti* and *smṛiti* scriptures, and practicing *nāmasankīrtana* and repetition of Rāma's name 100,000 times a day, Bodhendra was told by his guru to follow him to the holy city of Banāras, far away in the North, where the guru desired to bathe in the Ganges. Bodhendra was to travel with a young companion, Jñānasekharan. As they were leaving Kāñcīpuram the two made a suicide pact: if one died en route, the other would proceed to Banāras and inform the guru of the agreement, and then take his own life in the Ganges. As fate would have it, Bodhendra's friend Jñānasekharan died en route. Bodhendra wanted to live up to the agreement, but when he arrived in Banāras the guru dissuaded him, saying he could accomplish something better by doing good on earth. The guru cited a story from the *Rāmāyaṇa* to justify breaking the vow, and argued that the best alternative would be for the boy to become a dedicated *sannyāsin*, asserting that this change was also a kind of "death" at one's own hand, because it would be a signal of the end of one's current worldly *janma* or birth.[23]

Though most Hindus today would not share the value, Bodhendra's willingness to commit suicide is a sign related to the transcendent in Hinduism in those times. Taking an action which results in losing one's life in this world in pursuit of a higher purpose is a most dramatic indication of faith in a realm and life *beyond*. In the case of a religious vow, suicide means not just to "end it all" but to take leave of this for *that*—affirming the transcendent reality beyond this world. Jains fasting to death are another example of this practice in India. Ritual suicide in rivers is described approvingly in the *Matsya Purāṇa* and in other scriptures, and Chinese and Muslim travelers to India noted witnessing such acts. For example, Chinese pilgrim Hiuen Tsiang in the 7th century wrote of the

[23] R. Krishnamurthy acknowledges his debt to V. Raghavan for his accounts of the *Nāmasiddhānta* leaders in his book *The Saints of the Cauvery Delta* (New Delhi: Concept Pub. Co., 1979). See V. Raghavan's introduction to *Śāhendra Vilāsa*, and T.M.P. Mahadevan's *Seminar on Saints* (Madras: Ganesh, 1960), and S. Seetha, *Tanjore as a Seat of Music* (Madras: University of Madras, 1981).

Prayāg Kumbha Mela, "the sacred rivers confluence festival." Hiuen Tsiang reported that he saw ascetics clinging to tall posts embedded in the river while staring at the sun until blind, then jumping into the water. The idea was to enable one's own ultimate "confluence" with the divine at this auspicious site and occasion. Others deliberately plunged headlong from a sacred banyan tree, or entered fires of burning dried cowdung patties, seeking an auspicious end and transition to merging with the eternal. Philosophers and kings followed by their wives drowned themselves, and *sādhus* slaughtered each other in a frenzy of self-violent renunciation at certain times. A Muslim traveler of the middle ages described voluntary drownings in Cambay (Gujarat) and Śrī Laṅka. Self-inflicted death at a holy place or time—under the wheels of the Jagannath festival chariot, or in the flames of a widow's *satī*, for example—was for a long time a religiously approved way to transcend earthly conditions.[24]

It is significant that Bodhendra's contemplated suicide—the death he had accepted in principle—was transcended by an unexpected new life at the guru's direction. The ending became a beginning—one identity faded as another emerged. Bodhendra received a new lease on life, finding a different life from the one he sought, a life revealed through circumstances which were beyond his control.

The second extraordinary event recounted in Bodhendra's life story concerns a miracle demonstrating the power of the holy Name. This event is said to have occurred after Bodhendra became a *sannyāsin.* His guru told him to return to Kāñcī after stopping in Jagannātha *kṣetra* (in Puri, Orissa) to get a text on the Name from Lakṣmīdhara (who in fact is thought by historians to have lived during the 16th century).[25] Lakṣmīdhara was "away

[24] *Book of the Wonders of India: Mainland, Sea and Islands* by Captain Buzurg ibn Shahriyar of Ramhormuz, tr. G.S.P. Freeman-Grenville (London and the Hague: East-West Publishers, 1981), pp. 4, 71-72, 81; Eleanor Munro, *On Glory Roads* (London: Thames and Hudson, 1987), pp. 52-53; V.S. Pathak, *Smārta Religious Traditions*, pp. 78-79. "The German poet, Ferdinand Freilgrath (1810-1876), recounted for his readers how hundreds of Hindu pilgrims in Puri, India, crushed themselves to death in religious ecstasy under the wheels al the juggernaut (Jaganath) chariot . . ." (Joseph W. Elder, ed. *Chapters in Indian Civilization*, Vol. II [Dubuque: Kendall/Hunt, 1970], p. 28). See also S. Settar, *Inviting Death: Indian Attitudes Towards the Ritual Death* (Leiden: E.J. Brill, 1989).

[25] Not much is known about Lakṣmīdhara, author of the commentary on the *Saundarya Laharī.* In a colophon to his *Śiva nibandha* text he says he was a devotee of Śiva at Ekāmra—Bhuvaneśvar, Orissa, and that he lived in the court of Pratāparudra Gajapat of Orissa (C.E. 1497-1539). He was an advocate of "fiercely puritanical

from home" when Bodhendra arrived at midnight, so, being a traveler with nowhere else to go, he waited on the porch. Then a Brahman couple arrived, also seeking Lakṣmīdhara. It seems that during their travels the wife had been kidnapped from her husband by Muslims. She had found her husband again later, but by then had been "polluted" as a Hindu, converted by them Muslims to their faith, though not voluntarily. Lakṣmīdhara's son, the Jagannātha Pandit Lakṣmīkānta Kavi, told the couple that saying *Rāma-nāma* would be sufficient *prāyaścittam* or penance to expiate the loss of ritual purity and status. Surprised by this answer, Bodhendra asked the authority for the teaching and was told it could be found, supported by orthodox references, in Lakṣmīdhara's text *Bhagavannāma Kaumudi.* Bodhendra said, "If the Name is really that powerful, it should cause the woman's Muslim clothes and ornaments to be replaced by Hindu ones if she prayerfully says the Name while bathing in the Jagannāthasvāmī temple pool." Lakṣmīkānta did not disagree. He showed his guests the way to the pool. There, saying Rāma's name the woman bathed and emerged a Hindu *sumaṅgali* or "auspicious married woman" with her *maṅgala sūtra, tilak,* and her necklace of black beads and other emblems of Hindu tradition restored. The story goes that this miraculous occurrence

and Brahmin dominated Śrīvidya tantrism" whose work solidified views on the *Saundarya Laharī*—later commentators follow his cues. He is responsible for certain vocabulary usages (such as right/left) and some ideas in Śrīvidya that have persisted. But he advocated a ritual and theological *sādhana* especially involving Śrīcakra which has no following, though like the Kaulācāra Bhāśkarāya's followers, some *sādhakas* identify themselves with his work and views without strictly following his literal teachings. An "ardent proponent of the Śrīvidya Śākta tantric tradition, centering on the beneficent *Lalitāmahātripurasundarī*, the Śrīcakra, and the 15 or 16 syllable *śrīvidya mantra* known usually as the *pañcadaśī.* It is not uncommon in South India for Śrīvidya *upāsakas* to be Śaivas for 'public' purposes, Śāktas privately and socially and religiously rooted in Brahmin communities (such as the Ayyar communities of Tamil Nadu, strongly identifying themselves with the Śaṅkara maṭhs and the traditional ascription of Śākta works, including *Saundarya Laharī*, to Śaṅkara)." So *Śrī vidya upāsakas* such as Lakṣmīdhara could have written a Śiva *nibandha.* "There is precedent, in fact among other historical Śrīvidya adepts to 'cross' sectarian lines (artificial lines, for most part, when you speak of *smārtas*)." I am indebted to Prof. Douglas Brooks, University of Rochester, New York, for much of this information (personal correspondence, Jan. 20, 1988). Teun Goudriaan and Sanjukta Gupta, in *Hindu Tantric and Śakta Literature* (Wiesbaden: Harrassowitz, 1979), and C. Chakravarti, *The Tantras: Studies on Their Religion and Literature* (Calcutta: Punthi Pustak, 1963), p. 72, ff., also provide some information on Lakṣmīdhara's background.

convinced Bodhendra of the power of the Name and set him on his path of enthusiasm for spreading devotion to the holy Name.

The pilgrimage was thus for Bodhendra an initiation of sorts into full faith in the power of the Name. In this depiction of the origins of Bodhendra's belief in the power of the Name, it is noteworthy that the larger-than-life episode of Hindus seeking to recover their status and identity from the overpowering Muslim forces sets the stage for his later career. The story communicates an experience of wonder at the Name's power in the face of an anxiety- producing historical challenge: Islamic threats to the survival of Hindu traditions. It points to Kāverī delta *Nāmasiddhānta*'s origins and concerns for legitimate authority—scriptural citations on the Name—and it also has to do with hope for survival of a religious lifeway in a disturbing transition time.

A third sign of transcendence comes later, after Bodhendra had grown older, having composed one *lakh* (100,000) *ślokas* (verses) based on Lakṣmīdhara's work about the Name, writing that work at his guru's behest, and having succeeded his guru as head of the Kāñcīpuram monastery, serving for years in that capacity. An old man now, Bodhendra went to Govindapuram village, in the Kāverī delta, where he remained, living a life of renunciation and yoga. It is said he would go into *samādhi* after burying himself in the Kāverī river bed sands. (*Samādhi* is the meditative experience of transcendent consciousness—reaching beyond the usual mind characteristic of human conditioning.) In the evening, following the agreement they had made with the holy man, children would go to the riverbed and uncover him, waking him from his higher state of consciousness. One evening when the children came to uncover the holy man a divine voice told them Bodhendra had attained *mahāsamādhi*, final liberation. To commemorate this event, the voice advised, devoted people should build a memorial structure and perform an *arādhana* (worship celebration) yearly. At night the ethereal sound of the name "*Rāma*" is said to be audible there, according to believers.[26] Bodhendra died in 1692, leaving a legacy of scholarship, devotion, and a long life dedicated to service of the Name.

[26] The image of the yogi in *samādhi* underground is familiar in the North as well. For example, there is a Banāras legend of a yogi in trance in an underground cavern unearthed by engineers. Awakened from his meditation, he was shocked to hear Rāma and Sīta were gone and that is was now the Kali age. He plunged into the Ganges and vanished (Diana Eck, *Banāras: City of Light*, p. 247).

2. Āyyāvāl, as Śrīdhara Veṅkaṭeṣa Ārya came to be called, was born around 1650. He was a married Telugu *smārta* Brahman.[27] He refused when a Mysore rāja invited him to serve as minister, a position his father had held. Instead he went south, settling in Tiruviśanallūr village because of his fondness for the nearby Mahāliṅgasvāmī temple. Āyyāvāl met Bodhendra in Tiruviśanallūr, and, like-minded in their enthusiasm for the Name, they offered each other encouragement. Together they are considered the launchers of the *Nāmasiddhānta* tradition in the Kāverī delta. Āyyāvāl enjoyed the patronage of King Śāhajī II for reciting and expounding on the Sanskrit epics—the *Rāmāyaṇa* and *Mahābhārata.*

A miracle story told about Āyyāvāl demonstrates that genuine devotion partakes of a mode beyond forms and conventional sectarian categories. It seems that a Krishna devotee at first wanted Āyyāvāl to attend a Rādhākalyānam festival, in which Krishna's marriage to Rādhā is celebrated with song. Then, some time later, the Krishna devotee sent a message saying, "No, don't come, you're a Śiva *bhakta*, so we're starting without you and your disciples." The Krishna devotee and his guests realized the folly of emphasizing sectarian differences when they heard from observers that Krishna publicly appeared to Āyyāvāl soon thereafter, as proof of the holy man's worthiness. Genuine devotion transcends the petty-minded categorizations which humans habitually make, Krishna's appearance would seem to say. The story implies that one should not underestimate the non-sectarian or inter-sectarian *bhakti* of a devout *smārta*, and that Krishna's grace overflows the neat boundaries people habitually use.

Another story relates that when the Kāverī was flood-swollen, Āyyāvāl, instead of crossing as usual to worship in the temple, decided to pray at home, offering praise inwardly, and in so doing transcended ordinary space. That he overcame the distance between himself and the temple deity is shown in the story in which a priest from the temple appeared in Āyyāvāl's home and offered *prasād* to him. Āyyāvāl is said to have given the priest a shawl to protect him from the cool monsoon dampness. Later, the temple image was seen wearing the same shawl when the inner sanctum was opened, and the priest there seemed to know nothing about the shawl. It soon dawned on everyone concerned that it must have been the deity who visited Āyyāvāl in the form of the priest.

The third and most memorable miracle story—one for which Āyyāvāl is best known—concerns his feeding a starving outcast food intended for

[27] Oral tradition says Āyyāvāl was a Karṇāṭaka Brahman of Mysore. V. Raghavan calls him an Andhra; his father's name was Lingaryar. Śrīdhara is an *intiperu* or house name. Bodhendra, in *Nāmāmritaṛasāyana*, calls Āyyāvāl "Veṅkaṭeśa Śāstri."

śrāddha rites, which are rituals of homage to the ancestors. When local Brahmans criticized him for breaking caste rules by feeding an outcast, and pronounced as penalty a bath in the Ganges river to expiate his sin, Āyyāvāl stood his ground. He prayed at home and the Goddess Gaṅgā appeared in his backyard well, to satisfy any ultraconservatives' ritual requirements, and to prove Āyyāvāl's superior compassion toward a man starving to death.

All of the Kāverī *Nāmasiddhānta* saints must have experienced the distress of periodic famine which plagued Tāñjavūr during their lifetimes and they must have seen the effects of starvation, in the lower castes especially. In India, in modern times and before, the needy are a fact of life and this is reflected in religious expression. There are many stories of Śiva disguised as a beggar outcast, rewarding those who serve him in that form. The ideal response of Āyyāvāl to the need of a starving man was preserved in stories still current in the Kāverī delta. Devotees still celebrate the appearance of "Ganges water" in Āyyāvāl's well, and continue the practice of bathing in the *maṭh* which was built at that site, during celebrations on the annual Āyyāvāl *arādhana* day festival.

Āyyāvāl, as previously mentioned, wrote a long Sanskrit poem praising the Maratha king Śivaji for protecting Hindu tradition by destroying the invading Muslims, and praising king Śāhajī as divine. Thus, Āyyāvāl's life shows that his *bhakti* era led him to envision Śiva in both *cāṇḍāla* and rāja, with a sensibility which transcended usual social categories. Like Bodhendra, Āyyāvāl promoted *Nāmasiddhānta* in individual practice and group *bhajana* singing. Unlike the *sannyāsin* Bodhendra, the householder Āyyāvāl felt no qualms about accepting court patronage.[28] In fact, Āyyāvāl's life shows more dependence on the support of a king than is seen in the other leaders' lives. Rejecting one king's offer, he became poet-laureate of another. He profited from praise and his girth in portraits bears testimony to his being well-fed. Yet the overall evidence is not one-sided. The householder Āyyāvāl was also remembered for siding with the poorer and middle class, and almost colluding with Robin Hood-like outlaws: One harvest-time, it is said when *thivatti kolaikutam*—"robbers with torches"—threatened Tiruviśanallūr at night, Āyyāvāl told the poor

[28] Biographical traditions about Āyyāvāl are found in R. Krishnamurthy's *The Saints of the Cauvery Delta* (New Delhi: Concept Pub. Co., 1979), which follows Raghavan quite closely. See also V. Raghavan's introduction to *Śahendra Vilasa* (Tiruchi: Kalyan Press for Saraswati Mahal Library, 1952). Biographical traditions about Bodhendra are found in R. Krishnamurthy's *The Saints of the Cauvery Delta* and in Mahadevan's book, *Seminar on Saints*, p. 133.

and middle classes to gather and sing *nāma-bhajanas* on the Kāverī shore. They did so, while the rich busied themselves at home trying to hide their wealth. The bandits robbed the rich, but then approached the saint and the poor people singing by the river, and in the encounter the bandits had a conversion experience. To show their submission, they gave part of the loot they had stolen from the rich to be used at Āyyāvāl's discretion. He accepted it and gave it to Mahaliṅgasvāmī temple for a golden serpent ornament to be made for the deity. This ornament is still on display there.

3. Sadāśiva Brahmendra, or "Sadāśivendra, disciple of gracious Parama Śivendra," as he referred to himself, was born around 1675. His Telugu *smārta* Brahman father, Mokṣam Somasundara was a native of Tiruviśanallūr but he was born farther south in Madurai. He was also called Bhikṣu Guptan, a name meaning "gift of the Lord." He married young, but did not remain in the wedded state. At the feast held in celebration of his wife's attainment of puberty he grew hungry, and then became angry at being kept waiting so long for something to eat. Self-consciousness of this agitation, and disappointment at his own short temper, disturbed him so much he came to the conclusion that only a renunciate's life would be one of peace. He left home and studied first with Āyyāvāl, then with the Śaṅkarācārya of the Kāmakoṭi Pīṭha in Kumbakoṇam, who initiated him into the *sannyāsin*'s life. During his years of wandering he composed songs to Śiva, Rāma, and Krishna and wrote *advaita*-themed verses. An *avadhūta* ("discarder of worldly attachments") Sadāśiva Brahmendra was a renunciate without possessions—even foregoing ownership of clothes to cover his frame. Brahmendra has more "signs of the transcendent" clustered in his life story than any of the other *Nāmasiddhānta* leaders. That is, more episodes and symbolic images pointing to belief in experiences of a reality beyond the conventions and limited surfaces of this world are found associated with his life and works. He is thought of as enjoying transcendent consciousness—*sat-cit-ānanda*—as an experience more real to him than his physical life in the material world.[29]

Sadāśiva Brahmendra's vow of silence is a sign of awareness which is beyond language and discursive thought. The acts which conventional people would deem "overreactions" to worldly incidents, were spiritual

[29] V. Raghavan, "Sadāśiva Brahman," in *Seminar on Saints*, ed. T.M.P. Mahadevan (Madras: Ganesh, 1960). V. Raghavan, "Sadāśiva, Brahmendra," *The Hindu*, Feb. 18,1970. "Śrī Sadāśiva Brahmendra's *Ātmavidyavilāsa*," *Vedānta Keśari*, Dec. 1950, pp. 301-304. Shuddhananda Bharati, *Sadāśiva Brahman* (*The Silent Sage*) (Madras: Shuddhananda Library, [n.d.]).

occasions which pushed Brahmendra into the realm of the transcendent. Criticized by his guru for displaying clever debating skills to villagers, he took a vow never to speak again. His customary *nakedness*, which may have resulted from someone casually mentioning that possessions were a bar to release, represents a return to the primal simplicity which exists before and beyond ordinary social convention. Pictured in clothesless silhouette, Brahmendra is popularly called "the ghost" or "the shadow," and is remembered for his *avadhūta* childlike purity. He is described as sitting in *samādhi* for weeks at a time, so that a shifting riverbed covered him with sand in the natural course of its changes. The image of obliviousness to time and the elements of nature also indicates otherworldly experiences: Sadāśiva Brahmendra seemed so absorbed in *that*—the transcendent realm, that he lost all sense of *this*, the world we live in.

Sadāśiva Brahmendra blessed king Śarabhojī I (also known as "Serfoji"), who reigned in Tāñjavūr from 1712 to 1729, with the gift of a book on *Vedānta* which he had written, and this auspicious act of benediction is thought to have enabled the king to have the children he had long desired. Of course, from the king's view Sadāśiva Brahmendra was an aid in getting ordinary worldly desires satisfied—but his power was respected because it was extraordinary—it seemed to come from contact with a realm *beyond ordinary material control.* Vijaya Raghunātha Tondaiman learned the meaning of the *Dakṣiṇamūrti mantra* when Sadāśiva Brahmendra wrote it on the sand. The ruler kept the sand in a gold casket and venerated it as a sacred keepsake of the lesson; it is still kept in the Pudukoṭṭai palace today.

Brahmendra is remembered for showing a lack of concern for social status, political power, and other matters pertaining to this world. For example, it is said he fearlessly or absentmindedly entered the court of Chanda Sahib, Muslim Nawāb (or governor) of Arcot. The Nawāb interpreted the stranger's bold intrusion into these private precincts as a threat to his harem's safety, and attacked the intruding saint with a sword. Brahmendra is recalled in the tales about him as exhibiting detachment from both pain and physical comfort. When the Nawāb slashed Brahmendra's arm off, the naked saint calmly, almost absent-mindedly, re-attached it and went on as if he was used to such things happening. It is a story somewhat like the New Testament story in which Jesus restores the High Priest's servant's ear which Peter cut off (John 18.10, Luke 22.50-1). Brahmendra's life is depicted with characterizations of mysterious power obtained from beyond the ordinary man's realm. It is said that once he temporarily paralyzed some harvest workers who were about to attack him on a threshing floor. They had feared he was a bandit and so they struck out against him, only to find themselves immobilized. Later, after others begged the saint to break the spell, he released the human statues from their rigid stances.

Mistaken identity figures in the plot of yet another story about Brahmendra. This one is set in a village near Tiruchirāpalli. There, village officials were gathered to collect taxes, and fuel was being heaped up to cook food for them. The naked silent holy man was passing through just then and the arrogant officials mistook him for an outcast laborer because of his nakedness. They stopped him and made him carry a bundle of firewood on his head. When he arrived at the kitchen and dropped the wood, it burst into flames, damaging goods in the kitchen, and scaring everyone present, as well as causing the tax men to regret their presumption. In other stories the saint is pictured as the favorite visitor of little children, whom he often befriended and fed, and entertained with wonders—such as an instant trip to Madurai and back again. There are many signs of people's awe at this imagination-capturing figure, including a story of his reviving a dead bride.

Brahmendra's lyrical works are also marked with suggestions of a transcendent reality which he reached through deep inner realization. In one song, for example,[30] to clear up misconceptions about literalism and geographical interpretations of the Rāma story, he sang that Rāma is always playing in his heart; Rāma's lady is Serenity, and she rejoices in Ayodhyā, the unassailable capital which is *dahara*, the ethereal center of the subtle heart-realm, the "beyond within." Here transcendence is not found in the geography of this world, to which Brahmendra was often oblivious, or beyond the world, out there somewhere, but in the timeless inner realm. His poem *Ātmavidyavilāsa*[31] is full of descriptions of the realized soul absorbed in transcendental consciousness. For example, he

[30] Sadāśiva Brahmendra, song on Ayodhyā. *Compositions of Śrī Sadāśiva Brahmendra* (Madras: Semmangudi Srinivasa Iyer Golden Jubilee Trust, 1979). Also found in *Śivamānāsikapūjā Kīrtanāni Ātmavidyāvilāsa* (Madras: Śrī Kāmakoṭi Kośaṣṭhānena Prakāsitam, 1951), p. 47.

[31] Sadāśiva Brahmendra, *Ātmavidyāvilāsa* in *Śivamānāsikapūjā Kīrtanāni Ātmavidyāvilāsa*, p. 79 and ff. *Avadhūtas* are described in the *Bhāgavata Purāṇa* XI.7-8-9 and the *Avadhūta Upaniṣad.* An English translation of this is found in *Samnyāsa Upaniṣads*, Vol. 104 Adyar Library Series (Madras: Theosophical Society, 1978), pp. 1-7. *Manu Dharmaśāstra* VI.1 describes the life of a renunciate, and *The Crest Jewel of Discrimination* (*Viveka Cūḍāmani*), tr. Prabhavananda and Isherwood (N.Y: New Am. Lib., 1947), attributed to Śaṅkara, describes one continually illumined by consciousness of *Brahman*: "unattached . . . he may wear costly clothing or none. . . . He may seem like a madman, or like a child, or sometimes like an unclean spirit. Thus, he wanders the earth" (pp. 96, 111).

describes the ideal life as follows: "The sage wanders, desires crushed, knowing the universe is unsubstantial" and that it has come into existence from *māyā*, the clouding illusion of the mind (v. 12). The sage "sports like a child"; he has plunged into "the Ocean of pure Bliss" and is "delighted with the diverse actions of men, without any feeling of 'you' or 'I'" (v. 14). Wandering in jungle outskirts he is like a deaf, blind idiot, karma-less and delighting in the Self (v. 15). Immersed in bliss, "he remains in another world, as it were," and depending on his mood he thinks, sings, or dances (v. 21). Abandoning the dry "desert region" of the worthless world, the sage is a "good swan" who plays freely in the serene lake which is absolute bliss (v. 30). He meditates on riverbanks, withdrawn from names (v. 34).

More than any of the other great *Nāmasiddhānta* saints, Sadāśiva Brahmendra is pictured as reveling in a realm of awareness where names and forms are not taken seriously, and are left behind. He further depicts the life he lived in this manner: With the humor of poverty, bare existence is sufficient wealth to the desireless sage. The cupped palm of his hand is his begging bowl; under a tree he finds his resting place; he wears the "jewel" of non-attachment; the riverbank bush is his home, his bed is the sand (v. 36). "Having dissolved the entire world" under the power of the eternal, he puts in his mouth through *prārabdha karma* (reaping karmic results from actions before his realization experience) the food that comes his way (v. 40). The yogi does not unduly regard nor does he disregard anything (v. 41). He remains in a state of spiritual plenitude like an unflickering lamp, rid of conventional śāstraic injunctions and free from obligatory acts (v. 42). To him the universe is a grass-blade. His body is smeared with mud and decked with straw. He "enjoys secret Bliss in regions beyond death and old age" (v. 43). Not seeing, speaking, hearing, he is steady in bliss like a still log (v. 44). He wanders like a fool, unnoticed, seeing only perfection everywhere (v. 45). He rejects nothing as bad, accepts nothing as good (v. 50). He is unconcerned with past, future, and with what is in front of him; he is bliss (v. 51). The ascetic roams beyond the senses (v. 52). Independent of all, "mind lost in That which is beyond the entire universe of *Līlā*," divine play (v. 55), he becomes absolute *Brahman* (v. 58), the One Truth, the Ultimate Shore, *Tat*, shining unperceived by the senses (v. 62). If these and similar pointers toward transcendence do not indicate the values of being beyond the world, nothing does. Yet the sage plays a part in this world. People look up to him, find inspiration and guidance from his spiritual presence.

It is no wonder that the more Sadāśiva Brahmendra approximated his ideal, the more the folk memory immortalized him with such mysterious titles as "the shadow" and "the ghost," and pictured him simply as the empty silhouette of a naked man's form. Plainly, people remembered him as extraordinary. Such charisma also made people prize his catchy songs, which are still very popular in South India today, thanks to such seminal Karṇāṭaka musicians as Semmangudi Srinivasa Iyer, himself a *smārta* Brahman, and to others as well, including housewives and intellectuals, businessmen and professional Indians living outside India.

4. Nārāyaṇa Tīrtha, another Telugu *smārta* Brahman, is remembered in the *bhajana sampradāya* of South India—the intersectarian multilingual tradition which worships via codified *bhakti* songs from a variety of Indian languages representing different *bhakti* composers. The *bhajana sampradāya* which grew out of the *Nāmasiddhānta* movement was organized in group singing form by Sadgurusvāmī, the last of the five leaders to appear chronologically, as we shall see. Nārāyaṇa Tīrtha was born in the 17th century in Guntur, Andhra Pradesh, and died in 1735 or 1745. Nārāyaṇa Tīrtha is known especially for his Sanskrit lyrical drama *Krishnalīlā Taraṅginī* ("Waves of the Sports of Krishna"). He was an advaitin *sannyāsin*, like Brahmendra, who was his senior, and like Upaniṣad Brahmayogi, the guru and founder of a Kāñcīpuram *maṭh* who came later.

According to traditional stories,[32] Nārāyaṇa Tīrtha entered the *gṛihastha* or householder stage of life, and the first sign in his biography concerning the extraordinary is related to the manner in which he left the householder stage of life. Once, swimming across the Krishna river in Andhra Pradesh to be with his wife, Nārāyaṇa found that the current became so violent it threatened to drown him. He heard a *voice from beyond*, it is said, telling him to take the vow of *sannyāsa* immediately.

So, in panic, he discarded his sacred thread, pulled out a token hair (since he could not shave), and hurried through the necessary mantras which are recited by those taking vows of renunciation. But, much to his dismay, he survived the turbulent waters. He was now in the uncomfortable state of being a married *sannyāsin*, a renunciate with a wife. Being both, he could be neither. The *sannyāsin*'s role is one of asceticism, detachment from conventional roles and activities. The *sannyāsin*'s life is associated with the extraordinary—it is a life devoted to seeking *mokṣa*, beyond worldly conventions such as societal roles, responsibilities, parenthood, etc. The *sannyāsin* must be possessionless, dependent on the charity of others whose lives he passes through momentarily as he wanders. Nārāyaṇa Tīrtha longed for that life, but had tied the marriage bonds. What to do

[32] Nārāyaṇa Tīrtha, *Krishnalīlātaraṅgiṇī*, Telugu script version (Madras: Vavila, 1967).

in this state of confusion? Finally Nārāyaṇa Tīrtha's wife and her family generously released him from family obligations, so he could follow the new life he seemed destined to live. (Like Sadāśiva Brahmendra's wife, Tīrtha's wife was a person displaced by her husband's transformation, and her life does not seem to have been considered especially important, next to his. His wife got out of his way so he could fulfill his spiritual destiny.)

A second sign of the transforming influx of grace from beyond, or spiritual destiny becoming manifest, is found in the story of Tīrtha's stomach-ache. He was suffering from chronic intestinal pain in the village of Nadukkāverī, and he prayed for a cure. In a dream *a voice told him* to follow an animal which would appear to him when he awoke. If followed, it would lead the seeker to a place where he would be free of his ratcheting pain. A boar (*varaha*) appeared next day and ran along the banks of the Kodamurutti river, a branch of the Kāverī, for three miles, into Varahūr village (also known as Bhūpatirājapuram) with Tīrtha following. The boar disappeared into the temple of Veṅkaṭeśvara there. Nārāyaṇa Tīrtha believed he had been led by Viṣṇu's boar incarnation, through whose intervention he had been saved from a torturous affliction. The sign from beyond the human condition had come in the inspiring dream, in the form of a wild animal and the guiding voice, and in discovering a village with that animal's namesake, which would become his home. Through surrender to God's will (*prapatti*) his future was made known to him and peace was secured.

In Varahūr village, Nārāyaṇa Tīrtha established a *bhajana sampradāya*, composing many songs and teaching them to others. His disciples sang and danced the Krishna play he was inspired to write. Raghavan writes that Nārāyaṇa Tīrtha "augmented the *bhāgavata* (devotional) tradition in Tāñjāvūr with *bhajana* songs promoting *bhakti* through arts and discourse." In the *Krishnalīlā Taraṅgiṇī*, elegant Sanskrit lyrics express Vedāntic ideas as well as the ever-charming Krishna and *gopī* stories of love. In the first *taraṅga*, Nārāyaṇa Tīrtha encourages listeners to bathe in the supreme *prayāg* or confluence of the three great rivers of divine Names: the Name Rāma being the Ganges, the Name Krishna being the Yamunā, and the name Govinda being the Sarasvatī river. The inner processes of *bhakti* are said to give the same merit as the outer actions of ritual, and Nārāyaṇa Tīrtha, with verve and imagination cultivated these among the people of the Kāverī delta.[33]

[33] V. Raghavan, "Tīrtha Nārāyaṇa," *The Hindu*, Jan. 4, 1970. R. Krishnamurthy, *The Saints of the Cauvery Delta*, pp. 63-67. Saints Narasimha Mehta and Jñāneśvara

Promoting *bhakti* in popular forms (which are still being celebrated), Nārāyaṇa Tīrtha was later thought of as a reincarnation of Jayadeva, the 12th century author of Sanskrit love songs about Krishna. Yet Hindus never forgot Nārāyaṇa Tīrtha as the afflicted one transformed by unusual experiences. It would be speculation or overdetermination to suggest that the original pain of stomach ache was caused by historical famine or widespread food problems of the time, but symbolically the episode could stand for the problems and traumatic memories of many—a time of uncertainty and unease resolved by providential guidance. Again, the story tells of a turning point, a hopeful new start—survival, as well as inspired creative efflorescence.

5. Sadgurusvāmī was born in Tiruviśanallūr in 1776. At the start of the *bhajana sampradāya* or devotional song program performed by groups in many parts of Tamil Nadu, the singers recite verses on Bodhendra, Āyyāvāl, Nārāyaṇa Tīrtha, and Sadgurusvāmī. V. Raghavan calls these "the four *ācāryas*" or masters of this tradition which has preserved in recent centuries both the religious discipline of *bhakti* and the fine art of music in Tamil Nadu. Sadgurusvāmī believed that the Name alone would not suffice—*bhakti* song was also part of the full devotional regimen needed to provide salvation for Hindus in the present age, and so he organized and codified a program of singing to be followed, with the songs organized in a definite sequence.

An early sign of the transcendent in stories of Sadgurusvāmī's life is seen in the effect which the miraculous power of the Name of Rāma had upon him. As an infant and toddler it is said that he was unable to speak. Then, while still a child, he heard his guru whisper the name "Rāma" in his ear, and from then on he was able to speak. The extraordinary power of the Name allowed him to take part in the otherwise closed world of human language. It is a way of saying that he only spoke because he had been blessed by means of the Name.

In another episode from Sadgurusvāmī's life story, when Bodhendra's *samādhi* memorial was once washed away by river floods, Sadgurusvāmī went to the riverbank and sought a sign whereby he could locate the obliterated memorial. He attentively walked and listened until he could hear the still-vibrating echo of the transcendent name of Rāma. Thus he located the original site of his hero's resting place so it could be built anew. The story has symbolic meaning: Sadgurusvāmī is pictured as re-discoverer, renewer, rebuilder of an old faith.

used similar imagery in earlier centuries.

There are fewer miracles associated with Sadgurusvāmī, who appears as a more practical-minded organizer than some other leaders—he is much more of an institution builder than Sadāśiva Brahmendra, for example. If Brahmendra stands for spontaneity, Sadgurusvāmī stands for routine. He gave initiation in the Name to the weak Marāṭha King Sarabhojī II (also known as Serfoji), who was a puppet of the British East India Company, and received a Kerala king's help in building Bodhendra's memorial, as the architecture of the structure testifies. He also founded a "lay maṭh" and codified the *bhajanas* into a set program that included songs in various languages dedicated to various divine forms. He regularized practices and instituted the six rules to be followed in the tradition.[34] Perhaps Weber's "routinization of charisma" is a concept useful in understanding his function. That is, with his influence the institutional form of *Nāmasiddhānta* took on a shape closer to that of sects with their own set forms of community worship—yet it is important to remember that it also remains non-sectarian, very inclusive, in terms of intersectarian membership and multilingual expression in songs sung to various forms of the divine.

Sadgurusvāmī is said to have repeated his *Rāma mantra* 108,000 times a day. He was married, yet lived by *uñchavṛitti* or mendicancy, alms-gathering, receiving rice from supporters in the community, as Tyāgarāja, his contemporary, also did. This means of livelihood is intended to ensure humility, poverty, and dependence on the community of devotees rather than on the king. Though a householder, Sadgurusvāmī appears to be associated with a transcendence of worldly emotional attachments—he was not overcome by grief at his wife's death, according to his biographies. Sadgurusvāmī died in 1817, at the age of forty-one, thirty years before Tyāgarāja's death.

Reflections on *Nāmasiddhānta* Lives and Historical Context

Taken together as a cluster or "family resemblance" group, the *Nāmasiddhānta* leaders' life stories reflect faith in and religious experiences of several kinds of transcendence. Significant motifs recur. For example, varied indications of faith in the transcendent power of the Name, as would be expected; the river as a transformative presence in these saints' lives is

[34] The rules or practices are as follows: The devotee (*bhāgavata*) should remember to repeat the Name, ritually awaken and worship the Lord each day, live by alms, perform *pūjā*, sing the praise of God with others, and ritually put the Lord to sleep each night.

also noteworthy. Like Śaṅkara, two of these Brahmans became *sannyāsins* when they came into contact with the perilous waters. Appearances of divine beings—Krishna, the Goddess, the boar incarnation of Viṣṇu, Śiva disguised as a priest, etc.—are common episodes. For Kāverī delta hearers, stories told by *bhāgavatars* (performers of musical discourse on *bhakti* themes), such as the story of Bodhendra learning of the Name, and of Āyyāvāl witnessing the Goddess Gaṅgā in his own backyard, arouse faith and wonder in listeners. These make a higher reality present to the imagination of the hearers, inviting participation through faith. Such stories encourage practices offering hope that the *sādhaka* (aspirant) who likewise takes the Name as a path will reach similar ends.

In the gestalt of the saints' lives taken altogether, there is a symmetry or balancing effect. Sadāśiva Brahmendra has an experience with his guru which shuts his mouth for good; Sadgurusvāmī has a guru experience which opens his mouth to speak for the first time. Sadāśiva Brahmendra seems beyond all dependence: silent, bare, innocent, wise, and blissfully oblivious; Nārāyaṇa Tīrtha, at the mercy of a painful existence, relies on self-effacing trust in non-human intervention—complete surrender.

As a group these men were not exclusively *sannyāsins* or householders, but had involvement in both realms. They were *siddha*-like yogis, sometimes lost in *samādhi* and found by others, inspirers through contagious song, and yet they were able to function as builders of spiritual communities in a time of recovery. Thus, these saints combine dynamic contrasts. There are interrelations within the group—"members" were friends (Āyyāvāl and Bodhendra), helpers in a mutual enterprise (Bodhendra and Sadgurusvāmī), re-constructors supporting each others' works. Their interdependence, and the historical time in which they lived, both contribute to their identities, and dictate certain standards. Perhaps all saints fulfill an historical function, responding to some gripping needs of the time, appealing to contemporaries with archetype-developing lifeways. In the *bhajana sampradāya* movement, into which *Nāmasiddhānta* seems to have evolved, the saints' names and works are celebrated in the program of devotional songs. Their works live on, activating further religious activity, and in a sense, their lives still "work," promoting faith in the Name.

It was V. Raghavan, a *smārta* Brahman himself, who made a strong case for this cluster of unique individuals with similar backgrounds and concerns and divergent personalities, as a group of saints. Yet Raghavan was an intellectual spokesman who could articulate the leaders' importance only because the common people of the delta region already had accepted their teachings and kept popular the oral tradition of their lives, and because the *bhajana sampradāya* program maintained this self-composed sense of tradition, continuing to sing time-honored songs of name-reciters of the past. Unless they are embraced by the people who carry on the traditions, "saints" (whether Brahman or not) are the custodians of nothing vital. The ritual telling of their leaders' lives enacts a faith in the transcendent. Interactions between the folk and the intellectual guardians of tradition are dramatically illustrated by the process of the development of the life story of Tyāgarāja, who is said by V. Raghavan and others to be the culmination of the *Nāmasiddhānta* tradition.[35] This musician-saint's life, as told by the people of the Kāverī delta and in works of the Tamil Harikathā performers, became associated with motifs found in the lives of earlier *Nāmasiddhānta* and pan-Indian singer-saints.

The *smārta*-hood of the leaders is significant. Some Tamilians, including scholars and members of the tradition say it was "just a coincidence" that all five were *smārta* Brahmans, and insisted that saying and singing the Name is a religious practice which transcends caste and other bounds. Outsiders cannot help but notice, however, that traditionally *smārtas* had an unusual freedom to encourage worship of a variety of names and forms, a freedom which some Hindus now take for granted. Being *smārtas*, the *Nāmasiddhānta* leaders knew Sanskrit and wrote their works in that language, embodying high culture. But like some other *smārtas* they showed with their lives a love of popular and vernacular culture, including messages and melodies singable by all. Modern Hindus often downplay the old designations—of being a member of a *smārta* family, for example.[36] But for historians, there are reasons to point out the contributions of this community.

Smārta Brahmans such as Lakṣmīdhara, the five leaders, Tyāgarāja, and Upaniṣad Brahman (who founded a *maṭh* in Kāñcīpuram, wrote commentaries on 108 *Upaniṣads*, and composed *bhakti* songs) are all somewhat inconvenient in terms of sect categorization. The *smārta* option of choosing a favorite name and form for worship, the concept of images used in worship being non-absolute vehicles to a divine reality which is

[35] See my article, William J. Jackson, "A Life Becomes a Legend: Tyāgarāja as Exemplar," *Journal of the American Academy of Religion*, LX, 4, 1992, winter.

[36] In present-day India it is bad manners to ask someone in public if he is a Brahman, and *smārta* is a term fast becoming unrecognizable to many in the younger generation. Even the older generation of *smārtas* usually have had no particular connection with *smṛiti* texts (J.L. Mehta, personal correspondence, Jabalpur, July 23, 1987; S. Ramaswāmī, personal correspondence, Madras, Feb. 19, 1986; and Savitri Rajan, personal correspondence, Madras, March 9, 1986).

ultimately formless, can be traced to the *Upaniṣads.* In various Hindu traditions for many centuries, the relatively real (with names and forms) is used to attain the divine absolute (nameless and formless). As a thorn is used to remove a thorn, the guru uses *māyā* as an instrument—relatively real names, forms, and methods are used to dissolve worldly *māyā.* Practices propagated by *smārtas,* such as worship of the five focal points of *pañcāyatana pūjā* and the tradition of having a reservoir of various *iṣṭadevatās,* any one of whom may be chosen as a focus for devotion to the divine Name, gave a broad-based encouragement to the updating of pan-Indian Hindu faith, generating for the survival of their lifeway something like "a buffer of diversity that will protect the human being against obsolescence," to use Gregory Bateson's words.[37]

South Indian Hinduism in the time immediately preceding the period of the *Nāmasiddhānta* leaders—during the Vijayanagara era (1350-1600)—was a "faith that had undergone an ordeal." The ordeal was a series of violent Muslim invasions and a period of military occupation during the first part of the 14th century. Earlier heterodox challenges from Buddhists and Jains, as well as Hindu sect differences now seemed to Hindus to be relatively insignificant doctrinal divergences, compared with the conflicts with Muslim foes who invaded with force and put infidels to death. Hence, after personally experiencing this extreme enmity, Hindus developed a more tolerant mood toward the variety of sects within their own homegrown traditions. Vijayanagara rulers encouraged this spirit, and new sects found fertile soil for development. "The birth and evolution of *Smārta*s, the Bhāgavata community, Mādhavas, Viṣṇusvāmīs, Nimbārkas, Vallabhāchāryas, Rādhā-Vallabhis, Svamī Nārāyaṇis, Śrī Vaisṇavas, Sātānis [non-Brahman Vaiṣṇavites who cannot wear the holy thread and who are sometimes non-vegetarians], Menbhaus and Rāmānandis can be traced to this period," Job Thomas states.[38] In my view, members of already long-

[37] Gregory Bateson and Mary Catherine Bateson, *Angels Fear: Towards an Epistemology of the Sacred* (N.Y.: Macmillan, 1987), p. 52. In the 10th century a *smārta* named Bhaskara in his introduction to a *Bhagavad Gītā* commentary seems to carry over social elitism into soteriology—or vice versa. Thus, not all *smārtas* were invariably expansive and progressive in their philosophy toward the lower castes; some were rigidly conservative.

[38] Job Thomas, "Cultural Developments in Tamil Nadu During the Vijayanagara Period," in *Vjayanagara—City and Empire: New Currents of Research,* ed. A.L. Dallapiccola and S.Z. Lallemant (Stuttgart: Steiner Verlag, 1985). Farquhar, Van Buitenen, Pathak and others do not consider the *smārtas* to have originated at this time, but earlier. I agree with them. Perhaps Thomas means a noticeable phase of

existing *smārta* and *bhāgavata* traditions were in a position to know the needs of the time and responded creatively, appealed anew and gained momentum during that stimulating era. North Indian saint Narasī Mehtā's life also shows a progressive and creative *smārta* response in relation to *bhāgavata* enthusiasm.[39]

Nāmasiddhānta was one strand in the pan-Indian scheme of reformulation in early modernity. In the 15th century in North India, the saint Rāmānanda and a variety of others, at the dawn of a new age of popular piety, called for the illiterate, the downtrodden, and untouchables to partake more fully in the community life of religious devotion. Caitanya (1486-1534) taught his disciples that Krishna could become present through devoted voicing of his divine name, and that chanting the Name was a great purifier, helping win grace and release. Likewise, in other regions, Name enthusiasts with "non-sectarian" teachings transcended caste and community barriers. Kabīr, Purandaradās, Tulasidās, Annamācārya, Mīrābāī became voices to sing along with and exemplars to follow. The neat schemes of sects, *jatis*, and *varṇas* were not the final word or reality to these more free-floating agents. These border-crossers and tricksters confronting the rigidities of convention sometimes delighted in bursting barriers, or at least in challenging the ultimacy of caste boundaries with the anomalies of their devotion-centered existence. Whether with a mysterious smile or a brittle break, they eluded some of the old lines of demarcation and broke through crusty barriers which blocked free sharing, opening up the field of religion to all who could feel with heart-felt enthusiasm. *Nāmasiddhānta* leaders, like many of these other *bhaktas*, did not seek to destroy sect affiliations, but wanted to emphasize and promote a harmonious *bhakti* way open to the many through saying and singing holy Names. With an eye to the future and a rejection of short-sighted petty limits, *Nāmasiddhānta* answered exasperating social strictures through embracive expansiveness. The leaders performed a corrective function in the system of Hindu society as a whole, operating within the limits of their own world view. Though they did not achieve perfect impartiality there are signs of a vision of a more inclusive neutrality than is found in some earlier forms of Hinduism, such as availability of the name to all and songs in various languages calling on different holy names.

The impulse of openness, of declaring free access via the Name,

smārta development is traceable to this time.

[39] John S. Hawley, "Morality Beyond Morality in the Lives of Three Hindu Saints," in *Saints and Virtues* (Berkeley: Univ. of California, 1987), pp. 59-63.

seems to be in tune with developments in India which were coming to fruition in the 17th century; it seems more in tune with modern times and hence more viable than a narrow sectarian response. The old traditional tripartite division of society—Brahmans, clean non-Brahmans, unclean non-Brahmans—changed with modernization, developments in politics and economy, and such influences as *niyogis* borrowing from Western lifestyles. The way of the Name offered a stable and simple staple in the midst of complex change and spiritual hunger.

The earlier Kāverī *Nāmasiddhānta* leaders fulfilled the Marāṭha king's wishes to reaffirm and strengthen Hinduism against the Mughals and Europeans, and Āyyāvāl especially depended on the king for his livelihood. But some of the leaders saw the danger of too close a dependence on the king, who himself was soon to become a dependent of the British, and eventually a thing of the past. One sign of this is the fact that the leaders sometimes chose the path of renunciation and *uñchavṛitti*, which bound them to poverty. These saints, like other *bhaktas*, had their own tradition of skepticism, and sang scornful criticism, heckling devotional hypocrites, men of "belly *vairāgya*," and all who made a prosperous career of showing off their *bhakti*. To interpret their lives in purely political terms would leave out much that is significant, because their stance was spiritual, infused with love-inspired faith.

The Telugu *smārtas* of *Nāmasiddhānta* combined practical adaptability with ideals of preservation and creativity. They straddled the *householder-sannyāsin* ideals which still compel many conscientious modern Hindus at least in theory. The founding of a "lay maṭh" is an institutional example of this. Those leaders who were associated with the village of Tiruviśanallūr, near the temple town of Kumbakoṇam, were supported by the king, and felt free to co-operate with the court. They could bless the king with spiritual advice and, in the case of Sadgurusvāmī, seek a king's help in a building project. Those who were renunciates were free to abandon all dependence on the court. The composite portrait is of a group of men for all seasons, thermostats of Hinduism, popularizers of age-old spirituality. Women figure in their life stories. For example Bodhendra accepted a prostitute as a follower despite gossipers, and when she died it was said that her head burst and the people present could hear the name of Rāma resonating—dramatic proof of Bodhendra's rectitude. But no prominent woman saint came to rank among the great leaders. In the times after the singer-saint Tyāgarāja's death, Bangalore Nagaratnāmmāl became an important figure, a saintly promoter of *Nāmasiddhānta*, but no counterpart to Mīrābāī in the North shares the stage with the male leaders.

There is an ancient strand in Indian religious traditions, a sentiment which promotes tolerance for and encouragement of various faiths.

In Aśoka's 12th Rock Edict, for example, it is said that Aśoka wanted to encourage "growth in the qualities essential to religion in men of all faiths."[40] This characteristic strand or inclusive tendency affirms service to and support of religious practices not because they are Buddhist or Hindu, Vaiṣṇava or Śaiva, but because they tend to ennoble human life. In terms of the motivation behind the *Nāmasiddhānta* leaders' work, I see no reason to underestimate this motive, or the motive of sheer enjoyment which the creative participants found in composing devotional poems and songs; neither should we underestimate the genius and will of the Hindu spirit to hold to the sacred at all costs.

The *Nāmasiddhānta* teachers and their life stories demonstrate a spectrum of religious modes—for the harassed and overburdened any calling on the name is beneficial; for the devoted and musically inclined regular singing of enjoyable songs spreads joy and well-being; for the dedicated yogi or specialist, recitation of the Name many millions of times leads to *siddhis*, extraordinary yogic powers. Thus, with undemanding minimalism, enthusiastic celebration, and the promise of high attainments, faith in the Name offered defenses against invading forces and the loss of old Hindu forms. It promised a sense of continuity, a feeling of *communitas* and ultimately, access to *mokṣa*. Beyond the merely "within" of the lone ascetic, or the unsatisfying mundane—the public historical crisis—the Name partakes of transcendent glory, offering a way well-suited to unpredictable times, a flexible way to resolve dichotomies, a way bridging people and the ultimate through simple utterance in song or sigh. The leaders of *Nāmasiddhānta* were saints, charismatic renewers of faith whose lives seemed linked to a reality beyond chaos. Like the mythical Satyavrata, they fostered a way to keep a bond to the primordial sacred despite all else. Like earlier holy men—*riṣis* and yogis—their life stories preserve signs of transcendence.[41] The power of the sacred name is a simple link to the sacred, accessible to many in complicated times of crisis.

William J. Jackson

[40] Eugen Hultzsch, ed. and tr., *The Inscriptions of Asoka*, Vol. I of *Corpus Inscriptionum Indicarum* (Delhi, 1925, reprint 1969), Twelfth Rock Edict.

[41] In 1989, when I was researching the tradition in South India, it seemed that such expounders of the Name as Krishna Premi of Paranūr and Veṅkaṭarāmana Bhagavatar of Tiruvidaimarudūr, continue to keep up the tradition in the Kāverī delta and in Tamil Nadu generally. In the 21st century, as India modernizes, I have not been in touch with the people I met while doing my research, and so, I cannot report on the tradition's current state.

Part I

CULTURAL OVERVIEWS: V. RAGHAVAN'S ESSAYS ON THE NAME IN INDIAN CULTURE

1.

Indian Culture's Creative Revivers: Singer-Saint Integrators[1]

The thoughts and teachings of a culture have a two-fold basis, first, the spoken words and written texts, and the living exemplars who speak and write. In the most ancient stage, the two were represented by the *Vedas* and the seers or *ṛiṣis*. Then came as personal exemplars the avatars, incarnations such as Rāma and Krishna, and then the *ācāryas*, master teachers, such as Śaṅkarācārya, Rāmānujācārya, and Madhvācārya.

At all times, the person of the guru was emphasized, and even when one was literate and capable, the imparting of a mantra, the mystic formula of syllables to be repeated, or the teaching, *upadeśa*, had to be personally done. For when a thing is taken from a book, it is like firewood without a flame, but when the guru imparts it he transmits also a part of his power and grace. After the age of the great *ācāryas*, in the post-classical period, when Sanskrit and the Prākrits (regional languages) derived from Sanskrit were yielding place to Apabhraṃśa (the early medieval vernacular with incorrect grammar and corruptions in language), and the early phases of the modern Indian languages were yet to come into existence, there appeared all over the country a succession of men of divine grace and realization who mediated between the hoary heritage and the future generations, and who translated and interpreted the ancient heritage from the learned levels to the people at large, using for this mission the local languages and the art of music. If not for them the heritage would have been fossilized; they were as great as the original *ṛiṣis* or *ācāryas* for what they did. In the words of Sister Nivedita: "Greatness is but another name for interpretation. . . . Every profound truth waits for the life that shall be all its voice, and when that is found, it comes within the reach of multitudes to whom it would have remained inaccessible."[2] These saint-singers in the Indian languages had to appear to make the heritage live again, gaining in the process fresh dimensions and widening participation.

[1] From V. Raghavan, *The Great Integrators: The Singer Saints of India* (New Delhi: Pub. Div., Ministry of Information, Govt. of India, 1966, 1969, 1976, 1979), pp. 4-19.

[2] Margaret E. Noble (Sister Nivedita), *Kali, the Mother* (Mayavati [Almore]: Advaita Ashrama, 1950), p. 43.

Overview of *Bhakti* Scholars' and Saints' Emergence

The learned and popular traditions have had a parallel development from remote times, alternately blossoming forth and influencing each other. If the *Vedas* represented the former, the *Itihāsa* and *Purāṇas*, stories of the past and legends, stood for the latter. Within the classical tradition itself *Kāvya* (poetry) and *Śāstra* (scriptures and lawbooks) represented the former while drama and the arts addressed themselves to the people at large. The rise of temples and depiction of myths and legends in sculpture were a further attempt to take the masses into the sweep of this culture. Classifying the periods of Indian culture Śrī Aurobindo describes this post-classical period as "a lifting up of the whole lower life and the impressing upon it of the values of the spirit. This was the sense of the *purāṇic* and *tāntric* systems and the religions of *bhakti*."[3]

Popular religious movements and forms of worship prevalent or growing in various parts of the country were taken up, and they were given a proper setting and incorporated into the *Purāṇas*. As successors of the ancient *āśramas* of the *ṛiṣis*, *maṭhs* and cave-retreats associated with religious teachers, particularly the Śaiva saints, appeared in historical times. Śaṅkara's activities also led to the formation of orders of monks who moved about and ministered to the spiritual needs of the people. At this time the classical language had given rise to the Prākrits and their literatures and these in turn had ushered in the Apabhramśa dialects (derived from classical Sanskrit) in which literatures had begun to bloom. From earliest times, there was a floating popular didactic poetry, a mass of wise sayings, *subhāṣitas*, in simple Sanskrit, employing similes and other devices enabling easy memorization by the people. Part of this store of *subhāṣitas* went into Buddhism, part into Jainism, and the rest continued to be in the main stream of Sanskrit literature.

All these popular aspects of Sanskrit literature have to be borne in mind while tracing the origin and growth of the saints and their songs in the spoken languages of India. In Jainism, there was the mystic tradition represented by Yogīdu, author of the *Paramārtha Prakāśa*, and certain others, who, unlike the scholastic Jain dialecticians, spoke a universal language and freely referred to the Supreme Power in cosmopolitan terms such as Jina, Buddha, Brahmā, Haṃsa, Śiva, and Viṣṇu, and to the state of salvation as *mukti* and unity, without any sectarian differences. The Yoga

[3] Śri Aurobindo Ghose, *Renaissance in India* (Chandernagore: Prabartak Publishing House, 1920), p. 21.

which cut across the different contending schools and which was, as a *sādhana* or spiritual discipline, cherished by all of them was a great solvent of the differences. Along with yoga, *tāntra* was also resorted to by Jainism and Buddhism, as much as by Hinduism. While in the West of India the Jain mystics were producing this kind of eclectic literature, in the East the Buddhist *siddhas* of the *Sahāja* movement were composing in symbolic language (*Sandhā-bhaṣha*) philosophical songs called *Caryā-gītas.* As *padas* these *Caryā-gītas* were all set to music, and in a way, may be considered to have paved the way for the emergence of the Hindu saints and their songs in the Indian languages. From the allusions in the songs of the saints, and from records about some of them, we are led to relate the rise of these saints in the North to the *nāth* movement. One notable figure who popularized yoga was Gorakhnātha who stands at the threshold of the age of the popular saints. The whole of North India up to Nepal and the lower Himalayan areas were pervaded by Gorakhnātha and his teaching on Hathayoga and the esoteric practice of *nāda* or *śabda*—the spirituality of mystical vibrations in mantra and music. To all of these teachings we find references in the songs of the later North Indian saints, Kabīr, Nānak and others. Jñāneśvara, the pioneer in Mahārāṣṭra, is said to have belonged to the *nāth sampradāya.*

The Rich Traditions of Tamil Saints

In the South, the movement started with Pallava times when South India was a stronghold of Buddhism and Jainism. It was the effort to reclaim the country for the Vedic, Purāṇic, and devotional path that threw up the Śaiva and Vaiṣṇava saints in Tamil. This movement began in the 6th century and gathered momentum in the next few centuries by which time the whole of the South had been completely swept back into the older faith. This was a two-fold renaissance: one adopting the medium of Sanskrit, the other that of Tamil. The two streams of the new activity should be mentioned as the Sanskrit works composed at the time became masterpieces of the greatest import and played an unprecedented part in influencing the North and effecting its spiritual and devotional reclamation. The *Bhāgavata Purāṇa,* which was the equivalent of the Bible to the later schools of *bhakti* in the North, was a product of this momentous creative period in South India.

Śaṅkara towered above all the geniuses of these times in the South. The force of his personality and the spectacular success of his mission can be gauged by the reference made by another South Indian Śaiva saint, Māṇikkavāchakar, to Śaṅkara's philosophy as "raging in the country like a tempest."[4] After Śaṅkara, South India produced Rāmānuja, and it was a follower of the devotional school of *Vedānta*, Rāmānanda, who was responsible for the *bhakti* movements of the North, Kabīr, Tulasi, and others owing allegiance to him. Rāmānuja's work coalesced with the earlier work of the Tamil hymns of the Vaiṣṇava saints called *ālvārs* who had built up the movement of devotion to Viṣṇu. The *ālvārs* are ten in number counted also as twelve with the addition of two more, including the woman known as "the Lord's bride," Āṇḍāl. These came from different parts of the Tamil region including the Chera kingdom. They flourished between A.D. 700 and 900. Five of them may be said to be more important than the rest—Poihai, Pey, Bhūtam, Nammālvār, and Periyālvār. The songs of the twelve *ālvārs* are together called "The Divine Composition" (*Divyaprabandham*), as also "Four Thousand" (*Nālāyiram*) from the number of verses. Twenty-four separate compositions are included in the four parts in which the collection is arranged and a whole fourth of it is the composition of Nammālvār, called *Tiruvāimozhi*, meaning "sacred utterance" or the *Veda* (in Tamil). All these were collected and arranged by Nāthamuni from whom the Sanskrit tradition of Śrīvaiṣṇavism starts. The poems in the collection are all set to different *rāgas* or melodies.

The Śaiva saints, *nāyanārs*, are sixty-three in number and their period too ranges from 700 to 900 A.D. They were first listed by one of them, Sundaramūrti, and their detailed biography was written by the Chola minister Śekkizhār. The greatest of these are Appar, Sambandhar, and Sundarar, referred to as "the trinity" (*Mūvar*). With Māṇikkavāchakar, author of the collection *Tiruvāchakam*, they form the four Śaiva *samaya gurus*. Seven are the greatest composers of the Śaiva hymns called *Devāra*, meaning "adoration of the Lord," and of them the most prolific were the trinity. Appar sang 49,000 verses of which 3,110 are extant, Sambandhar 16,000 of which 3,840 are available, and Sundarar 38,000 of which only 1,000 have survived. As in the case of the Vaiṣṇa hymns, the Śaivite ones, too, had to be salvaged and organized; this was done by Nambi Andar Nambi, at the instance of Rājarāja Chola I in the 10th century A.D. Including the hymns of the first three *nāyanārs* and the poems of Māṇikkavāchakar, the entire Śaiva religious poetry as then available was arranged in twelve books, the last one being Śekkizhār's biography of the saints. These books included the hymns of seven later saints too. (Recently a set of eleven hitherto unknown *Devāram* hymns has been discovered in a 12th century temple inscription.[5])

[4] IV. *Porri-t-tiru-ahaval*, II. 54-55.

[5] *Annual Report of Epigraphy* (Madras, 1918), p. 149.

The hymns of the *Devāram* are not only rich in their devotional fervor and religious and philosophical ideas, but they were all composed as music, set in different *rāgas*, and as such form the earliest corpus of South Indian music compositions. Endowments came to be made very early for their regular recital in temples with flute, string, and drums accompaniments—from the time of Pallava Nandvarman III (844-66 A.D.). Even to this day the moving strains of the *Devāram* songs are to be heard in the temples and in concert halls; conferences are held and research is being done on their *rāgas* known as *pan*. In Sambandhar's songs alone a hundred rhythmic varieties are to be found. The three peaks of South Indian spiritual revival, Śaṅkara (32 years), Sambandhar (16 years), and Sundarar (18 years), all passed away very young, after galvanizing the people. The poetry and music of *Devāram* and *Divyaprabandham* are closely linked to South Indian temples, the building of which was taken up on a large scale by the Pallava rulers and on a larger scale by the Cholas later. The temples proved to be the physical citadels of devotion and the arts also were sources of inspiration to other saints and their devotional outpourings. The service that the *nāyanārs* and *ālvārs* rendered cannot be estimated merely by their life-work or their hymns; for the spirit they generated gathered force through the centuries. New galaxies of saints came into being and new geniuses arose to add further impetus.

The Tamil *siddhas*, of whom little is known outside Tamil Nadu, must be mentioned. The Tamil *siddha* tradition is seen in medicine, alchemy, and religion. Among the religious *siddhas*, eighteen in number, there were Tirumūlar, the vedāntin author of the *Tirumantra*, and counted also among *nāyanārs*, Paṭṭinattār, known too for his saintly life and compositions, Śivavākyar, the largest composer in this group and considered to be identical, in his earlier life, with the Vaiṣṇava saint, *ālvār* Tirumazhiśai, and a group of mystics who have fanciful names and sobriquets based on the characteristic features of their songs, e.g., "the Snake-Charmer *siddha*" whose songs are couched as addresses to the dancing snake. The *siddhas* adopt symbolic language. It is interesting to note that in the South Indian *siddha* tradition there was one Bhoga who lived in Kāñcīpuram talking a strange language according to saint Appar; Bhoga is considered to have been a Chinese.

The 15th century produced the most remarkable personality—Aruṇagirināthar, whose heart, bursting with devotion to Kumāra, broke out into 16,000 songs on Him as enshrined in 225 temples in Tamil Nadu and Śrī Laṅka, which shrines the saint-singer visited. His songs are set to a marvelous variety of rhythmic patterns in which South Indian musicians, adept in *laya*, are continuously exercising their imagination and rhythmic skill. Aruṇagiri handled also a unique language which freely passed from Tamil to Sanskrit and without the mechanical appearance of the well-known mixed bi-lingual diction in Tamil and Malayalam called *maṇi-pravāla*.

The passage of time did not mean that the ages of the great saints were over in South India. The 17th century produced Tāyumanāvar, belonging to a family of officials of the Nāyak Court in Madurai; this saint was a prolific composer and he has left a legacy of songs of vedāntin-cum-Śaivite flavor which are full of his Sanskrit and Tamil erudition. The latest was Rāmāliṅgasvāmī, a contemporary of Rāmakrishna Paramahaṁsa. Born in 1823 near Chidambaram, he disappeared in 1874; but many devotees and admirers believe that he will appear again. His annual festival is celebrated. He was a Pillai by birth but drew followers and admirers from all classes. At Vadalūr near Chidambaram, he built a temple with only a lamp as symbolic of the Great Light of Divine Grace (*arut-perum-jyoti*) and poured forth a large volume of songs on Divine Grace (*arutpā*). He desired to establish a Brotherhood of Man and his school is called *Śuddha samarasa mārga*, the pure path of harmony.

This sustained spiritual and religious fervor in South India which led to the long and continuous flowering of saintliness, devotion, hymns and songs in the Tamil region may be studied against an all-India background. Its North Indian contacts were many. The appellations *nāyanār* and *ālvār* mean the same thing as *nātha*, and the *siddha* is an all-India phenomenon. There were affiliations between South Indian Śaivism and Vaiṣṇavism and the forms of these two sects as practiced in Kashmir and other parts of the North. Saints and scholars like Tirumular and Nathamuni were from the North. Aruṇagirinātha, author of the *Tiruppughazh* on Kumāra, belonged to a Bengali family from Varendra and settled in the days of the Vijayanagara empire at Mulluṇḍrum near Aruṇāchala.

The Creative Saints of Karṇātaka

The new impulse spread from Tamil Nadu to adjacent Karṇātaka, where comparable to the *nāyanārs* and *ālvārs*, two groups of saints arose, the Vīraśaivas or Liṅgāyats, and Haridāsas. The former movement began in the 12th century with Basava the Brahman Minister of the Kalachuri King Bijjala of Kalyāna, or as it is held by some, with Ekāntada Rāmāyya. Besides Basava, other noteworthy figures in this tradition are Allama Prabhu and the "God's bride" in this school, Akkā Mahādevī; but from sayings left by the saints of this school we come to know of over two hundred of them, men and women. That this was a popular movement which transcended all caste-distinctions among its votaries is borne out by the variety of avocations from which the saints were drawn: from the Brahman Minister and the intellectual Allam to cobbler, washerman, cultivator, oil-monger, watchman, weaver of mats, etc. The literature of this school is of special significance, as it took the form of aphoristic prose, called *vacana.* These *vacanas* show that Vīraśaivism was a call to get over all formalism, ritual, and castes and to vow for oneself the higher life of virtues. The name Vīraśaiva underlines their being worshippers of Śiva; their other name, Liṅgāyata refers to their wearing always on their body a replica of the Śivaliṅga. The organization includes monasteries, gurus, and reference of the five founders, Ekorāma, Paṇḍitārādhya, Revaṇa, Marula, and Viśvāradhya. Wandering Vīraśaiva mendicants, the *jaṅgamas*, chanted the *vacanas* in simple tunes. (The musical affiliation of the *vacanas* may be seen in these lyrics from a *vacana* of Basava: "My Lord Kūḍala Saṅgama! make my body the *daṇḍi* of the *vīṇā*, my head the sound-box, and my nerves the strings, and play the thirty-two *rāgas* on me.")

The Karṇāṭaka movement based on Viṣṇu-devotion, that of the Haridāsas, became widely known in non-Kanarese areas also, chiefly through its association with music. The greatest of the devotional lyric or *pada*-singers of this school, Purandaradāsa (1480-1564), is revered as the founder of modern Karṇāṭaka music. The Haridāsas became affiliated to the *dvaita* or dualist school of Madhvācārya, and thus, too, the songs of the Haridāsas spread in other areas. Purandara is believed to have composed an incredible number of simple devotional songs known as *padas*— 475,000. What has survived is itself large in number and distinguished by a variety of forms of musical composition. His *padas*, the model and the source of inspiration for Tyāgarāja, are remarkable for their devotion, moral teachings, popular sayings, wit and satire, and philosophical truths. There were other *dāsas* ("servants of the Lord") in this group, the *Dāsakuṭa*, who composed *padas*: Kanaka, Vijaya, Jagannāttha, and Gopāla. That Kanakadāsa was a shepherd and that this teacher was the pontiff Vyāsarāya shows that the Haridāsa movement, too, was a popular one. The *dāsas* also popularized in South India the practice of holy mendicancy, going about with the *tambura* on the shoulders, bells on feet, the *chipals* (jingling percussion clappers) for rhythm in hand, singing the *padas* and receiving handfuls of rice (*uñcha-vṛitti*) from willing house-holders. Similarly, in the Western world William James quotes an Italian mystic who says: "The true monk takes nothing with him but his lyre."[6]

[6] W. James, *The Varieties of Religious Experience* (New York: Random House, 1902), pp. 266-7.

Mahārāṣṭran and Gujarati Singer Saints

The sweep of the *bhakti* movement over Mahārāṣṭra and the areas of old Rajasthāni, Hindi, Bengali, etc., has been made known by scholars by systematic historical accounts, monographs, and translations into English. The activities of the Mahārāṣṭra saints, who number about fifty, cover a period of five hundred years. The saints of this region, too, are drawn from the highest intellectual classes as well as the "lower" classes including outcastes, and some women and Muslims too. Jñāneśvara, the pioneer and the foremost among these, who wrote his gloss on the *Bhagavad Gītā* in 1290 A.D., is advaitic. The work of Bopadeva on the elucidation and popularization of the *Bhāgavata Purāṇa* under the Yādavas of Devagiri, under whom Jñāneśvara too flourished, gave to this part of the country devotion to Krishna oriented to *advaita*; Jñāneśvara adopted this approach. The most important of the Mahārāṣṭra saints are, besides Jñānadeva, Nāmdeva (1269-1344), a tailor, Tukārām (1608-49), a shopkeeper, and Samārtha Rāmdās (1608-81) author of *Dāsabodha*, and Śivājī's guru, who popularized devotion to Rāma in Mahārāṣṭra. There are many edifying and miraculous stories related in the *Bhaktamālā* of Mahīpati about these saints, each of which has its own significance, exemplifying as it does a truth or a tenet of the doctrine of devotion or of knowledge. There are some parallelisms in the lives of the saints of the different regions, e.g., Ekanāth feeding a hungry *mahar* (menial laborer) at his house and Veṅkaṭeśa Āyyāvāl of Tāñjavūr District (C. 1700 A.D.) feeding a *caṇḍāla* (untouchable) with the *śrāddha* food for his ancestor-rite, and the story of the Tamil pariah saint Nandanar and that of Cokamela with reference to entering the temple. The message of these stories is that true devotion alone matters and that caste, station, pomp, and mere learning are of little moment. The Mahārāṣṭran devotional institution of musical *sankīrtan* had far-reaching effects, and the new stimulus to the practice of *bhājana* or congregational singing of the Lord's name or of songs of devotion which Tāñjāvūr District in Tamil Nadu got especially, was largely the cultural outcome of Marātha rule in Tāñjāvūr in the 17th and 18th centuries.

In Gujarat too, the same typical devotional activity and poetry manifested themselves; there were the twin strains of *advaita* and Krishna-*bhakti*. The two most important figures who sanctified this part of the country are Narasimha Mehtā of Junagadh, author of the song dear to Mahatma Gandhi, *Vaiṣṇava jana to*, and Mīrābāi of Rājasthan, the princess who became Lord Giridhar's bride. This spirit pervaded Sindh also, as the lives of Shah Karim and Shah Inayat, and the poems of Shah Abdul Karim show.

Kashmīri, Punjābi, and Other Northern *Bhaktas*

Kashmir was the home and meeting-place, in classical times, of different systems of philosophy and religion, Buddhism, Śaivism, and *advaita*, and held the premier position as the touchstone of Sanskrit scholarship for centuries. At the end of the classical period, Kashmir gained a new position as the meeting-place of traditional Hindu thought and culture and the new Islamic thought and culture. Sufism and *Vedānta* provided the bridge and mystics arose who spoke in a language which drew followers from both sections of the people. Lallādevī, the lady mystic of the 14th century, whose monistic utterances form a large collection, is the best representative of Kashmir's contribution to this corpus of the poetry of *Vedānta* and *bhakti* in the Indian languages.

Punjab's outstanding contribution is Nānak and the Sikh faith. As Toynbee says: "The Sikh religion might be described, not inaccurately, as a vision of this Hindu-Muslim common ground. To have discovered and embraced the deep harmony underlying the historic Hindu-Muslim discord has been a noble spiritual triumph; the Sikhs may well be proud of their religious ethos and origin."[7] After Nānak (1469-1539), there was a succession of nine gurus, Angad, Amar Dās, Rām Dās, Arjan, Har Govind, Har Rai, Har Kishan, Tegh Bahadur, and Gobind Singh, down to 1708. The songs of these gurus are collected in the *Granth Saheb* which, after the tenth guru, became the permanent "guru" for later generations. The *Granth Saheb* is a storehouse of songs of the Sikhs, some of them from the earlier saints of Mahārāṣṭra, Vārāṇasī, etc., all of them glorifying divinity, in an impersonal form, without any particular name, advocating the higher forms of abstract and non-sectarian worship and the sincere practice of spiritual *sādhanas*.

The ultimate inspiration of all the saints of the Hindi-speaking areas is Rāmānanda, who had twelve disciples. The greatest figures of this tradition were Kabīr and Tulasi; both of them were Vedāntins and adored Rāma, but Kabīr was more strictly advaitic. In the words of Sir G. Grierson: "The words of two men of the past can be still heard in every village of Hindustan. These are Tulasi Dās, the abandoned child of a beggar Brahman tribe, and Kabīr, the despised weaver of Benāres."[8] Kabīr's influence extended up to Punjab, his songs being included in the Sikh sacred writings; other sects,

[7] *The Sacred Writings of the Sikhs* (New York: UNESCO and Sahitya Akademi, 1960), Foreword, p. 10.

[8] F.E. Keay, *Kabīr and His Followers* (Calcutta, 1931), p. 67.

besides individual writers, inspired by Kabīr are the Dādūpanthis, Lāldāsis, Bābālalis, Sadhu Charandāsis, Garibdāsis, Rāmāsanchis, Paltupantis, Prānnāthis, Rādhāsvāmis. Different from the schools of Rāma-devotion which had an *advaita* background and denounced forms and rituals, there were schools of Krishna-devotion of which Vallabhācārya was the inspiration. Sūrdās, the blind-singer of Agra, was the greatest personality in the tradition of Krishna-devotion. The most prominent feature of the popular movement in the area was the background of Hindu-Muslim relations; as a result, many of these popular saint-singers became the apostles of a synthesis and rapprochement, aided by the common points in *advaita* and Sufism. This commingling produced also Krishna-devotees among Muslims who sang fine lyrics in their Krishna-*prema* (love), for example, Raskhan and Abdul Rahim Khankhana.

If we turn East, it is the land of Krishna and Śakti. The early stirrings of Rādhā-Krishna devotional literature go back to Jayadeva and his masterpiece of Sanskrit lyric, the *Gītagovinda*, which became the main inspiration of a flowering of musical dance-drama composition all over the East, the Deccan, and South India. Krishna-*bhakti* bloomed in Western India too. In the East, Vidyāpati of Mithilā (14th century A.D.), a distinguished Sanskrit writer, was the pioneer of the *pada* compositions in the spoken languages on the theme of Rādhā-Krishna *bhakti*; his songs were sung by Caitanya and they form the common heritage of Bihar and Bengal. He was followed by Śaṅkaradeva of Assām whose literary output as well as the organization of devotional institutions in his part of the country was most impressive. Śaṅkaradeva (1449-1558), son of a Kāyastha local chief, became learned in Sanskrit; under the influence of the *Bhāgavata Purāṇa*, he turned from his family tradition of Śakti-worship to Krishna. He propagated Krishna-*bhakti* versions in his language of portions of the *Bhāgavata Purāṇa*, by composing songs and creating a type of drama of *Bhāgavata Purāṇa* themes called *Aṅkia-Nat*, by writing prayer-formulae for congregational recitation (*nāma-ghoṣha* and *kīrtana-ghoṣha*) and by setting up centers for devotional exercises called *sattras* and *nāmghars*. His pilgrimage included South India and the influence of his work extended beyond Assām and embraced areas of Tibeto-Burman peoples. Here again the movement was cosmopolitan and Śaṅkaradeva had Brahmans as also Muslims as pupils.

Bengali Singers and the Return to the South

In neighboring Bengal where already the Buddhist *caryāgītas* and later different kinds of *mangal* songs had paved the way, the new *pada*-compositions on Kālī or Krishna arose with Caṇḍīdās (14th century), who was a Śakta and then became a Vaiṣṇava. The Caṇḍīdās or *Devi-mahātmya* in Sanskrit was the ultimate source of inspiration for the Śakta lyrics of Bengal. Rāmāprasad (1718-75), of whom Sister Nivedita, after comparing his songs with aspects of the writings of Blake, Burns, and Whitman, observes that "the radiant white heat of childlikeness" in his songs, has really no parallel,[9] is perhaps the best of the Śakta *pada*-composers of Bengal. However, Rāmāprasad was not an exclusive worshipper of Devī as his Krishna and Śiva *kīrtanas* show. A fresh upsurge of Krishna-*bhakti* in Bengal flowed from Caitanya (1486-1534). Caitanya wrote only two short Sanskrit *stotras* (poems) but his disciples and followers put out a large body of literature in Sanskrit and Bengali in song, poem, play, aesthetics, and biography of Caitanya which attest to the hold of his gospel of Krishna devotion on the Bengali people. Caitanya's sway extended to Orissa also.

The cycle came full circle and reached South India again. Through music, dance, and dance-drama, the influence on Jayadeva spread southwards and in Telugu, Kannada, Tamil, and Malayalam, musical stories and plays on devotional themes were composed in Sanskrit and these languages. *Kīrtana* and *bhajana* flowed from Mahārāṣṭra chiefly, and from Bengal to some extent, so that on a soil [which was] already the seedbed of *bhakti* the flow of these fresh waters from other areas led to a rich new crop of devotional music and dance-drama. With Nāyak and Maratha rule at Tāñjāvūr, many devout teachers and gifted music-composers from Āndhra and Mahārāṣṭra went there; it was as if for a time all literary and cultural roads led to Tāñjāvūr. This was the golden age of Karṇāṭaka music. In Āndhra, Bhadrāchala Rāmādas was a local officer under the Sultans of Golcanda. For spending the revenue collection on Lord Rāma in the temple at Bhadrāchala he was thrown into prison, from where he sang his songs on Rāma. In his footsteps and those of Purandaradāsa of Karṇāṭaka, Tyāgarāja, a Telugu domiciled in Tāñjāvūr District in Tamil Nadu, followed. Tyāgarāja, the greatest of the Karṇāṭaka music-composers, was also a great devotee of Rāma. His compositions take an important place in the Rāma-literature of India. Among music-composers or saint singers who adopted a single theme, Tyāgarāja stands foremost for literary appeal, richness of ideas and fancies, endless emotional variations, and intensity of feeling.

The Name, the Guru, True *Bhakti*, and Oneness

In an over-all comparative study of this song-literature of the saints, we find some common features in the religious and philosophical doctrines as

[9] Margaret E. Noble (Sister Nivedita), *Kali, the Mother*, p. 48.

well as expression. Firstly, all the saints, from the 7th century *nāyanārs* and *ālvārs* of the South to the most recent ones, inclusive of the Muslim mystics who sang on Krishna or Rāma, hold the name of the Lord, *nāma*, as the savior and as fundamental to their approach. Many ideas and illuminating analogies are offered by the saints to bring out the importance of the Name (*nāma*) and its relation to the form (*rūpa*) of the Lord.

Second, is the uniform emphasis on the guru which we find even in the songs of Muslim devotees. Here again many striking and suggestive similes are used to bring out the nature and role of the guru in relation to God and realization. The third is the stress on the uniqueness of *bhakti* as a democratic doctrine which consolidates all people without distinction of caste, community, nationality, or sex. The fourth is the repeated clarification of the true form of devotion or worship. The fifth is their reformist zeal and denunciation of sham and deception as also of empty formalism. The sixth is the comprehension, catholicity, and the sense of unity of all paths. Nānak adopts not only a Hindu-Muslim eclecticism but also assimilates Buddhistic terms from Tibet like *Māyā* and *mahaśūnya*. The seventh is, barring some stray cases of exclusive allegiance to Śiva or Viṣṇu, the generally prevailing *advaita* tone and the preference for monism and, ultimately, unity. Not only are many descriptions of the abstract Brahman in the *Upaniṣads* echoed or adopted, but actual assertions are made with this conviction. Some of the saints like Tulasidās try to harmonize the concepts of *jñāna* and *bhakti*, and of *sākāra* and *nirākara*, the Personal and the Impersonal, with the aid of meaningful analogies. This is one of the many integrations of the faiths, paths, modes, and *sādhanas* which the saints achieved by repeated emphasis on this old and principal Indian belief. In doing this, they did only what mystics of all climes have done. Says William James in his *Varieties of Religious Experience*: "Mystical states of mind in every degree are shown in history, usually, though not always, to make for a monistic view."

2.

Praise of the Name from Ṛg Vedic Times to Tyāgarāja[1]

What is there in a name, one may ask. It is name that is everything. Name is fame. It is by using somebody's name that one has to get on. When one is highly enraged or highly pleased, one calls names, of abuse or of praise. In the excess of one's hate or love, what comes out of one is mere name. In those short exclamations that break forth, the entire surcharged feeling stands compressed.

A name is therefore a condensed "tablet" form of a *guṇa*, an attribute of a person. The *Viṣṇu sahasranāma* ("Thousand Names of Viṣṇu" in the *Mahābhārata* epic) says that *nāmas* are based on *guṇas*, the qualities or strands of nature. The *Bhāgavata Purāṇa*, a *bhakti* text, says that the names of the Lord are each marked with fame, exploit, and quality of the Lord.[2] And of the Lord who is possessed of infinite excellences, the names are also infinite.

The earliest outpourings of man praying to the divine powers are seen in the Ṛg Vedic hymns, in the form of praises of the names and qualities of different deities, Agni, Indra, etc. In the *Śatarudrīya*, the same deity Rudra, who is conceived as everything, is praised with different and numerous names. Even in the *Upaniṣads*, *Brahman*, which is really without qualities (*nirguṇa*), is yet characterized by expressions like *satya*, *jñāna*, *ananta* [truth, knowledge, infinity].[3]

It is a matter of common experience, as the *Bhāgavata Purāṇa* says, that when one keeps on muttering the name of a thing, one's mind develops a love for it and a gradual absorption in it.[4]

[1] This text was first published as part of *The Spiritual Heritage of Tyāgarāja*, by C. Ramanujacari with an introductory thesis by V. Raghavan (Madras: Srī Ramakrishna Math, 1966), pp. 109-137; revised edition 1981, pp. 99-124. I have reduced the Sanskrit passages and replaced some with English translations for the sake of easier reading.

[2] *Nāmānyanantasya yaso'dkitāni* (*Bhāgavata Purāṇa*, I.4.11).

[3] Paramaśivendra Sarasvatī, the guru of Sadaśiva Brahmendra, collected together as *Upaniṣan-nāma-sahasra*, to be of help in the contemplation and realization of the *svarūpa* of *Brahman*.

[4] "*Rāma nāma śravanamu valla nāma rūpame/hṛidayamuniṇḍi prema buṭṭa jeya-*

It is with the help of a word, the name of an object, that one can recollect and fix an object in one's mind. Names, therefore, serve as fasteners attaching the Lord's personality in our mind and heart.[5]

In seeking a person through praise, there are three forms: firstly to describe in varied and poetic manner the greatness of the person sought; secondly, to refer to his varied glory by several significant attributes in the form of manifold names; and lastly, to call him forth for our help by the repetition of only one name of his. Under the first category come all poetic hymns. Under the second come the *sahasra nāma*, *astottara nāma* hymns and the *nāmāvalis* sung in *bhajans*, and under the last comes *nāma pārāyaṇa* or the repetition of a single name: Rāma, Śiva, Krishna, or the Goddess.

It has been held that with the gradual deterioration in the faculties and abilities of men, as ages passed on towards the *Kali yuga* (the fourth age, an age of strife in the Hindu time cycle), the sages devised further and further easier paths, for the salvation of suffering humanity. It is with this purpose in view that the path of *bhakti* or devotion was developed. *Kali* is predominantly an age of emotion and it is through this emotion that man has to be saved. This is achieved by turning the flow of his emotion in the direction of a Supreme saving Personality. To draw man's heart in love towards the Supreme Being, the emphasis was shifted from knowledge to devotion and from an abstraction to a Personality endowed with infinite excellences, in fact the human form itself in which Divinity frequently incarnated. When *bhakti* was thus evolved and developed, further processes of simplification were introduced, so that anybody and everybody, in whatever standard of equipment of mind and character,

ga ledā." Tyāgarāja similarly says, in his song *Smaraṇe sukhamu*, that the constant listening to *Rāma-nāma*, establishes the form of that name in the heart and fills the heart with love. "Listening to Rāma's name and filling the heart with the form being named, this causes love to be born, doesn't it?" In one of his visions of realization, the song *Nājivādhāra*, Tyāgarāja exclaims of his Lord, "Are you not the letters of the Name I repeat in my *japa*, taken shape like this?"

[5] "*Nī nāmāmṛta-pānamu yanu sōpānamu dorikenu.*" Varying the metaphor, Tyāgarāja in his song *Veṅkaṭeśa ninu*, compares the drinking of the nectar of the Lord's Name to something that lifts one to the presence of the Lord, verily the flight of steps leading one to God: "By drinking the nectar of Your name I have found that very staircase." The imagery is based on the local fact of the numberless steps of the Seven Hills of Tirupati which devotees mount and traverse uttering the Lord's Name.

might have some means to take to.[6]

Along with temples, worship of images, adoration with acts of worship, singing the Lord's glory, reading and listening to writings on divine glory, and even mere recitation of divine names developed. Thus were the Himālayan waters of the *Upaniṣads* brought to the plains, to irrigate the hearts of the masses of the entire country. All glory to these spiritual engineers who undertook these works, the *paurāṇikas*, the *bhāgavatas*, the *ālvārs*, and *nāyanārs*, the saints and *bhaktas* and musicians of this country, to which galaxy Jñāneśwara and Rāmānanda, Caitanya and Tyāgarāja belonged.[7]

The literature of *bhakti* bearing in particular on the doctrine of the Lord's Name as the supreme means of salvation is quite considerable. Besides some of the later *Saguṇa Upaniṣads*, portions of the *Mahābhārata*, the *Bhagavad Gītā*, the *Viṣṇu Sahasranāma*, the *Purāṇas* and especially the *Viṣṇu-* and the *Bhāgavata Purāṇas* form the main authorities of this school of thought. A number of religious writers contributed treatises on the theory of the subject of *Nāmamahātmya* (praise of the glories of the sacred Name), in which they seek support not only in the above-mentioned texts, going up to the later minor *Upaniṣads*, but also to the Ṛg Vedic hymns themselves. The basic Vedic text on which they take their stand is *Ṛg Veda*, 2.2.26: "O Praisers, knowing them, express every one of his names. O *Viṣṇu*, we desire the goodwill of you who are great."[8]

Of the *Upaniṣads* referred to, I shall mention briefly here only one, the *Kalisantaranopaniṣad*, which specially concerns itself with the means of salvation appropriate or most efficacious in the *Kali* age or to get over *Kali*. According to this text, at the end of the *Dvāpara* age and the opening of *Kali*, Nārada asked his father Brahmā how he could cross over the *Kali* age. Brahmā gave him the remedy: "You can shake off *Kali* by reciting the

[6] That the doctrine of Name redeems the humble and the learned alike is expressed by Dīkṣitar in a song of his on Rāma, *Māmava raghuvara*: "*pāmarapaṇḍitapāvanakara-nāmadeya.*"

[7] Like the Maharatha saints in the South West, and Rāmānanda and his followers in the North, Śrī Caitanya in the East was responsible for making the whole country resound with "Hari-bōl." In their doctrines, the Caitanyaites hold "Name" itself as a form of the Lord; and though capable of other significances also, two passages in Tyāgarāja may lend themselves to an interpretation that the composer knew the tenet that *nāma* was itself a *rūpa* of the Lord: "My prayer is Your form (*Nā japa varṇa rūpama*) in his song *Nājīvādhāra* and "The very form of your name is in my heart" (*Nāma rūpam hṛidayamuninḍi*) in his *Smaraṇe sukhamu.*

[8] I am indebted to Professor Robert Hueckstedt for this translation.

Name of the Lord Nārāyaṇa, the Prime Being."

The *Bhagavad Gītā* added its weight to this school of thought when it said that of all forms of *yajña*, the Lord was of the form of *japa-yajña*: "Among sacrifices, I am the sacrifice of repeating the mantra."

The full significance of this exaltation of *japa-yajña* in the *Bhagavad Gītā* is brought out later in the *Mahābhārata* epic, in the introduction to the *Viṣṇu Sahasranāma*. Having listened to all sorts of *dharma*, Yudhiṣṭhira, still not satisfied, asked Bhīṣma again: "What do you consider to be the greatest, the *dharma* of all *dharmas*, the most righteous action of all? By reciting what will beings as such be liberated from the cycle of birth and transmigration?" Bhīṣma replied that in his view, the devoted adoration of the Lord with hymns of praise and through the thousand divine Names is the *dharma* which is superior to all other *dharmas*. It was in reply to this question of Yudhiṣṭhira that Bhīṣma gave the world the thousand Names of the Lord. (See the translation of the *Viṣṇu Sahasranāma* in a later part of this book.)

The superiority of this *japa-yajña*, sacrifice of repetition, or *nāma-stotra*, hymn in praise of holy names, over other *dharmas and yajñas* which is meant here is well explained by the master teacher *ācārya* Śaṅkara in his commentary on the *Viṣṇu Sahasranāma*. Śaṅkara says: "What is the ground of superiority of this adoration in the form of the hymn? Its superiority over other kinds of *yajñas* consists in the following points in its favor: it does not involve injury to a being in the form of sacrifice; it is an *ahiṃsā yāga*, a sacrifice of non-violence. For doing it, you need no collection of men, money, or material, nor need you observe any particular time, place, or procedure."[9]

And Śaṅkara then quotes a large number of verses from several *Purāṇas* to bear out his explanation. The *Viṣṇu Purāṇa* says: "Meditation in *Kṛita Yuga*, sacrifices in *Tretā Yuga*, worship in *Dvāpara Yuga*—what these give, that one attains in *Kali Yuga* by merely uttering the Name of the Lord."[10]

> One can cast off this sheath of sin by uttering the Lord's Name even as one walks, stands, lies down, drinks, eats or bends down. In every *karma*, gaps or lapses occur and expiations for them have

[9] *asya stutilaksanasya arcanasya ādhikye kim kāraṇam?/ucyate himsādipuruṣāntara-dravyāntara/deśakālādiniyamānapekṣatvamādhikye kāraṇam.*

[10] *dhyāyan krite yajan yajñaistretāyām dvāpare 'rcayan/ yadāpnoti tadāpnoti kalau samkīrtya keśavam* (*Viṣṇu Purāṇa*, 6.2.17).

> to be done; if those expiations are further *karmas* of penance etc., further lapses are in store and there is infinite regress, *Avavasthā*. So, the expiation of all expiations is the thought of the Lord with the uttering of His Name. The singing of His Name reduces all sins, even as fire, all dross. In *Kali*, Name alone is the means; there is no other path.[11]

Furthermore, there is the insistence that "You need not recite Vedic chants—the *riks*, *yajus*, or *sāmans*. Sing the Lord's Name. There is the Lord's name available to men, there is the human tongue which men themselves can control—still, men fall into hell—what a wonder!"[12]

The *Bhāgavata* is the *Purāṇa* of *Purāṇas* for this school of *bhaktas* and worshippers of the Lord's Name. Owing to the great facility of attaining salvation through Name, the *Kali* age becomes meritorious, in spite of its many defects and indeed those that know hold *Kali* in great regard for this.

> Indeed there is one great virtue which the *Kali* age possesses, O Parikṣit, though it is the storehouse of all the evils that exist. By merely chanting the names and glories of Lord Krishna, one is released from all one's attachments and reaches the ultimate. . . . Mature and discriminating persons who appreciate the merits of the Kali age and recognize the essence of things, extol this age, in which by merely chanting the names of the Lord one can attain all the desired objects (which could otherwise be attained through efforts in a variety of other ways).[13]

According to the *Bhāgavata Purāṇa*, even the great *jnānins* (wise men) and *paramahaṃsas* (great sages, who, like the mythical swans of their namesake, separate milk from water, the eternal from the temporary) though they have nothing to do or gain, revel in the Personality, Names, and songs of the Lord. In fact, the *Purāṇa* holds that the liberated state of pure *jñāna*, without any act, if it is to be devoid of the love of the Lord, is not good. To sing of the Lord's glory is the only beautiful thing; it is eternally fresh and charming; it is an incessant festivity for the mind; it alone removes men's sorrows completely. The speech and writing, in

[11] *Viṣṇu Purāṇa*.

[12] *Viṣṇu Purāṇa*, XII.3.51, XI.5.36.

[13] *Bhāgavata Purāṇa*, XII.12.49.

which the glorious Names of the Lord are imbedded, is the flood that washes away the sins of humanity, though every verse of it may be full of grammatical lapses. That literature, however wonderful, which is barren of the glorification of the Lord, is like the pool where crows splash dirty water, not the *mānasa* lake in which the swans of liberated souls sport and delight.

> That speech alone is pleasant, which constantly gives newer and newer delight, that alone is a perennial source of great rejoicing to the mind, and finally that is the only means of drying up the ocean of man's grief, through which Viṣṇu's glory is continuously being sung. Speech, which though full of figurative expressions, never utters the praises that possess the virtue of sanctifying the whole world, is considered to be the delight of voluptuous men who wallow in the pleasures of sense like crows that feed upon the dirty leavings of food. Like swans, which are believed to have their abode in the lotus beds of *Mānasarovar* lake, devotees who have taken shelter at the lotus feet of the Lord and therefore ever abide in His heart never take delight in such speech (v. 10). On the other hand, that composition which, though faulty of diction consists of verses each of which contains the names of the immortal Lord, bearing the impress of His glory, wipes out the sins of the people; it is such composition that pious men love to hear, sing, and repeat to an audience (v. 11). That wisdom too which is free from blemish and is a direct means to the attainment of liberation does not adorn one's soul so much, if it is devoid of devotion to Lord Acyuta. How then, can sorrow at every stage (both while it is being performed and at the time of its fruition), and even disinterested action that has not been dedicated to God serve to heighten one's glory (v. 12).[14]

It is in accordance with this that great advaitic teachers from Śaṅkara onwards have all been *bhaktas* and have sung many a hymn of devotion. It is in accordance with this that many distinguished scholars, *bhaktas*, and *sannyāsins* gave a fresh stimulus to the school of *Nāmasiddhānta* in Cola Deśa, the Southern areas including Tāñjāvūr District, in the seventeenth and eighteenth centuries. The most noteworthy amongst these propagators of this *Nāma bhajana* is Śrīdhara Veṅkaṭeśa, popularly known

[14] *Bhāgavata Purāṇa*, I.5.10-12.

by the revered name "Āyyāvāl" who wrote the *Ākhyāṣaṣṭi*, or "Sixty Verses" on the Lord's Name, and another treatise on this subject entitled *Bhagavan nāma Bhūṣana*. He was accompanied in his enthusiasm by Śrī Bodhendra, a *sannyāsin* who wrote four works expounding the details of this doctrine, using titles associating the name with nectar: the *Nāmāmṛita Rasāyana*, the *Nāmāmṛita Rasodaya*, the *Nāmāmṛita Sūryodaya*, and the *Bhagavan Nāmamṛitārṇava*. The guru saluted by Tyāgarāja in his *Naukā Carita*, Śrī Rāmakrishnānanda, was also probably an expounder of this *Nāma māhātmya*. "*Nāma-paras*," adherents of the path of the Name, are mentioned separately from those who take to the six philosophical systems, by Tyāgarāja in his piece *Nijamarmamulanu*. And it is significant to note here that one of the manuscripts in Tyāgarāja's library, which has come down to us, is of a work called *Devatā Nāma Māhātmya*.

It is necessary to look more closely at this kind of background to understand the literary and historical influences on Tyāgarāja, which helped form his devotion to *Rāma-nāma*, and the ideas he expressed on this subject in the course of some of his songs.

* * *

It is well known that in the wake of the *bhakti* movement, the worship of Rāma attained great importance, and the movement spread widely and gave rise to a considerable literature taking the form of *Upaniṣads*, sections of *Purāṇa* and independent purāṇic compilations called *Samhitas*, philosophical and devotional versions of the *Rāmāyaṇa* epic such as the *Adhyātma Rāmāyaṇa*, the *Adbhūta Rāmāyaṇa*, and the *Ānanda Rāmāyaṇa*, and independent digests on the methods and details of worship, recitation of Rāma's name, and so on. In the process of this magnification, stories came up to explain such incidents in Vālmīki which obviously called for an explanation; thus a series of "earlier stories" arose, some of these being necessitated by the supposedly vulnerable points in the acts of Rāma. The mass of such stories of praise of Rāma's glories, *Rāmamāhātmya* grew so much and got spread over so wide a literature that today anyone who wants to have a collection of all these is faced with the formidable task of collation of material scattered in numerous works, many of which are in manuscripts. But fortunately for the student of Rāma literature, a recluse named Rāmabrahmānanda Sarasvatī set himself to the task and produced a compendium of such Rāma stories in a work called the *Tattva-saṁgraha-rāmāyaṇa*. This work is very useful to votaries of Rāma and students of history and the development of Rāma stories and their impact on the literatures of the different parts of the country, particularly works like the *Rāma-carit-manasa* of Tulsidās, produced under the spell of the Rāma movement that gained a momentum at the hands of Rāmānanda of Banāras. In South India one of the greatest and most popular figures to follow this movement of *Rāma-bhakti* and to have attained *siddhi* or spiritual realization by the prescribed mode of repeating Rāma's name was Tyāgarāja. His elder, Upaniṣad Brahman was another devotee of this tradition, a pupil of Vasudevendra. Another disciple of Vasudevendra, who taught Advaita and *Rāma-bhakti*, was Svayamprakāśānanda. Svayamprakāśānanda was the guru of the author of the *Tattva-saṁgraha-rāmāyaṇa.*[15]

* * *

Of the later *Saguṇa Upaniṣads*, three deal exclusively with Rāma: the *Rāma Rahasya* and the *Pūrva-* and *Uttara Rāma Tāpaṇī-Upaniṣads.* In those as well as in the *Kali Santaranopaniṣad,* the doctrine of *Nāma* is given to us in the form of *Rāma-nāma.* After Brahmā told Nārada that *Kali* could be crossed over by the recital of the Lord's Name, Nārada asks again: "What is that Name?" and Brahmā replies: "*Hare Rāma Hare Rāma Rāma Rāma Hare Hare/Hare Krishna Hare Krishna Krishna Krishna Hare Hare.*"

In the *Rāma Rahasyopaniṣad,* which is one of the later ones, Rāma says that one escapes from all sins by repeating his Name, nine hundred and sixty million times. (The detailed procedure to be followed for the performance of the *koṭijapa* of *Rāma-nāma* is set forth in the *Tattvasaṁgraha Rāmāyaṇa, Kiṣkindhā Khāṇḍa,* 9, *Śiva-Parvatī-samvada.*) Towards its close, the *Rāma Rahasyopaniṣad* expounds the significance of the syllabic constituents of the name, Rāma. It is said Śiva knows this significance well. The name Rāma is a synthesis of the essence of the Nārāyana eight syllable mantra and the Śiva five syllable mantra, its two syllables being extracted from the two separate mantras.

It is because *Rāma-nāma* is dealt with so fully in the *Upaniṣads* that Tyāgarāja describes that Name as *Vedavarṇanīyamau nāmamuto* in *Evarikai* and as *Vedasāramau nāmadheyamunu* in his song *Talacinantané.*

The *Rāma uttara tāpanī* says that *Rāma mantra* is called *tāraka,* "enabler of the crossing," because it traditionally has been the utterance empowering aspirants to cross over *saṃsāra,* the sea of worldly existences, to the other shore of ultimate reality. (Rāma has been adored as the *nāma-*

[15] I have inserted this relevant paragraph from V. Raghavan's article on "The *Tattvasaṁgraha-Rāmāyana* of Rāmabrahmānanda," *Annals of Oriental Research, University of Madras,* Vol. X, part 1.

tāraka par excellence, by Muthusvāmī Dīkṣitar also in his song on Rāma, *Rāmacandram bhāvayāmi—Nāma-kīrtana-tārakam.* In the song *Raghupate Rāma,* Tyāgarāja characterizes Rāma as "*tāraka-nāmadheya*" meaning "He whose name saves one"). In fact *tāraka nāma* is a very common epithet of Rāma, found for example in the song *Sujana jīvana. Tāraka* is *Brahman* and Rāma is *Brahman.* And this *Rāma tāraka mantra* is given to every person who dies at the *Avimukta kṣetra* ("Sacred field of Liberation") in Banāras, at the *Maṇikarṇika tīrtha* shrine or any part of the Ganges bank, imparted by Lord Śiva Himself. Banāras or Vārāṇāsi, where the two rivers Vārāṇa and Asī meet, is an external correlative of the juncture of the brows and the nose, and here is the spot to be concentrated upon by yogis. The imparting of the *tāraka mantra* of *Rāma-nāma* by Śiva at Banāras is further dealt with in the *Kāśīkhaṇḍa.*

The poet Kalidāsa wrote that when the guru Vasiṣṭha gave the name "Rāma" to King Daśaratha's first son, he was prompted to suggest that name because of the charming personality of Rāma; and the poet immediately adds that the name became the foremost auspicious thing of the world. Tyāgarāja sang that the name chosen was as charming as the person: *Rāmabhirāma rāmanīyanāma. Rāma-nāma* is also the Victorious Name which bestows success in the mundane as well as spiritual spheres: *Jayakara-nāma,* Tyāgarāja sings in *Dīnajanāvana.*[16]

As already observed, one of the tenets of the worshippers of the Lord's Name is that the *Nāma* itself is the *Rūpa,* the Form. Accordingly, to the worshippers of Name with such a belief, the Name is not merely an *upāya,* a "means" to reach the Lord, but is *upeya,* the "end"—the holy goal itself. This tenet of Name itself being first the means and then the end, both *upāya* and *upeya,* is expounded in the treatise just referred to, the *Upeya nāma-viveka* by Upaniṣad Brahman, which Tyāgarāja must have read.

The Name has two phases even as the *Brahman* has the two phases, *saguṇa* and *nirguṇa,* with form and formless. The former is the *upāya,* the means, and the latter, the *upeya,* is the Absolute to be attained.

The *upāya-nāma* of the Name as normally understood has itself four phases, from the gross to the subtle: *sthūla* ("gross"), *sūkṣma* ("subtle"), *bīja* ("seed"), and *turīya* ("fourth"), each of which forms, in an ascending order, the object of worship as the aspirant evolves higher and higher. In the fourth, the *turīya,* the devotee sees no difference between himself

[16] Cf. the custom of *pārāyaṇa* ("summary") of the *Rāmāyaṇa* or the *Sundarakāṇḍa* that we do according to formulae like *rāghavo vijayam dadyāda mama sītāpatiḥ prabhuḥ.*

and that state which *Rāma-nāma* would endow him with; that is, he has reached the non-differentiating advaitic stage here. On the attainment of this fourth stage, the aspirant becomes qualified to realize complete oneness in which the body and the world cease to exist for him and he is just the "disembodied consciousness" itself, *vikalebaracaitanya*; this is the stage of *nāma* itself as the *Brahman* and the goal, the *upeya*.

The first three stages of adoration of *upāya-nāma* are stages of duality of the worshipper and the worshipped; the fourth is a stage of unity but the next stage of *upeya-nāma* is the final realization where there is no question of duality or non-duality; it is the absolute impartite state of realization.

This detailed introduction is needed to understand Tyāgarāja's practice of *Rāma-nāma japa* and the full meaning of his songs on *Rāma-nāma*. Just as the wanderings and doings of Śrī Sadāśiva Brahmendra along the Kāverī banks, which are still a fragrant memory with us, are a proof to us in recent times of the glory of the high *avadhūta*[17] state, so is the life and *siddhi* (extraordinary yogic power) of Tyāgarāja, the master of music and *bhakti* saint, a proof of the efficacy of *Rāma-nāma* as a potent means of salvation.

Tyāgarāja was an exponent of the school that the *Nāma japa* of the Lord is the most effective path and that the devotee of the name need not be concerned with other paths: *Rāmanāmamu sārame gāni anya-mārgavicāra meṭike,* O *manasā*, he sings in the song *Sārame*. "O mind, only the name Rāma is most precious and all worthy—why be concerned with other roads and various ways?" According to a tradition of the Umayālpuram village "school" of Tyāgarāja's pupils, Tyāgarāja embarked in the prime of his youth, his twentieth year, on the great *tapas* of reciting *Rāma-nāma* nine hundred and sixty million times; and it took him twenty-one years and fifteen days to finish this *japa*. In the end Tyāgarāja had the *darśan* or vision of Śri Rāmacandra and he sang his first inspired piece, *Ela nī dayarādu,* according to this school.

In this connection, we may bear in mind that the *Rāma Rahasya Upaniṣad* lays down that *Rāma-nāma* has to be chanted ninety-six crores [one crore is ten million] times for the attainment of *siddhi* or extraordinary powers. Whether the form of the tradition in the Umayālpuram School is true exactly or not, there is no doubt that Tyāgarāja did attain *siddhi* through practicing the *japa* of *Rāma-nāma*. In more than one song does Tyāgarāja refer to his having had the visit of Rāma or his sight; for example in the songs *Kanugoṇṭini* and *Bhavanuta*. To utter the Lord's Name became

[17] *Avadhūta*: a possessionless, realized soul, from whom all extraneous worldliness has "fallen off."

a second nature to him. If the Tamil Śaiva saint prayed to his Lord that even if he forgot the Lord, his tongue should go on repeating the Lord's Name,[18] Tyāgarāja prays for nothing more than that his tongue should become used to continuous repetition of the Lord's Name, in his song *Śrī Raghuvara.*[19]

In *Ūrake*, another song, he affirms that this king of mantras, *Rāma-nāma*, was ever "shining" (*rājillu*) on the tongue of Tyāgarāja. He must have developed this practice of *nāma japa* very early. Attention may be drawn in this connection to those songs of his in which he himself tells us that he was devoted to Rāma from his early years, and even from birth. He was thus a *garbha-bhāgavata*, "a devotee while still in the womb," like Prahlāda. In fact, his familiarity with devotion to the name from the time of his birth, is not unlikely, when we recollect the fact that his father Rāma Brahman was a classmate of Śrī Upaniṣad Brahman and both of them were Rāma *bhaktas*, and Upaniṣad Brahman Yogi, the author of the treatise on *nāma* called *Upeya-nāma-viveka*, was one of the teachers of the *bhakti* movement devoted to *Rāma-nāma* in South India.

In *Pāhi mām hare*, Tyāgarāja says that he secured early in his life the precious pearl of *Rāma-nāma*. (*Pāhi rāma nāma muktāphalamul riti.*)

One of the doctrines of this *Rāma-nāma siddhānta* which we saw mentioned in the *Rāma Upaniṣads* is that Śiva knows the value and taste of the sweet name of Rāma and that He imparts it to people dying in Banāras. This tenet is basic to the entire body of Tyāgarāja's songs. When the composer introduces his *mudrā* or signature at the end of all his pieces in expressions like *Tyāgarājanutuni*, the expression means "Rāma praised by both poet Tyāgarāja and by Lord Śiva," Tyāgarāja being the name and form of Śiva worshipped in the main temple at the composer's birth place. Tyāgarāja makes an explicit and full reference to this in a song (*Inta saukyamani*):

> Is it possible for me to describe the *ānanda*, the divine bliss one derives from chanting *Rāma-nāma*? Who knows its measure and quality? Only true and great devotees know it. Lord Śaṅkara, who delights in drinking the nectar of music with the sugar-candy of *Rāma-nāma*, knows it well.[20]

[18] Editor's note: I have been unable to identify the "Tamil Śaiva saint" referred to here. It may have been Maṇikkavācakar.

[19] Cf. John Damascenus: "We must learn to invoke God's Name more often than we breathe, at all times and everywhere and during all our labors."

[20] In *Pāhi mām hare*, a *Divyanāma* piece, Tyāgarāja says he was born into this

At the end of Tyāgarāja's song *Rāma raghukula jalanidhé*, there is another reference: "You made Śaṅkara utter your *tāraka mantra* in the ears of the people who live in this *Kali* age." In the song *Nityarūpa* Tyāgarāja says, "The Lord Śiva of Kaśi knows your name." In *Kana kana rucirā* he cites Śiva as a witness to the efficacy of *Rāma-nāma*: "Śiva, the one who lives in Kailāsa, is a witness. . . ." In the well known piece *Vādérā Daivamu* Tyāgarāja says that Śiva initiates the ignorant folk of the world in this *tārakamantra* so that they might cross over the sea of *saṃsāra. Sārame gāni* is another piece in which he cites the example of Śiva. By making reference to the initiation of Vālmīki in *Rāma-nāma* by Nārada and to Śuka teaching *Hari-nāma* to King Parīkṣit, the song emphasizes to us the primary position which we should give to the *Rāmāyana* and the *Bhāgavata Purāṇa*.

> Did not Śiva, the delighter in *Sāma gāna*, music of the *Sāma Veda*, drink with all earnestness the nectar of *Rāma-nāma*, besides unceasingly uttering it to his holy consort Pārvatī and explaining to Her its great efficacy and significance?[21]

We noted above that the interpretation of the significance of *Rāma-nāma* given by the *Rāma Rahasyopaniṣad*, considers it an essence extracted out of both the *Nārāyaṇa aṣṭākṣarī* (eight syllable mantra) and Śiva *pañcākṣari* (five syllable mantra). The doctrine is set forth fully by Tyāgarāja in his song *Evarani*:

> What do people determine you to be and how do they worship you? As Śiva, Mādhava, Brahmā, or the Supreme Absolute? I prostrate before those wise ones who found the solution by extracting and combining the soul of each of the two mantras, "*Rā*" from "*Om Nāmo Nārāyaṇāya*" and "*Ma*" from "*Om Nāma Śivāya.*"

world with the name Rāma on his lips and had steadfastly kept it up. *Pāhi rāma yanucu bhuvini bāgabuṭṭidi! Pāhi Rāma yanucu gaṭṭi paṭṭu baṭṭiti* ("Protect me; I was born uttering the name Rāma and have always kept saying it— save me").

[21] Compare the words of the Christian St. Bernard: "The Name of Jesus is not only light; it is also nourishment. All food is too dry to be assimilated by the soul if it is not flavored by this condiment; it is too insipid unless this salt relieves its tastelessness. I have no taste for thy writings if I cannot read this Name there . . . it is honey for my mouth, melody for my ears, joy for my heart, but it is also a *medicine.*"

In the song the actual order of the syllables as set forth by Tyāgarāja is not *Rā-ma* but *Ma-rā* which according to some imaginative interpreters is a reference to the sage Vālmīki of whom Tyāgarāja is adored as an incarnation and the story of Vālmīki, who unable to utter *Rāma*, was going on uttering "*Marā-marā*" so that in the concatenation, the correct name *Rāma* was automatically formed; even such an utterance is considered efficacious according to *Nāma-siddhānta*, as explained here below. This "*Ma-rā*" episode is mentioned in a Purandaradāsa song too.

A further point in this process of extraction of the essences of the two mantras is also suggested by Tyāgarāja when he sings *I vivaramu delisina* (literally "knowing this specification or detail") and calls the two extracted syllables the "*jīva*" or life of the two mantras. This *vivara* or further "detail" of how these two syllables constitute the *jīva* or life of the two mantras is that if "*Rā*" is taken out of "*Nārāyaṇāya*," the word becomes "*Nāyaṇāya*" which means, "It helps not as the path for the aspirant" and if "*Ma*" is taken out of "*Namas Śivāya*" the expression becomes "*Na Śivāya*" meaning "not for good." This is all set forth by Upaniṣad Brahman at some length in his *Upeyanāmaviveka*.

One of the further developments in the direction of the glorification of *Nāma* as the easiest of means is the view that just as fire burns even if it is touched without knowledge, the Lord's Name saves one, if it comes from any quarter and in any form, even if it is uttered unconsciously or in play, in ridicule or whatever. Even if the letters constituting the name Rāma, Śiva, Krishna, or the Goddess, occur as part of other sound-combinations in sentences of other meanings they are salvific. The *Viṣṇu Purāṇa* asserts this power of the name: "by the repetition of [Viṣṇu's] name man is undoubtedly liberated from all sins, which fly like wolves that are frightened by a lion" (VI.8.19). This and other similar verses are quoted by Śaṅkara in his *Viṣṇu sahasra nāma bhāsya*.

The *Bhāgavata Purāṇa* also upheld this view and illustrated it with the classic story of Ajāmila, who, having spent his life in dissipation, called out at the time of his death, the name of his last beloved son, which was Nārāyaṇa. The moment the sound "Nārāyaṇa" came out of that sinner's mouth, all his sins vanished, and the emissaries of Viṣṇu rushed to prevent those of Yama from claiming Ajāmila. It is declared on that occasion that whatever the spirit or manner in which one uttered the Lord's name, he is saved. The medicine does not require the sick man to have much knowledge about it to give him the cure.

> The wise know that saying a name of Viṣṇu is able to cleanse all one's sins, even if it is intended to denote another, or when

> it is spoken in jest, or as an exclamation during a song, or even disrespectfully (*Bhāgavata Purāṇa*, VI.2.14). A man who says the word "Hari" involuntarily, spontaneously as he stumbles or falls, when suddenly bitten (by a snake or other creature), in fever, when an arm or leg is broken, no longer deserves to undergo sufferings (VI.2.15). . . . Just as a medicine with the most potency is certain to produce the best effect, even if taken by chance, so too does the name of the Lord reveal its power to purify, even when someone is ignorant of it, and is uttered casually (VI.2.19).

Ajāmila, a character in the *Bhāgavata Purāṇa*, uttered the whole name, though he was only referring to his son. To illustrate the case, *bhāgavatas* (expounders and lead singers of devotion) tell stories and offer illustrations. One is the conversion of Vālmīki by Nārada, which incident is referred to by Tyāgarāja in *I menu galigi nanduku*. But the *bhāgavatas* say that Vālmīki the hunter could not, as already mentioned, utter "*Rāma*," but, as a man of the forest, could utter "*Marā*," the name of a tree. Therefore, Nārada ingeniously asked him to repeat quickly "*Marā-Marā-Marā*," so that in the sound chain the name "*Rāma*" automatically sounded.

Ayyāvāl, the predecessor of Tyāgarāja and one whose teaching on the subject of *Nāma-mahātmya* held the field in Coladeśa, the South land, subscribed to this view and in some verses in his hymn on the Lord's name, *Ākhyā ṣaṣṭi*, he referred to the name Śiva as saving one even if its sounds were somehow introduced in the everyday speech of a man, for instance, "Where does he l*ive*?" asks one; "On the bea*ch*," says another; in the answer, something similar to the sound combination "*Śi-va*" occurs, even though the syllables are reversed.

This, Tyāgarāja felt, was carrying it too far. The uttering of the Lord's Name, he insisted, should be informed by love for the Lord. Those who do not love the Lord know not the relish of His Name. "O Rāma, will people without love for you know the flavor of your name? O Sītā!" (*Rāma nīyeḍa prema rahitulaku/nāma ruci delusunā*).

Besides, "Rāma" means the essence of Śiva and Viṣṇu; Rāma is *Brahman* itself; what is the use of repeating the sound Rāma, without any knowledge of its meaning or as referring to another person or object? Tyāgarāja elaborates his view by means of a series of telling similes in his song *Telisi rāma cintanatō*:

> The Name must be uttered with a knowledge of its significance and with contemplation of Rāma. Closing the senses up for a

> minute and realizing the real truth of the *tāraka-rūpa* of Rāma, one should utter the Name.
>
> Rāma means a woman; that leads to lust, etc. Rāma is the name of the Supreme *Brahman* too; that removes all the distress of mortal birth. *Arka* is the name of a poisonous plant; *Arka* means the Sun that dispels all darkness. *Aja* means a goat; *Aja* means also *Brahman*, who would bless you with success.

That *nāma kīrtana*, singing the divine names, is not a mechanical process, that a real practice of this means a full equipment of knowledge, self-control, purity of mind, devotion, concentration, etc., has also been emphasized in the books. In his comments on the name *Viśva*, (literally meaning "all") which leads the one thousand Names of Viṣṇu, Śaṅkara says that it is only one who has realized the truth that God is *Viśva*, Everything, who can utter the *nāma*. Śaṅkara's teaching in his comments on the Name *Viśva* is summarized by Tyāgarāja in the last part of his song *Intakanna yānanda—Nī japamulu vela nī jagamulu nīvai rājillunaya*—"Whenever I murmur again and again your name, the worlds seem to shine with your presence." Such a realization would make one completely refrain from *hiṃsā* (violence), etc., and such a person deserves to sing the Lord's Name. Some texts go so far as to say that only the realized souls who have become one with the Lord can take the Name; others should not vainly take it. . . .

Upaniṣad Brahman says in his *Upeya nāma viveka* that the repetition of *Rāma-nāma* should be attended with the non-dual contemplation, *advaita-bhāvanā*.

In the *Padma Purāṇa*, ten pitfalls for enthusiasts of *nāma-kīrtana* are set forth and their avoidance is insisted upon. They are characterized as ten offences against the Lord's Name, *nāma-aparādhas*. The first is the deriding of good men, *nindā* of *sādhus*. The second is to see difference between one form of Deity and another, e.g., Śiva and Viṣṇu. Then, disregard for gurus, denouncing the *Vedas* and *Śāstras* as needless, considering that the glorification of *Nāma* is in fact an exaggeration, committing sins on the strength of the *Nāma*, absence of purity of mind achieved through refraining from injury to others, from lying, stealing, incontinence and receiving gifts. The next is to desist from all *karmas* and *dharmas* on the excuse of the *nāma-japa*. Then, teaching the Name to the faithless and the uninterested. And lastly, failing to cultivate benevolence and continuing to be dominated by *ahaṁkāra* and *mamakāra*, the sense of "I" and "mine."

Tyāgarāja was one of those who considered the recitation of *Nāma* a high form which only qualified people should resort to, if they are to reap the benefit. To the second and partly to the seventh *aparādha* referred to above, Tyāgarāja's *Sukhi evarō* gives expression:

> Who is the blessed one that enjoys the bliss of *Rāma-nāma*, the highest of *mantras* calculated to save men from bondage? Who is that blessed one who, unflinching from truth, serving all humanity and free from hatred towards other deities, sings sweetly the *Rāma-nāma*?

There is again reference to the second *aparādha* in the essentials of a true devotee described by Tyāgarāja in his *Bhaktuni cāritra* ("Conduct of the Devotee"), *Śiva mādhava bhedamu jeyagarādu* ("You shouldn't make any difference between the names of Śiva and Viṣṇu"). In his song *Vinatāsuta*, Tyāgarāja condemns disputes about different faiths as useless. In the song on the Goddess, Dharmasamvardhanī, opening with the words *Karuṇa jūdavamma*, Tyāgarāja addresses the Goddess as being both Śiva and Rāma.

In a song on Śiva, *Śambho Śiva Śaṅkara*, he describes the Lord as one who always puts down the pride of those inferior people who revel in sectarian differences: "God is the destroyer of the pride of a person who has fallen into the pit of differences of religions" (*Mata-bheda-patita-mānava-mada-santata-bhaṅga*).

In *Itaradaivamula*, Tyāgarāja says that without any prejudice against other faiths he is devoted to Rāma—*matabheda-muleka sadā madini marulu gonna tanaku.* "[I am] one whose mind without harboring any prejudice against other faiths is constantly and passionately in love with you. Only such a Rāma *bhajana* as is done with a mind free from the six inner enemies, lust, anger, and the others, will bring salvation, and free one from the ills of this world."

In the true spirit of one who, while adoring one form as his dearest, held in respect the rest as but other forms of Divinity, Tyāgarāja praised Subrahmaṇya as "unequaled among the Gods" (*Nīvanti daivamu sadanana*), and Devī as the "refuge of Tyāgarāja's family"—"*Tyāgarāja kulasaranye*," in his song *Ammadharmasamvardhanī*.

The very fruit of *nāma-japa* is that the Name purifies one's mind: "My mind has been cleansed by chanting your holy name" (*Nī nāmamuce nāmadi nirmalamainadi*, in the song *Jñāna-mosagarādā*).

And hence is *Rāma-nāma* "the most sanctifying name" (*Paramapāvana-nāma*) as he sings in *Rāmaramaṇa*. "If there is one who thus worships the Lord truly with His Name—surely, who can equal him?" he asks in *Dāśarathānī ṛiṇamu*:

> Who can equal that worshiper of the Lord's Name, who has cleared his mind of all its manifold lumber, who has steadfast

> devotion, who discards sectarian disputes, who longs for the Lord, who has established the Lord's feet in his heart, who shuns like poison the company of those who do not enjoy this happiness, and who values the company of true devotees? Who can equal those who are transported to ecstasy meditating on the Lord?

And he asks what can equal our own human birth if we do this adoration of the Lord with the flowers of divine glorious names. "O mind, that human life is blessed in which the Lord is installed on the golden throne of thought and is worshipped with flowers of his holy names" (*Nāma kusumamulace pujiñce*). It is necessary to understand fully the significance when Tyāgarāja speaks more than once of *nāma-kusuma*, of the name of the Lord as the flower of His worship. According to the prescribed directions for the adoration of *Rāma-nāma* (*Rāma mantra puraścarana* and *Kriyāyoga*) *Rāma mantra* itself is to be used as the flowers for the *pūjā* (worship); *nāma-japa* is the flower worship (*puṣpa-arcana*).[22]

And if one cannot have true love for *Rāma-nāma*, of what use is his life—"Of what use is a life without true love for your holy name, O Rāmacandra?" he asks in *Pāhi paramātma*. The Lord's Name brings prosperity here, and leading one on the right path, it brings one to the abode of Divinity or is itself all prosperity, all austerity and the abode eternal. "The name of Rāma brings one welfare, leads one always on the right path, and is the abode of divinity," he asserts in *Vandanamu*.

The most elaborate expression or exclamation relating to the joys of uttering *Rāma-nāma* is of course the long *Divya-nāma* in the auspicious *Saurаṣṭra rāga* in which Tyāgarāja simply loses himself as it were. The song begins with the words *Melu melu Rāma-nāma-sukham ī dharalō manasā*:

> Ah Mind! Exceedingly superior in this world is the bliss of Rāma's Name to the joy of a thirsty man getting water to drink, of a pauper coming by a treasure, of getting water in draught, of a frightened person getting courage, of a hungry man getting a sumptuous feast, of an angry man calming down, of an ignoramus becoming suddenly learned.

Indeed, Tyāgarāja in this song exalts the bliss of the utterance of the Lord's Name above sweet devotional music, above even the bliss of

[22] See *Tattvasaṁgraha Rāmāyaṇa*, Sundara, Cantos 13, 14.

contemplating God, or spiritual experience, or the realization of *Brahman* itself:

> The pleasure one derives in meditation on Śrī Rāma the Bestower of prosperity, O mind! The happiness that *Rāma-nāma* gives to one is *higher than that*!
>
> The pleasure one derives after successful Vedāntic inquiry, O mind! The happiness that *Rāma-nāma* gives to one is *higher than that*!
>
> The bliss which one derives from the realization of *nirguṇa para Brahman*, O mind! The happiness that *Rāma-nāma* gives to one is *higher than that*!

3.
Perennialism and the Name: V. Raghavan's Foreword to Frithjof Schuon's *The Language of the Self*[1]

> "'Internally' every religion is the doctrine of the one Self and its earthly manifestation, as also the way leading to the abolition of the false self or the way of the mysterious reintegration of our 'personality' in the celestial Prototype."
>
> —Frithjof Schuon

The Perennialist Scholars

There is a class of writings which has contributed in a unique way to the true understanding of Hinduism in the West. This is a class of writings different from the more widely known one of the Orientalists, but may be considered the consummation of the work which these "Orientalists" had done since their discovery of Sanskrit and their subsequent study of the East by editing and translating Eastern classics and tracing the development of the different branches of Oriental thought. To adopt the language of the *Muṇḍaka Upaniṣad*, all that they have done may be called the *aparā vidyā*, non-transcendent knowledge, while the class of writings dealt with here may be deemed the *parā vidyā*, transcendent knowledge. An eminent figure who easily passed from the former to the latter[2] and who is not only well known in this country but widely admired is Ananda K. Coomaraswamy. Another name that comes in this line is that of the French savant René Guénon, the quintessence of whose teachings Coomaraswamy himself brings together in his essay, "Eastern Wisdom and Western Knowledge."

[1] This introduction by V. Raghavan is dated August 18, 1959. Frithjof Schuon, *Language of the Self*, tr. by Marco Pallis and Macleod Matheson (Madras: Ganesh and Co. 1959). Elements of the introduction not bearing on *Nāmasiddhānta* have been omitted, and the selections from Schuon's *Language of the Self* have been made on the basis of their relevance to Name traditions.

[2] Like Truth, the same *sādhaka* or spiritual aspirant, may have modes and levels; and one can pass from one kind of study to the other without looking down upon the other, or fearing the loss of caste by mixing with those of another school, or being accused of having as if two distinct brains.

Yet another member of the elite of authentic exponents in the West of Eastern wisdom is Frithjof Schuon.

In the works of these authors the words Tradition and Orthodoxy—quite unfashionable these days—have been used. At the outset a certain distinctiveness and distinction were also claimed for the class of writings these perennialists produced. What are the chief features of their approach?

Seven Features of Perennialism

Firstly, these writings bring out the fact that underlying the different religions of the world there is a common tradition and a basic unity. To quote Schuon, "explicitly to practice one religion is implicitly to practice them all."[3] This common tradition is the gnosis or the *philosophia perennis* which is the connecting link between the different religious languages.[4]

Secondly, while Truth is one, Revelation or Tradition or Form is naturally diverse, thanks to the infinity of divine possibility.[5] While orthodoxy, which represents divine necessity, is the conforming to this basic gnosis, originality, which represents divine freedom,[6] comprehends the different forms this gnosis puts forth at different times or in different parts of the world: "the diverse revelations do not really contradict one another, since they do not apply to the same receptacle and since God never addresses the same message to two or more receptacles."[7] In the words of Guénon, "differences in doctrines, in order to be legitimate, can only be a mere matter of adaptation, modifying the more or less external forms of expression but in no wise touching the principles themselves";[8] according to men's varying capacity, God "taught them at one time one thing and at another time another, as circumstances required."[9] ". . . Every traditional form is superior to the others in a particular respect and it is this

[3] Frithjof Schuon, *Gnosis* (London: John Murray, 1959), p. 33.

[4] Ibid., p. 27.

[5] Ibid., p. 29.

[6] Frithjof Schuon, *Language of the Self*, p. 100.

[7] Frithjof Schuon, *Gnosis*, pp. 29-30.

[8] René Guénon, *Introduction to the Study of Hindu Doctrines*, p. 201. Compare Schuon, *The Transcendent Unity of Religions* (New York: Harper Torchbook, 1975), p. 124: "Every tradition is necessarily an adaptation. . . ."

[9] Frithjof Schuon, *Language of the Self*, p. 101.

characteristic which in fact indicates the sufficient reason for the existence of that form."[10]

Thirdly, while a search in the writings of the different religions of the world has shown that this gnosis or knowledge of the Self forms the core of all religions, it is in Hinduism that it is found in a most pronounced form and has never been forgotten. Also, the Hindu heritage is precious for another reason: it is not only "the most ancient of the living traditional forms" but "it possesses a certain superiority or 'centrality' with respect to later forms."[11] "Hinduism has the faculty of combining all the perspectives which elsewhere are mutually exclusive." While combining through the doctrine of *adhikāra-bheda* (different paths depending on one's talents and tastes) and *ruci* (spiritual temperament) the different perspectives (*darśanas*), "Hinduism does not lose sight of unity; it has a tendency to see unity in diversity and in each element of this diversity."[12]

Fourthly, the highest of these perspectives is Gnosis, the metaphysic of the Self, the *Vedānta*. "That the way of Knowledge, *jnāna-mārga*, is among spiritual ways the highest, and in a still more ultimate sense, that it is the spiritual way as such, the one in which all other ways finally must merge, is a fundamental truth to which all traditional teachings bear witness either openly or else by implication." Of "those doctrines and methods that keep closest to true knowledge as the 'highest' ways open to man," "the Hindu *Vedānta* provides an example that conforms in its presentation, as near as conceivably possible, to the goal it sets itself, which is Deliverance total and unqualified."[13] As to Śaṅkara and the Sufis, to these writers too, knowledge alone delivers. The doctrine of *bhakti*, Hindu or Christian, does not contradict that of *jñāna*, for "the conceptions of Rāmānuja are contained in those of Śaṅkara and are transcended by them." "Rāmānuja affirms against Śaṅkarācārya truths which the latter never denied on their

[10] Frithjof Schuon, *The Transcendent Unity*, p. 50. To be more precise one should rather say that every traditional form specializes in a particular aspect. "That one enunciation may be less direct in its form than another is no proof whatever of a lesser wisdom but solely of a lesser receptivity on the part of the particular environment" (*Language of the Self*, p. 68).

[11] Frithjof Schuon, *The Transcendent Unity*, p. 51 (Cf., p. 107, fn., "Hinduism represents the Primordial Tradition. . .").

[12] Frithjof Schuon, *Spiritual Perspectives and Human Facts*, pp. 66, 68.

[13] Frithjof Schuon, *Language of the Self*, p. 46.

own level."[14] Like faith (*Sraddhāvān labhate jñānam* ["The man of faith discovers wisdom"], *Bhagavad Gītā*, IV.39. Cf. "It is for certain men who have been allowed to pass from faith to gnosis."—Clement of Alexandria), devotion is a pre-condition of knowledge; there have been no greater hymnists in India than Śaṅkara; for, to one who has realized the Self, it is more natural than not, as the *Bhāgavata Purāṇa* says, to be singing of the Lord.[15] Not only Rāmakrishna, but many a forebear of his has been this *bhakta jñānin*, devotee-sage. Also, when the *Upaniṣad* says of the Supreme Self, *yam evaiṣa vṛiṇute tena labhyaḥ tasyaiṣa ātmā vṛiṇute tanūm svām* ("The supreme Self reveals itself only to the soul who embraces the Self as the Master within the heart"), there is, as it were, a synthesis of *jñāna* and *bhakti*. It is in this light that statements such as that of St. Macarius of Egypt, "Love is inseparable from knowledge," are to be understood. Between different approaches, e.g., *bhakti* and *jnāna*, it is, therefore, not a question of error and truth, but one of lesser truth and greater truth or of different gradations of the universal reality.[16]

Fifthly, between the subject to be realized which is *Sat*, *Cit*, and *Ānanda* and the objective world superimposed on it, "there is interposed a direct objectivation of the subject" which mediates in the re-integration, the trinity of the *avatāra*, the guru, and the revelation or mantra.[17] "The Absolute reveals itself also, to the same sage, in an objective manner, by springing up suddenly in the mind in the form of sacred words; and the Absolute reveals itself also in the giving of inspired Texts which are to be the support of life and of spiritual realization to an entire civilization; in such a case the Absolute never reveals itself in subjective mode, except in the case of certain *avatāras* whose body and mind manifest the Self in a manner eminently more direct than with the ordinary sage."[18]

Sixthly, the East and Hinduism in particular are noteworthy for

[14] Ibid., p. 24.

[15] See Ch. XLII, "From Bhakti to Jñāna and Back" in the *Call of the Jagadguru*, lectures by the Śaṅkarācārya of Kāñcī (Madras: Ganesh & Co., 1961).

[16] *The Transcendent Unity*, p. 38. "Reality affirms itself by degrees, but without ceasing to be 'one,' the inferior degrees of this affirmation being absorbed, by metaphysical integration or synthesis, into the superior degrees. . . . Furthermore Being Itself, which is none other than the 'Personal God,' is in its turn surpassed by the 'Impersonal' or 'Supra-Personal Divinity'" (*The Transcendent Unity*, p. 53).

[17] *Language of the Self*, p. 18.

[18] Ibid., p. 57.

preserving not only this tradition of gnosis, but what is very important today, the "'techniques' of realization." For "knowledge is not merely a matter of right theory . . . but is something to be 'actualized' with the help of a method running parallel to the doctrine. . . ."[19] Foremost among these techniques is yoga, which as described by Patañjali includes the virtues and that unique mode called *japa*, repetition of a holy name in a *mantra*, which runs like a golden thread through *karma*, *bhakti*, and *jñāna*, and assimilates the former two to the last.

Lastly, "as the *spiritual technique* is essentially the art of concentration,"[20] the traditional ideology favors art, which in origin was the imitation of the divine act or the analogy used by revelation for exegesis, as a direct aid to spirituality; "the spiritual efficacy of aesthetic supports is in the very nature of things," for "apart from the intrinsic value of beauty" the efficacy of art is "to be found in the unifying power of aesthetic experience."[21] As Schuon says in his *Spiritual Perspectives*: "There is something in our intelligence which wants to live at rest, something in which the conscious and unconscious meet in a kind of passive activity, and it is this element to which the lofty and easy language of art speaks. The language is lofty because of the spiritual symbolism of its form and the nobility of its style; it is easy because of the aesthetic mode of assimilation."[22]

A Vision of Underlying Unity

Perhaps the greatest gain from this study of world religions is the discovery of their underlying unity and of the fact that they are but diverse "paths that lead to the same summit." It is also clear that this unity could lie only in the doctrine of gnosis, for it is knowledge that has no history. The realization of this truth would obviate the evangelistic obsession of certain faiths, which by admixture of violence, exploitation, or corruption of one kind or another or by dilution of the teaching, carry out their expansionism. As Aldous Huxley says: "Like any other form of imperialism, theological imperialism is a menace to permanent world peace. The reign of violence will never come to an end until, first, most human beings accept the same true philosophy of life; until, second, this perennial philosophy is recognized

[19] Ibid., p. 229, 48.

[20] Ibid., p. 89.

[21] Ibid., p. 78.

[22] *Spiritual Perspectives*, p. 29.

as the highest factor common to all the world religions; until, third, the adherents of every religion renounce the idolatrous time-philosophies, with which, in their own particular faith, the perennial philosophy of eternity has been overlaid."[23] This does not mean a watering down of faith or the growth of a religious indifference; it is only a curative of sectarianism. Every religion is unique and the aspirant devoted to it should strive within it with that faith; but when he has reached the goal, he no longer sees any diversity. This has been affirmed so far as the manifold perspectives within the Indian tradition are concerned continuously by the Veda, the *Upaniṣad*, the *Bhagavad Gītā*, and the hymns of saints and devotees, but it was left to Rāmakrishna Paramahaṃsa in modern times to demonstrate this in respect of the non-Indian religious traditions too, Christianity and Islam. For a correct estimate of Rāmakrishna, the following from Schuon cannot possibly be excelled. "In Rāmakrishna there is something which seems to defy every category; he was like the living symbol of the inner unity of religions; he was, in fact, the first saint deliberately wishing to penetrate 'foreign' spiritual forms. . . . In the present time of confusion, disarray, and doubt, he was the saint called to 'verify' forms and 'reveal,' if one can so express it, their single truth."[24] In 1926, a European student of *Vedānta* met his Holiness Śrī Śaṅkarācārya of Śringeri and at the end of the conversation wanted to know if Hinduism took converts. "No, rather it is needless for Hinduism to take converts," so saying, His Holiness explained why Hinduism was called *Sanātana Dharma*, the Eternal Law. The European said that he had no idea when he came that he would be going away from his Holiness with a desire to be a better Christian. His Holiness observed in conclusion that an artist howsoever capable required a stable background of canvas for his painting. "Apply your God-given gifts on the stable background of your own God-chosen faith, Christianity. When the painting is over and you are contemplating the beauty of the picture, the background may face away from your view of its own accord. . . ."

The Service of Perennialists to East and West

The service that this group of perennialist writers in the West has done is both to the East and the West. The integration they have achieved on the basis of a traditional and spiritual outlook is not exactly Oriental, for as they

[23] Aldous Huxley, *The Perennial Philosophy* (New York: Harper & Row, 1970), p. 229.

[24] *Language of the Self*, p. 37.

have shown, this outlook is common to the medieval and scholastic West. "What we have in mind for the Christian," says Schuon,[25] "is a return to his own sources and not an orientalization of the West." "If Guénon wants the West to turn to Eastern metaphysics, it is not because they are Eastern, but because this is metaphysics. . . . It is only because this metaphysics still survives as a living power in Eastern societies, in so far as they have not been corrupted by the withering touch of Western, or rather modern, civilization . . . and not to orientalize the West, but to bring back the West to a consciousness of the roots of her own life and values . . . that Guénon asks us to turn to the East."[26]

The message of these writers is not less needed, nor ever more opportune than today, for the East, which under the impact of different forces from the modern West is either "sleeping over its truths," or indulging in a "spiritual demogogy" busy preparing versions of its teachings acceptable to the modern West, or committing suicide by working itself up into a frenzy that it had been terribly mistaken down the centuries and that, cutting itself completely from its hoary moorings, it should now set itself, in the wake of the modern West, to work for the Utopia of increased production, improved standard of living, and an equality instead of quality. That India and the greater part of the East are now free from Western colonialism is no guarantee that their traditions would be conserved. As Gai Eaton observes: "It is far too early to tell how profoundly Western ideas may have penetrated the basic structures of life in India, but it is clear that the process of penetration has by no means ceased with the abdication of the British Rāj; the country, now regarded as politically mature, because its traditional forms have been more or less undermined, has been left to the tender mercies of Westernized Indians who are unlikely to show such moderation as we did in tampering with the old way of life."[27] Both Guénon and Schuon have taken special pains to criticize modern Indian scholars or teachers who have had to "present," so to say, the orthodox tradition of India for Western acceptance. But one may not consider this the chief sin of modern India when one reflects on the long history of Hindu thought, during almost the whole course of which it had been submitted to the impact of forces both internal and external, and finds

25 Ibid., p. 229.

26 A.K. Coomaraswamy, "Eastern Wisdom and Western Knowledge," *Isis*, XXXIV:3, pp. 359-363.

27 *The Richest Vein: Eastern Tradition and Modern Thought* (London: Faber and Faber), p. 17. See also *Language of the Self*, p. 198).

that, without sacrificing its fundamentals, Hindu tradition had always put forth adaptations of forms, and that indeed it is these diversified forms which justify the claim of this culture to "formal amplitude."

On the other hand, the real danger is from that total Westernization in which the East is fast, thoughtlessly, throwing away its precious heritage. In their denunciation of Western civilization and in the way to regeneration that they have pointed out through the recovery of the traditional spirit, it is the East that these savants have shown as supplying the key to that treasure of spiritual wisdom. To many modern Indians and their leaders who are intensely allergic to the words Tradition and Orthodoxy, this growing school of Western thinkers should act as a shock-absorber. Their re-affirmation of the value of this ancient, in fact timeless, wisdom should lead to a reawakening in the East, and to an arrest of the spreading decay of its tradition. Let not that contingency arise in which, for this ancient wisdom, as for our antique artware, we would one day have to go to the West where it has been taken and treasured by a band of *vivekins*! (cognoscenti or discerning knowers). And for awakening us with their true and revealing exposition of this knowledge, these *vivekins* of the West are entitled to our gratitude and respect. "They resemble *ṛiṣis* and are venerable" (*ṛiṣivat te'pi pūjyās syuḥ*), as Garga of yore said of the *śāstra-jñās* of the West.

[The following passages from Schuon's book shed light on the place of the Name as an integral part of Hindu traditions.]

The Guru, the Name and the Self[28]

> According to certain people's expressed views, the crucial question is not that of tradition, of initiation, or of method, but the question of the Guru's own realization. Such a view leaves us with only two alternatives: either a man is not a perfect Sage, and in that case he has no means of knowing whether the Guru is a perfect Sage or not; or else a man is himself a perfect Sage, in which case he has no need of a Guru. All that the disciple can know is that the Guru is spiritually superior to himself; and he is only able to know this thanks to the tradition to which he belongs and from which the Guru has issued. When the disciple has attained the degree of his Guru, he is at liberty

[28] Excerpts selected from Frithjof Schuon, *Language of the Self*, tr. by Marco Pallis and Macleod Matheson (Madras: Ganesh & Co., 1959).

to seek another Guru, and so on, as is shown by the example, among others of Śrī Rāmakrishna whose spiritual realization surpassed, not only that of the Brāhmini Bhairavi, but even that of his second Guru, the *jñānin* Totāpuri. In every case the one thing which is indispensable is an immediate relation with the embodied Absolute, which "embodiment" can and must in fact assume different forms and cannot depend on anything as conjectural as the personal realization of such and such a man. The Veda, the *praṇava* Om, the divine Name (Śiva, Hari and others), and the Guru, both as such and in virtue of his function, are so many embodiments of the Absolute.

We have heard it said that the Hindus are not in agreement as to the degree of realization of Śrī Rāmakrishna; one can thus have different opinions on this matter, which shows precisely the falsity of the principle according to which it is for the disciple to judge the spirituality of the Master and to determine the degree of his realization. On the other hand, it is evident that the disciple will seek a guru whose teaching, reputation, and personal radiance betoken the highest wisdom. In any case, the fact that the guru Totāpuri was surpassed by his disciple Rāmakrishna in no way indicates that Śrī Totāpuri was a false guru or that Śrī Rāmakrishna was mistaken in allowing himself to be guided by him.

In the same line of thought is the question of the universality of tradition, which amounts in the last analysis to knowing whether the founders of great religions, such as the Buddha, Christ, Muhammad, possessed perfect wisdom, and whether as a consequence one finds within these religions the methods and Masters necessary to guide one towards the realization of the Self. Now the doctrine of the Self (in other words that which in Hinduism is called the *Vedānta*) is plainly enunciated in certain teachings of these *avatāras*, and their identity with the Self has been affirmed by them with the greatest clarity; if this be so, there is not the slightest reason to doubt, first of all their own "realization," and secondly the existence, within the respective traditions, of doctrines and methods the purpose of which is to lead those qualified to the same perfect realization: such a doubt cannot possibly arise in any balanced mind. In actual fact among the Buddhists as among the Sufis, and also in the ancient Christian churches, there have always been sages who have proclaimed their identity with the Self, even though they have necessarily been rarer here [in the West] than in the Hindu world where the most profound truths are enunciated much more openly and more directly than anywhere else. Be that as it may, the thing which matters is not the form but the meaning of the enunciations; that one enunciation may be less direct in its form than another is no proof whatever of a lesser wisdom but solely of a lesser receptivity on the part of the particular environment. The sage stands above forms and moreover no form as such is perfect; one cannot, therefore, measure wisdom according to the mental forms which it assumes. Whether one says "Who am I?" or "What am I?" is a matter of indifference, only the meaning is important.

We venture to hope, in any case, that there does not exist in India a guru who believes himself superior to the Buddha, the Christ, or the Prophet. The extrinsic proof of their identity with the Self resides not only in their own affirmations and in the existence of spiritual ways which derive from them, but also in the possibility of invoking the redemptive Name of the *Avatāra*. Thus, the fact that one can attain Deliverance by invoking Śrī Rāma, proves the perfection of his Wisdom; the avataric Name, whether isolated, or included in a formula, is the immediate vehicle of the eternal *sadguru*.

It is clear that, compared with the Truth, theory amounts to nothing; but in order to be able to say this one must take one's stand above theory, and not below it. For one who is not even capable of understanding it, theory will be his immediate need; it is theory which for him will represent the Self. If such a one presumes to scorn theory and to concern himself only with the realization he will be wasting his time. Only he who understands the doctrine can know that in the face of Reality it also counts for nothing.

If, as some maintain, the Self is so easily understood, how is it that It is not understood by all men? If on the other hand It is hard to understand, then it follows that one must possess in the first place rare intellectual and human qualifications in order to conceive of It, not to mention realizing It, if not to explain It, which may take on forms both subtle and complex, as well as apparently simple ones.

In conclusion, we are minded to add a few further remarks about the spiritual uses of Invocation, *japa*, as found in the great traditions practically without exception. Persons affected with intellectual pretensions have been prone to look down upon those who follow this method, whether in India or elsewhere, describing it as only suitable for the spiritually immature. This opinion, based as it is upon a complete failure to understand either the operative principle behind *japa* or the "technical" conditions governing its use at various degrees, is in its way rather characteristic of certain mentalities and will therefore provide a fitting conclusion to the present discussion; besides which the subject is of great importance in itself, since it relates to a spiritual means particularly related, as all the traditions agree, to the conditions of humanity in the latter days of the cycle.

How can one deny that the practice of *japa*, when it is accompanied by appropriate meditation, is able to bring about Self-realization, in view of the fact that the *Mānava-dharma-śāstra*, the books of yoga, and other sacred texts bear witness to it? In order to understand that *japa* is not by definition a bhaktic method only (contrary to what certain people affirm) and that it can constitute an aid to the realization of Reality, one must understand that the divine Name does not refer by definition to an "objective God," but that it objectivates and actualizes the Self, exactly like the *sadguru*, and that it is thus an embodiment of the Absolute; in Sufism, the divine Name (*Allāh*) corresponds exactly to the *praṇava* "Om" with its mantras. *Japa* is not properly speaking a rite, otherwise the sacred texts would not say that for him who practices *japa* rites are no longer required. A rite is an act having a purificatory or sacrificial purpose; a Brahman could be, so to speak, crushed beneath an accumulation of rites; when it is said that rites cannot deliver from ignorance, it is evidently these sacrificial and purificatory rites which are in question, and not methodical invocation which even renders an elaborate ritualism impossible. *Japa* cannot be opposed to knowledge—which alone delivers—because it is a relative support of it; apart from the fact that the divine Name "incarnates" the divine "Ego," absolute and infinite, of which it provides us *a priori* with the virtuality, it removes *a fortiori* all such obstacles as are opposed to knowledge, that is to say such obstacles as separate us in illusory fashion from That which we have in reality never ceased to be—That which we are. If Śrī Śaṅkara says that knowledge is the only direct means of obtaining Liberation, this indicates implicitly that there are other means, indirect no doubt, but none the less efficacious. For us human beings knowledge always presents itself, at least *a priori*, in association with a support which is its vehicle; such a support can never be contrary to its own end. If the *japa* of a *jñānin* who has already obtained *tattva upadeśa* [instruction in the truth] constitutes an aid to preserving what has been assimilated spiritually, this also proves that *japa* is in no way opposed to knowledge, no more than the respiration with which *japa* moreover must eventually become merged. It is clearly evident that, after a certain stage, the "materiality" of the divine Name becomes secondary; but this likewise implies no condemnation of *japa*, quite the contrary. The jñānic *japa*, as practiced in certain Islamic religious orders, is accompanied by meditations on unreality and reality and after that by pure and unitive contemplation, which means that in Sufism, as in *Vedānta*, it is knowledge which always and alone delivers.

Śrī Śaṅkarācārya says in one of his hymns: "I do not ask of Thee, O Mother! riches, good fortune, or salvation; I seek no happiness, no knowledge. This is my only prayer to Thee: that, as the breath of life forsakes me, still I may chant Thy holy Name." And also: "If one who feeds on the flesh of dogs can learn to speak with honeyed words, a beggar gain uncounted wealth and so live long and fearlessly, simply from hearing Thy magic Name, who can describe what must befall one who repeats it day and night?" And again: "Chanting *Brahman*, the Word of Redemption, meditating on *Aham Brahmāsmi* ("I am *Brahman*"), living on alms and wandering freely, blessed indeed is the wearer of the loin-cloth." And finally: "Control the soul, restrain the breath, sift out the transient from the True; repeat the holy Name of God, and quieten the restless mind within; to this, the universal rule, apply yourself with heart and soul."

* * *

There is a dispassion which transcends all conditions of existence: this dispassion, or this deliverance, lies to some extent at the center of existence like a kernel of peace and light; it is like a drop of redemptive spray in an ocean of flames. "The whole universe is on fire," said the Buddha; our misfortune lies in our not knowing that the substance of existence is fire, this substance into which we are woven while yet remaining alien bodies. For the "naive and unrepentant," the world is a neutral space from which he chooses the agreeable content while believing he has the power to avoid the disagreeable, provided he be clever enough and meets with good luck; but the man who does not know that existence is an immense brazier has no imperative reason for wanting to get out of it, and that is why an Arabic proverb says, "The crown of wisdom is the fear of God"—that is to say, the fear of divine afflictions, which are the fatal price of our state of remoteness.

The kernel of light at the center of the current of forms is essentially the "remembrance of God"—which in the end demands all that we are—as the words of Muhammad declare: "All that is to be found on earth is accursed, save only the remembrance of God," and "There is no fault greater than that of existing." "None is good but one: God," said Christ. This implies that what comes from God—His Name—and what leads to Him—remembering His Name—share in his goodness. The virtual fire through which we live withdraws from things to the extent that we are centered on the mystery of this remembering; things then become transparent and transmit to us the rays of their immutable and blessed archetypes.

It could also be said that existence is fiery in so far as it is regarded as being outside God and, by this fact, it also leads to fire; it is a consuming blaze for the perverted will and illumination for the contemplative intelligence, and it is, thus, at once threat and "consolation," enslaving seduction and liberating vision. It is the changeless and blessed archetypes that man is seeking (did he but know it) when he attaches himself to shadows here below; and he suffers cruelly, first when these shadows disappear and later when, at death, he perceives the archetypes, from which his love for shadows had turned him away. (Music, like dancing, is the art of bringing terrestrial shadows back to celestial vibrations and divine archetypes. In the plastic arts an analogous function is performed by stylization.)

* * *

The divine name is thus a manifestation of the supreme principle, or to speak more plainly, it is not therefore in the first place a manifestation, but is the principle itself.[29]

[29] Cited in C. Ramanujachari and V. Raghavan, *Spiritual Heritage of Tyāgarāja* (Madras: Sri Rāmakrishna Math, 1966).

Part II

LEADERS OF KĀVERĪ DELTA *NĀMASIDDHĀNTA*

4.

Bodhendra and Sadgurusvāmi (by N. Raghunathan)[1]

Bhajana and *nāma-sankīrtana* are among the most prominent items of congregational devotion practiced by Hindus. Chanting the many auspicious names of the Lord with form, *saguṇa Brahman,* who is the object of worship even of those who believe in the advaitic Absolute, the formless One without a second who is beyond word and thought, has been regarded as the most acceptable form of praise of the Most High. It is calculated to invoke His Grace and, by reminding the devotee of God's infinite Wisdom, Goodness, Beauty, and Power, to instill in his mind a longing for intimate and loving communion with Him. For the past two hundred years neither the group singing of devotional songs (*bhajana*) nor the musical recital of litanies (*nāma-sankīrtana*) composed in honor of different aspects of the Godhead—Śiva, Viṣṇu, or Śakti—nor the repetitive chanting of the names of the great *avatārs,* Rāma and Krishna, has been begun in the Tamil country without the following panegyric verses being first sung in honor of the saints who are the subject of this paper:

> We beseech the Grace of Śrī Bodhendra, the prince of yogis and most glorious of spiritual preceptors, who was the embodiment

[1] First published in T.M.P. Mahadevan, ed. *A Seminar on Saints* (Madras: Ganesh and Co., 1960). N. Raghunathan was a colleague and friend of V. Raghavan. This essay completes and complements the other sketches of *Nāmasiddhānta* leaders by V. Raghavan. It was influenced by V. Raghavan's studies, though it was not written by him. Without this piece a gap would be left in the study, and because it was written by Raghunathan after consultation with, and guidance from, V. Raghavan, I have included it here. The *bhajana* program sequence codified by Sadgurusvāmī is as follows, according to Veṅkaṭaramana Bhāgavatar, the elder *bhajana* leader of Tiruvidaimarudur village, with whom I spoke in July 1989. First, Gaṇeśa invocation and verses invoking Bodhendra and Āyyāvāl. Then, 1. *Todayamaṅgalam kīrtanas* by Chinnayya Tāllappakka. 2. Songs celebrating the gurus Bodhendra and 3. Ayyāvāl and 4. Sadgurusvāmī. 5. *Gītā Govinda* lyrics. 6. Nārāyaṇa Tīrtha songs from Krishnalīlātaraṅgini. 7. Bhadrācalam Rāmadās *kīrtana.* 8. Purandaradāsa song. 9. Sadāśiva Brahmendra songs. 10. Gopala Krishna Bharati song in Tamil. 11. Tyāgarāja songs in Telugu. Then songs in other languages: Kabīr, Tulsidās, Mahārāṣṭra *abhaṅgas.* Chidambaram Natarāja *kīrtanas,* Śaiva and Vaiṣṇava songs, *divyanāma sankīrtanas,* and finally a ritual in which the singers sing while circumambulating a lamp with five flames.

of the inexhaustible riches of the soul which is the empire the Lord's Name brings.

We bow at the feet of Śrī Veṅkaṭarama [Sadgurusvāmi], the prince of spiritual guides, who was the incarnation in one person of the two great souls: Śrī Bhagavan-nāma Bodhendra and Śrīdhara Ārya.

Bhagavan-nāma Bodhendra, to give him his full *āśrama* name and Śrīdhara Veṅkaṭeśa Ārya, universally venerated as "Āyyāvāl" in the Tamil country, were contemporaries who spent many years in the opening decades of the 18th century in adjacent villages near Kumbakoṇam in the Tāñjāvūr District on the banks of the Kāverī. They were chiefly responsible for the renaissance of *bhakti* in the South and of art as its handmaid, a movement which in due course produced many a flower of spiritual perfection, including the great saint-composers, Tyāgarāja, Śyāma Śāstri, and Muttusvāmi Dīkṣitar who are among the peaks of Karnāṭaka music.

From the chronicles of Śrī Kāñcīpuram Kāmakoṭi Pītham, the monastery which was founded by Śaṅkarācārya, it appears that Śrī Bodhendra, a *sannyāsin* and Rāma *bhakta*, was a Telugu Brahman born in Kāñcīpuram who succeeded his guru in the headship of the Kāñcīpuram Kāmakoṭi Pītham. While on a pilgrimage to Rāmeśvaram, from Kāñcīpuram, which was then the home seat of the *math*, he met the great scholar, saint, and Śiva *bhakta*, Āyyāvāl. The two godly men found such satisfaction in each other's holy company and in the propitious conditions for spreading the teaching of the divine Name which they found in the Tāñjāvūr countryside that Śrī Bodhendra spent the rest of his life in and near Tiruvidaimarudūr, the great Śiva *kṣetra* or holy site. He attained beatitude at Govindapuram, a nearby village where his monument still attracts crowds of devotees every year at his anniversary.

Āyyāvāl, who came of a family of Telugu Brahmans originally domiciled in Mysore, lived in Tiruviśanallūr, a village across the river, which was famous for its scholarship and piety. It had been founded by Śāhajī, the son of Ekojī of the Mahāraṣtra dynasty. Āyyāvāl too was an advaitin, but he lived the householder's life. He had won the king's regard in his early years by his attainments as a poet and scholar and by his character. Settling down in the village of which his father was one of the original grantees, he composed many hymns in praise of Śiva, his *iṣṭadevatā* or favorite form of the divine, and other deities. He composed a treatise of the efficacy of the divine Name as a *tārakamantra*, a saving utterance.[2] From references

[2] A *mantra* or incantatory word or group of words which is believed to help the earnest seeker who repeats it to transcend the ocean of *karma* or transmigratory existence.

to it in Śrī Bodhendra's tracts on the same subject we know it was called *Bhagavan-nāma bhuṣana* and was distinguished by its devotional fervor, learning, and insight. Unfortunately no manuscript of the work has come to light.

Āyyāvāl is a household name in the Tāñjāvūr countryside because of a remarkable legend connected with his life. On a *śrāddha* day a starving untouchable came to his back-garden and piteously wailed for food. Without a moment's hesitation, the saint ordered the food cooked for ceremonial offering to the Brahmans to be given to him, though that involved a great violation of rule and practice. When the villagers remonstrated he prayed to the holy Gaṅgā, and forthwith the well in his back-yard began to rise and overflow. The onlookers were convinced that the holy Ganges stream had indeed issued from its Northern home, appearing here to testify to the loving compassion that had welled up from a good man's heart, and thus proclaimed to the world his superior sanctity.

A few decades after the passing away of both these saints there was born in another Telugu Brahman family of Tiruviśanallūr a child who was named Veṅkaṭarama, but who was known to fame as Śrī Sadgurusvāmī. An intense yearning for God developed in him from his earliest youth. Well-versed in the *śāstras* and endowed with an extraordinarily fascinating personality he was cut out for success, but his mind turned away from worldly pursuits. He dutifully lived a householder's life for a short while, following the *uñchavṛitti dharma;*[3] and when he lost his dependents he went about the countryside, a real *mukta* (liberated soul), incessantly singing the glory of God and the power of the divine Name, in all of the divine aspects and *avatārs*, thus consciously carrying on the combined mission of Bodhendra and Āyyāvāl. It is to his self-dedication to the task of resuscitating the *bhāgavata dharma* that metaphorical reference is made in the verse I have quoted above, which speaks of him as the incarnation of these two sainted men. After some years of itinerant ministry he came to rest at Marudānallūr, another village near Kumbakoṇam, where he established the Rādhākrishna *Bhajana* Maṭh and initiated large numbers into the divine mystery of *Rāma-nāma*. The heads of that lay *maṭha*, whose succession he established in the family of the disciple who first welcomed

[3] This had originally referred to the vow that a man would live by picking up the stray unregarded ears of grain that had fallen in the field or by the wayside while harvesters were at work. Later it came to mean the practice of accepting the small offerings of rice the devout made as the *bhāgavata* (one who dedicated himself wholly to the life of devotion) went along the village street of a morning singing or chanting the praises of the Lord.

him to that village, are looked upon as having authority, through the grace of Śrī Sadgurusvāmī, to initiate the aspirant in *Rāma-nāma japa*. That *maṭh* and other *bhajana-maṭhs* founded by his disciples in the Tāñjāvūr District and elsewhere carry on the *bhajana sampradāya* established by Bodhendra and Sadgurusvāmī and propagate the *Nāma-siddhānta* which teaches that salvation may be obtained by putting one's trust in the mercy of the Lord and the infinite potency of the divine Name. Though they were all mystics of a high order, Bodhendra was a philosopher as well, while Āyyāvāl was primarily a poet—his *Ākhya śaṣṭi*, on the potency of *Śiva-nāma* and his *Daya śaṭakam* (an invocation of the Compassion of Lord Śiva) show imagination as well as learning and piety, and Sadgurusvāmī was ecstatic with the power to impart a touch that transforms.

Before he became a *sannyāsin* Bodhendra had been to Banāras and traveled widely in the North. Age-long tradition credits him with having received the text of *Bhagavan-nāma kaumudi* from the family of its remarkable fifteenth-century author Lakṣmīdhara, who may be said to have been the first theoretician who systematized the philosophy which is familiarly known as the *Nāma-siddhānta* and who, as the picturesque legend has it, prophesied that it would be given to a great *sannyāsin* to spread the faith in the divine Name in the Southland (*dākṣiṇa deśa*). Bodhendra was familiar with Ananta Deva's commentary on Lakṣmīdhara's work as well as works by later writers on the subject.

Lakṣmīdhara, who is described as a great authority on *pūrva mimāṃsā*, the philosophical theory of ritual, seeks to establish in his terse treatise, by reference to scriptures— *Śruti* (*Vedas*), *Smṛiti* (Law books), *Itihāsa* (history and legends), and *Purāṇa* (devotional narrative scriptures), that there is no such large difference of opinion as had been supposed to exist between *Smṛiti* and *Purāṇa* in regard to the efficacy of the divine Name as the instrument for the destruction of sins and the opening of the way to salvation. He resolutely maintains that if the *Smṛitis* should differ from the *Purāṇas* in regard to any vital matter we would be justified in preferring the *Purāṇas*, because their recognized purpose, the "*upabrahmana*," making clear and explicit the teaching of the Veda, shows that they are superior to the *Smṛitis* which are merely ancillary and derivative. He traces thus the orderly evolution of spiritual progress by means of the practice of repetitions of the divine Name:

> The recital of the divine Name leads to the extinction of sin: the continued repetition of the Name strengthens the good tendencies (*vāsanas*) connected with the connotations of the name and the elimination of the bad *vāsanas* which had

> strengthened the tendency to sin; this generates the impulse to serve the devotees of the Lord; their infectious zeal in describing His manifold glory induces *naiṣṭikī bhakti*, unshakable devotion; then follow in succession the abolition of sorrow, the exaltation of the soul, the realization of the Highest, which is Truth and therefrom *mukti*.

Lakṣmīdhara bases his view mainly on the *Bhāgavata Purāṇa*, which is the *bhakti* scripture par excellence. He describes *bhakti* as *rati*, love for the Divine. There is not, however, in his work any reference to the Rādha-Krishna devotional movement or the refinements of the teachings of *prema-bhakti* or devoted love which the Caitanya school developed. Lakṣmīdhara traces the exaltation of the divine Name to its source in the Veda itself, quoting the Ṛik of Dirghatamas: "O praisers, knowing them, praise every one of his names. O Viṣṇu, we desire the good will of you who are great."

> *āsyajānanto nāmacidvivaktana*
> *mahatte viṣṇo sumatim bhajāmahe*

This is relied upon by Śrī Śaṅkara also in his commentary on the *Viṣṇu sahasranāma* to establish the potency of *Nāma-japa* and *Nāma-kirtana*.

Bodhendra, in his turn, reinforces the authority of the Ṛig Vedic verse with a Yajur Vedic verse.[4] And he also relies largely on the great *ācārya* Śaṅkara's *Gītā Bhāṣya* and *Sahasra-nāma Bhāṣya* as on the *Bhāgavata Purāṇa*, the *Viṣṇu Purāṇa*, the *Bṛihan-naradīya*, the *Brahma-vaivarta* and other *Purāṇas*, to support a thesis which is broadly the same as that of Lakṣmīdhara. He does this with massive erudition, a logical subtlety and nimbleness of mind which extort admiration. His mastery of *pūrva mimāṁsā* and *nyāya*, and his undoubted authority as a great advaitin who has written his own commentary on Śrī Śaṅkara's *Bhagavad Gītā Bhāṣya*, as well as the saintliness of his life, must have made him a formidable foe to the "frogs in the well" as he contemptuously terms those who thought that the exaltation of the Name as divine incarnation, *Bhagavan-nāma*, had no philosophical basis. One of them, in particular, roused his ire by writing a book which apparently gained some vogue even in areas outside the Tamil country, though even its name has not come down to us. His *Nāma-amṛita Rasodaya*, in six chapters, the longest of his treatises on the subject—he

[4] *patatte adyasipivista nāmāryassamsamiva yunnani vidvān.* (This passage from the *Yajur Veda* is not identified by number in the original article.)

seems to have written many, as seen from the tribute of panegyrists who speak of him as *Nāma-nibandha-śatakarta*—is a superb example of his polemical gift as well as of his practiced skill as a teacher; he uses iteration with great virtuosity. Of his other extant works, the *Nāma-amṛita rasāyana* is the most compendious as it seems to have been one of the earliest. It marshals the six reasons given by this school of thought for regarding the utterance of the divine Name as superior to other means prescribed in the scriptures. (1) the practice of *nāma-japa*, which is open to everybody irrespective of caste, stage of life (*āśrama*) or sex, involves no injury; (2) it needs no ancillary aid; (3) it is not dependant on the intercession of another person; (4 to 6) its practice is not regulated by restrictions and prohibitions regarding time, or place, or ritual. This tract also describes the ten kinds of "*nāma-aparādhas*" or sins which retard the efficacy of *nāma-kīrtana*. These sins include that of caviling against perfected men. Expiation for these sins is to be found only in the continued chanting of the divine Name till the propensity to sin is extinguished.[5]

Among these ten "*nāma-aparādhas*" figures another which is of peculiar significance for a true understanding of the teachings of Bodhendra and his followers. The sectarian who exalts his *iṣṭa-devatā* at the expense of others comes in for vigorous trouncing as being guilty of *nāma-aparādha*. Śrī Bodhendra is credited with two other works, *Hari-hara bhedadhikkāra* and *Hari- hara-advaita-bhūṣaṇam*, which aim to show that the scriptures which seem to exalt Viṣṇu and cry down Śiva, and vice versa, do this merely with a view to strengthening people's faith in the deity of their own allegiance and that the depreciation of others is not intended to be taken too seriously. By an elaborate review of all the relevant authorities he shows that the fundamental intention of all the scriptures is to emphasize the unity of the Godhead, the essential identity of Viṣṇu and Śiva. No less remarkable is the insistence, in an advaitin and a *sannyāsin* too, that *Mūrta-brahma upāsana*, the meditation or worship of the *Brahman* with attributes, is essential as a preparation for *advaita-anubhava*, the realization of oneness. He indeed stoutly declares that the foolish who deride *saguṇa upāsana* (devotion to the divine with qualities) can never hope to realize the *nirguṇa*, supreme formless reality. In this Śrī Bodhendra does not depart

[5] Bodhendra is no formalist. He suggests that the man who has developed passionate devotion and would like to spend his time doing *nāmasankīrtana* could legitimately restrict himself to the minimum of ritual observances and duties enjoined by the *Smṛitis*, provided he at the same time gives only the minimum of attention to worldly affairs and the earning of a livelihood.

from the spirit of the great Śaṅkara's teaching.

The influence of the *bhakti* movement started by Bodhendra and Āyyāvāl, strengthened by Sadgurusvāmī, and fortified by the living example of many a realized soul still keeps alive the flame of spirituality in the hearts of the people. And it has been a most potent force for true toleration. This catholicity of outlook indeed characterizes all the mystics who have exalted the divine Name from the early beginnings of the movement. It can be traced to Lakṣmīdhara himself. One of the closing verses of *Bhagavannāma kaumudi* effects a magnificent imaginative identification of Śiva and Viṣṇu with each other, with the guru and with the *iṣṭa-devatā.* With that characteristic expression of the Indian synthesis this short account may appropriately end:

> He who (as Viṣṇu) was the creator of the holy Gaṅgā, which flowed from his lotus feet, fell so much in love with its redemptive virtues that (as Śiva) he bore it on his own head: he is our Guru, he is the divine ruler of our race.[6]

[6] Lakṣmīdhara, *Bhagavannāma Kaumudi* (Kasi: Prakāśasthānam Acyutagranthamālā Kāryālayaḥ, 1907). A copy of this book is available at Widener Library, Harvard University.

5.

Śrīdhara Veṅkaṭeśa Āyyāvāl: Poet and Legendary Enthusiast of the Name[1]

"He who has pure knowledge and strong devotion toward the
Almighty and the Almighty's Name,
He who has love for the devotee, who is a worshipper of the
Name,
He who has detachment from all else, his heart turned toward
the Lord, steadfast in his loving kindness—
I give my veneration to that human form of the divine *Parameśvara*,
whose name is Śrīdhara Veṅkaṭeśa Āyyāvāl, the Guru."

It is with this prayer that *Bhajana sampradāya* sessions in South India begin. The divine form of Śrīdhara Veṅkaṭeśa Āyyāvāl is worthy of this veneration; it is well known that this saintly man was referred to both by the common people and by the learned as "Āyyāvāl," meaning "the honored one, the respected sire." That he was known by this name shows their deep regard for him. Śrīdhara Veṅkaṭeśa and Śrīmad Bodhendra were two important souls who gave life to the *bhajana* tradition and Name repetition movement throughout Chola Deśa.

The Mahārāṣṭran rulers of Tāñjāvūr patronized the arts and education on a large scale. Tāñjāvūr flourished very well during the reigns of Śāhajī, Śarabhojī, and Tukojī, sons of Ekojī, who founded the Mahārāṣṭra dynasty there. The arts developed greatly during their reigns. Of the three rulers, Śāhajī (1684-1710) was foremost. Not only did he encourage talented poets, but he himself was also well-versed in arts and literature. He composed poems and musical dramas in Telugu, Marāthi, and Sanskrit, and his devotion and generosity toward learned saints show that he was filled with spiritual discernment and yogic determination.

[1] The first two paragraphs and the last two paragraphs of this piece I have taken from V. Raghavan's introduction to the *Ākhyāṣaṣṭi* (Kumbakonam and Madras: Kāmakoṭi Kosasthānam, 1944), No. 15 in the series. The rest of the article (except for the translations from the *Ākhyāṣaṣṭi*) is from the introduction to *Śāhendravilāsa*, ed. V. Raghavan (Tiruchi: Tanjore Saraswati Mahal Library, 1952), pp. 60-74. I have had to omit some details because of space limitations.

In 1693 King Śāhajī donated the sacred place of Tiruviśanallūr village to 46 learned families who were well-versed in various specialties of knowledge, and the place was renamed Śāhajirājapuram. Śrī Rāmabhadra Dikṣitar, Bhaskara Dikṣitar, Veda Kavi, Mahādeva Kavi, Periappa Kavi, Nallakavi, Śivarāmakrishnar alias Sadāśiva Brahmendra, are all great people who belonged to these families. Among them were certain families from what is now Andhra Pradesh, too. Among the Telugu families one was that of Mokṣam Somasundara, and another was that of Śrīdhara Liṅgayariar. The great saint Śrī Sadāśiva Brahmendra was born of Somasundara, and it is thought by some that Śrīdhara Veṅkaṭeśa was born of the latter, namely Liṅgayariar.

It is not known for certain if Śrīdhara Veṅkaṭeśa, who was patronized by King Śāhajī, was one of the forty-five primary donees of the village of Tiruviśanallūr or not. That he was a resident of that village is amply borne out by the existence in that village of his house and the annual festival that takes place there in his honor. It would therefore appear that he was a subsequent donee. Śrīdhara Veṅkaṭeśa, as his prefixed house-name shows, was evidently a member of a family originating in what is now Andhra Pradesh. It is definitely known that there were pandits from the Telugu country among the donees of this village; but none of these is noted in the list of donee names in the grant with his house-name. Our author was known to his contemporaries as Veṅkaṭeśa or Veṅkaṭeśvara Śāstrin, as can be seen in Bodhendra's references to him.[2] If Śrīdhara Veṅkaṭeśa was one of the donees, he can only be the Veṅkaṭeśvara Śāstrin mentioned as the 24th in the list, but the likelihood is that the *Nāmasiddānta* author named Śrīdhara Veṅkaṭeśa is different from this Veṅkaṭeśvara.

Śrīdhara, as has been pointed out, is his house name; and in his colophonic verses in *Śāhendravilāsa* ("The Illustrious Acts of King Śāhajī") he mentions his father as Liṅgārya. That this Telugu Śrīdhara was

[2] Among the donee names, we have one Venkateśvara Vājapeyayājin (21st), one Veṅkaṭeśvara Śāstrin (24th), one Samavedi Veṅkaṭeśvara Śāstrin (39th), and one Veṅkaṭeśvara Kavi (42nd). Of these the Sāmavedi Veṅkaṭeśvara Śāstrin is evidently the same as the son of Ikkiri Appā Śāstrin alias Śrīnivasa, later Pūrṇānandayati, of Prayāga family, Kauśika gotra and Kaṇḍaramāṇikkam village (*Ind. Ant.* 1904, pp. 127, 191). The Vājapeyin and Kavi Veṅkaṭeśvaras are not likely to be our author; the latter, mentioned as Kavi, is as shown above, the pupil of Rāmabhadra Dīkṣita and author of the *Patañjalicaritavyākhyā* and *Ūṇādinighaṇṭu*. There is also a Veṅkaṭeśvara Śāstrin found as one of the collaborators with our Śrīdhara Veṅkaṭeśvara in the compilation *Padamaṇimañjari*.

patronized by the Tāñjāvūr court is evident from the *Cakorasandeśa* of Navīna Patañjali Śrīdhara Peru Suri.[3]

His Life

As mentioned before, Śrīdhara Veṅkaṭeśa is more popularly known as "Āyyāvāl," meaning "the respected sire." In fact, few indeed will be the South Indians with any pretentions to culture or religious faith who have not heard of "Āyyāvāl" and the annual festival that is held in his name—the Āyyāvāl *utsava* at Tiruviśanallūr. There is hardly any *bhajana math*, or prayer hall, where his portrait is not venerated; there are not only prayer-verses on him, but songs composed on him and sung regularly as part of the *bhajana* program. He, along with his contemporary Bodhendra, was responsible in the Kāverī delta region for the great spread of that phase of the *bhakti* devotional movement which believes in the singing of the Lord's glory and the repetition of the divine name, *Nāmasiddhānta*, as the most efficacious means of salvation, particularly in the present age. It is not only by his writings on this subject, both in the form of devotional hymns and critical treatise, but also by the high devotional and spiritual attainments of his life that he came to occupy this leading place in the pantheon of devotees of the Lord.

Several anecdotes are traditionally handed down in respect of Āyyāvāl and his spiritual attainments. It is said that with one of his hymns, the *Kulīrāṣṭaka*, he brought rains at a time when they had failed, and the last verse of the hymn itself has a bearing on this incident. With this hymn *Tārāvalīstuti*, he is said to have brought back to life or saved from imminent death a child, and the second half of each verse in this hymn has a direct reference to it.

More celebrated than these two miracles is the incident of Āyyāvāl and the hunger-stricken *caṇḍāla* or untouchable, which "canonized" Āyyāvāl and gave birth to the annual Āyyāvāl festival on the new-moon day in the month of Kārttika (November-December). Once, on the day on which he had to perform the annual *śraddha* ceremony for his departed parent, Āyyāvāl, while going to the Kāverī river for a bath, saw a *caṇḍāla* in the throes of death as a result of starvation; Āyyāvāl who saw the oneness of life everywhere and realized the universal presence of the Lord, was moved by the sight, and asked the consecrated *śraddha* food made ready at his house for the Brahman invitees to be made over to the *caṇḍāla*.

[3] Tāñjāvūr Ms. No. 3863.

Custom demanded from him an expiation in the form of a bath in the Ganges; for this he uttered forth a prayer to Mother Gaṅgā.

Of contemporary references to Śrīdhara Veṅkaṭeśa, two have come to my notice: As shown below, Bodhendra cites him in his work on *Nāmasiddhānta*. In the play, *Śṛingāramañjari Śāharājīya* by Periappā Kavi alias Vainateya, the author refers to himself in the Prologue as having received approbation from Śrīdhara Veṅkaṭeśa, among others. Our author is mentioned by Appākavi as a respected friend of the same age.[4]

Of the distinguished writers of the age who sat at our author's feet, we know now only one, Vīṇai Ayyaṇṇa Dīkṣita, a Telugu scholar and expert player on the *vīṇā*. Ayyanna's *Vyāsatatparya Nirṇaya* is a well known tract on *advaita*, conveying the correct import of the *Brahma sūtras*.[5] The author was the son of Veṅkaṭeśa Kavi, author of Rādhāmādhavasamvāda and other Telugu *prabandas* and younger brother of Nṛihari, author of Telugu *prabandhas* like *Sudantā Kalyāna*. In the second introductory verse, the author salutes his guru, Śrīdhara Veṅkaṭeśa Āyyāvāl.

His Works

As is only to be expected from the above given account of the life of Āyyāvāl, his devotional hymns became most popular. As early as 1895 the Śrī Vidyā Press of Kumbakonam, brought out a *grantha* script edition of all the *stotras* composed by Śrīdhara Veṅkaṭeśa. This collection which was edited by the well known Nṛisimha Bhāgavatar and Bhattaśrī Nārāyaṇa Śāstrigal consists of

1. Ākhyāṣaṣṭi
2. Dāyaśataka
3. Matṛibhutasataka
4. Stutipaddhati
5. Śivabhaktikalpalatikā
6. Śivabhaktalakṣaṇa
7. Tārāvalīstotra
8. Ārtiharastuti
9. Kulirāṣṭaka
10. Jambūnāthāṣṭaka
11. Dosapariharaṣṭaka
12. Krishnadvādaśamañjarī
13. Acyutāṣṭaka
14. Dolānavaratnamālā

[4] Madras Ms. R. 1843.

[5] It was published by the Vani Vilas Press in 1910 on the basis of two manuscripts from Mysore but neither of which contained the informing colophon in the Madras manuscript of that work (D. 15276). Two other works written by Ayyanna Dīkṣita are *Praṇavārthasudhodaya* and *Yajñaśāstrārthanirṇaya*. See New Catalogus Catalogorum, I, p. 271A.

and was based on manuscripts of these works collected from several places. Not only did the same Press subsequently reprint this collection, but other agencies too brought out similar collections.[6]

It is said that there is a hymn of his on Gaṅgā, (the Ganges) associated with the miracle narrated above but, as already stated, it has not yet been recovered and identified.

On the subject of the sanctity and efficacy of uttering the Lord's Name and attaining salvation thereby, i.e., on the *Nāma-siddhānta* school of devotion to which he gave a great stimulus in the Kāverī delta, he had made contributions in the form of hymns mentioned already, the *Ākhyāṣaṣṭi* being particularly a work of importance in this respect. Besides these, Śrīdhara Veṅkaṭeśa wrote a regular treatise called the *Bhagavan nāma bhūṣana* on this subject. This work has unfortunately not yet been found in manuscript. (The fifth *Śaṅkarabharaṇa-rāga* song in Gopālakrishna Bhārati's *Rāgamālikā* is on Śrīdhara Veṅkaṭeśa and refers to this work of our author.)

Another work with which Śrīdhara Veṅkaṭeśa was connected is the list of words called *Padamaṇimañjari* which he and two contemporaries and co-villagers of his, his namesake Veṅkaṭeśvara Śāstrin and Nallādhavarin, compiled at the behest of their beloved patron, King Śāhajī.[7]

At the end of each canto of his *Śāhendravilāsa* he refers to himself as proficient in all *śāstras*, particularly in *nyāya*, but no work of his in this line has yet come to light.

The only *kāvya* or lengthy narrative poem of his is the *Śāhendravilāsa* on his patron Śāhajī.

The question has been asked, how was it that the great saint and devotee of the Lord Āyyāvāl composed the poem on King Śāhajī? That is,

[6] The Vaidika Vardhani Press at the same place started issuing with Tamil meaning the hymns of our author in a series called the Śrīdhara *Stutimaṇimāla*, and the most famous ones among these, the *Ākhyāṣaṣṭi* and *Dāyaśataka* appeared in 1900. In *Devanāgarī*, the Vani Vilas Press, Śrīraṅgam, began publishing them in their Stotra Booklet Series: the *Ākhyāṣaṣṭi* and the *Śivabhaktikalpalatikā* appeared in 1908; *the Dāyaśaṭaka* and the *Mātṛibhutaśataka* in 1911. Of the other hymns, the same Press published in Vol. V, No. 17 of the *Journal of the Saṅkaragurukulam* (pp. 3-5) the *Kulīraśataka*, the *Tārāvalīstuti*, and the *Ārtihara-Umeśastotra.* With English and Tamil translations, Tamil notes and Introductions, V. Raghavan brought out the *Ākhyāsaṣṭi* and the *Dāyaśaṭaka* in the Kamakoti Granthavali. *Nāmāmṛitarasāyana* was published by Poornachandrodayam Press, Tanjore, 1926.

[7] The compilation, of which two manuscripts exist in the Sarasvati Mahal Library in Tāñjāvūr (Nos. 5011 and 5012).

why did he indulge in *nara-stuti*, "praise of man" as it is usual to put it? It is hardly necessary to offer in explanation of this that the *Śāhendravilāsa* was, as is clear, a production of the earlier years of Śrīdhara Veṅkaṭeśa. Even if the poem was written by him in his later years, there is nothing inappropriate in it. The close association of learned men and even *sannyāsins* with rulers has been a constant feature of Indian literary history; and as it happens quite often these rulers have been active litterateurs themselves. Rāmabhadra Dīkṣita, who was an exclusive devotee of God in the form of Rāma and would praise none else, was the most intimate author friend of Śāhajī and has praised him many times. Bhāskararāya, also known as Bhāsurānandanātha, one of the senior and much respected personalities of this time, and an acknowledged *ācārya* of highest attainments in Śakta-worship, composed, as has already been pointed out, a eulogy of eight verses on Śāhajī, in which he anticipated the same criticism that we are considering here.[8]

Apart from his zeal for fostering culture, Śāhajī, as all his court-poets have pointed out and as the works ascribed to him show, was deeply imbued with devotion. He was such an ardent *bhakta* of God Tyāgarāja of Tiruvārūr that when a reference is made to his demise, it is said that he attained oneness with Tyāgeśa.

The *Śāhendravilāsa* is primarily a poem, though it incorporates a few historical facts and narrates the two important military events of Śāhajī's time, the aid given to the Setupati and Rājarām at Gingee. As is usual in such compositions, poetic descriptions progress in the well known order: childhood, youth and marriage, hero's prowess and the march of the army, hunting and sporting in garden and water, city and palace, sunset and sunrise, love and separation, and seasons and scenes of nature.

Śāhajī came to the throne very young and died young at 40; except for the few events already referred to, there was not much of political unsettlement to disturb the peace and prosperity of the decades during which Tāñjāvūr was under his rule. Our author by speaking of him not only as an incarnation of Śiva, but also by expressing it in so many words that the God-appointed role of his life was to free the country from the harassment caused by the Muslims (VII. 10) reflects but correctly the security and stimulus that the resilient Hindu Chiefs of the South from the Vijayanagar times onwards gave to Hindu religion and culture. At this time there was the new menace of the Christian missionaries masquerading as Roman Brahmans, weaning away the masses and reviling Hindu faith

[8] Tāñjāvūr Catalogue XIV, p. 6411.

and worship. The European historian Manucci vouchsafes to us, in his reference to Śāhajī's persecution of the Christians, that our hero's zeal for the safeguarding of the country's religion was really comprehensive in its sweep. No wonder that Nallā alias Bhūmināṭha takes Śāhajī's biography as a holy chronicle and record of *dharma* in his *Dharmavijaya Campū*. The concluding eulogy in that work presents a true picture of the plenty and all round richness of life that was vouchsafed to the people of the Kāverī delta in this period. The tradition of the cultural richness of this area goes indeed to the Chola times and even earlier, but credit is due to the successive rulers who realized the value of this culture, and not only preserved it but enriched it considerably. If the Nāyaks reinforced it with elements of value from Telugu, the Marāthas breathed some fresh life into it with the elements from the Mahārāṣṭra. In arts and letters, devotion and spiritual endeavor, the culture of the Kāverī delta attained a marvelous complexion, varied, brilliant, and uplifting. In the making of this Kāverī river delta culture, the fragrance of which has not yet died out, Śāhajī played no small part, Śāhajī whom Āyyāvāl rightly hailed in this poem as "himself the heart and soul of the Muse."[9]

Āyyāvāl in Praise of the Name

Śrī Āyyāvāl praised the holy name, which like a mother pours out so much welfare, love, generosity, and nurturing care toward Name devotees, especially in verse like the following from the *Ākhyāṣaṣṭi*:[10]

> Some who contemplate that divine form of Śiva enjoy some good things in this world; others, O Mother, Compassion of Śiva, thanks to your support, delight in enjoying the ambrosial billows of Śiva's Name and casting away all anguish (v. 4).
>
> O Compassion! When will the floods of your excellences, in which are immersed Śiva Himself, engulf me with the ambrosial billows of the auspicious Names incessantly recited, Names like Smararati (Enemy of the Love-god), Śambhu (Auspicious),

[9] Editor's note: I have omitted a detailed critique of Āyyāvāl's poetry because it does not bear directly on our topic of *Nāmasiddhānta*.

[10] Editors note: I have selected these from V. Raghavan's translation of the *Ākhyṣaṣṭi Śatakam* of Śrīdhara Veṅkaṭeśa Āyyāvāl (Kumbakoṇam and Madras: Kāmakoṭi Kosasthānam, 1944), No. 25 in the series. They are not in the original introduction to *Śāhendravilāsa*.

Purahara (Destroyer of Tripura), Śiva, Umādhava (Lord of Pārvatī), Hara, Murari (Enemy of the demon Mura), Govinda, Chief of Gods, Mukunda (v. 22).

O Compassion of Śiva! You are capable of granting immediately the state of Brahmā or the fortune of Viṣṇu; why don't you give me the state of sitting somewhere, rid of all distress and concentrated in the continuous recital of the Name of Śiva? (v. 29).

"Let this man utter once the Name of Śiva even if it be through the guise of words like (*a*)*hara* ('Bring') and I shall take away all his distress." Which man, not stupid like me will not, without thought of another thing, resort to you who are thus constantly wakeful, O Compassion of Śiva? (v. 32).

O Compassion! If I am not taken up for support on the ground that I am a sinner, tell Śiva there will be ruin to his reputation as the protector of the distressed and as one the occasional utterance of whose Name destroys all sins (v. 56).

O Compassion! The occasional contemplation of Śiva, doing obeisance to Him or the mention of His Name, becomes the supreme means of removing the transmigratory toil, because of you. O Mother, your way is great indeed! (v. 91).

O Compassion! Give me that steadfast mind that Śiva and Viṣṇu, who are both like Śiva to me, may never leave my mind; even so, make this tongue of mine utter "Śiva, Śiva," for, barring these two, there is nothing else that is the object of my desire (v. 99).

O Compassion of Śiva! In my last moment, by your grace, may this much appear in my heart: this two-syllable Name, "Śiva, Śiva," your abode, the giver of Release, a Name that is auspicious to the whole universe (v. 101).

There are few in South India who have not heard of the Āyyāvāl Festival, which is still celebrated on Kārttika new-moon day in Tiruviśanallūr village, where Āyyāvāl spent so much of his life. Devotees continue to celebrate the episode in Āyyāvāl's life when he offered food to a starving untouchable, and then, ordered by offended Brahmans to bathe in the Ganges, saw the river goddess Gaṅgā arise from the well in his yard; devotees celebrate the event with a ritual bath at the well and with other festival ceremonies suitable to his memory.

There are many other interesting stories told about Āyyāvāl which show him as one who had attained great spiritual wisdom: he used to worship daily in a temple across the Kāverī river in Tiruvidaimarudur where Mahāliṅga Svāmī was the presiding deity. On two occasions floods obstructed this worship. Both times it is said that the Lord himself came to Āyyāvāl: once in the form of a priest, to deliver the divine offering (*prasād*) to him, and another time in the form of a boat-man, to take Āyyāvāl across the river.

6.

Sadāśiva Brahmendra: The Silent *Avadhūta*[1]

Who in Tamil Nadu has not heard the songs *Mānasa sañchara re* ("O mind, be occupied with *Brahman*"), *Brūhi mukundeti* ("Chant Mukunda, o my tongue"), and *Piba re rāmarasam* ("Taste the nectar of Rāma's Name")? Their composer is no less renowned than the celebrated composer Tyāgarāja. While Tyāgarāja and Dīkṣitar sang of the personal divinity, *saguṇa Brahman*, "the Supreme Being with qualities," the *sannyāsin*-author of these songs sang of the Impersonal Absolute, the *nirguṇa Brahman*, "the Supreme Being without qualities." He sang in the fullness of his own realization of the one Godhead, beyond all names and forms and of the very nature of *sat-cit-ānanda*, ultimate Existence, Knowledge, and Bliss. He was the bard of *advaita*, the philosophy of non-duality, divine oneness. Sadāśiva Brahmendra was his name.

Sadāśiva Brahmendra Sarasvatī, who was roaming as an *avadhūta*, one from whom worldly things have "fallen off," on the banks of the Kāverī river, is a memory still fresh in the minds of all truth seekers there; in the intellectual and devotional life of the Kāverī delta, he is still a force. Sadāśivendra, before he renounced life, was the native of the well known village, Tiruviśanallūr on the Kāverī near Kumbakoṇam, which Śāhajī, the Mahrātta king of Tāñjāvūr, A.D. 1684-1712, gave away as Śāhajīrājapuram to 46 scholars. Among these was Mokṣam Somasundara Avadhani who was father of our saint whose civil name was Śivarāma. Śivarāma as a student was in the company of three outstanding personalities of the time, Rāmabhadra Dīkṣitā, Śrīdhara Veṅkaṭeśa Āyyāvāl, and Gopālakrishna Śāstri, the last of whom later became, at Sadāśivendra's insistance, the preceptor of the Tondaman Chief of Pudukoṭṭai. A vexatious delay at his father-in-law's house on a festive occasion produced a sudden revulsion in the keen mind of young Śivarāma; an excuse, as it were, suddenly marked a predestined turn in life; the scales fell; awakening beamed forth, and Śivarāma renounced life, sought the feet of the *sannyāsin* Paramaśivendra Sarasvatī, and himself entered the order as Sadāśivendra Sarasvatī.

To Brahmendral, as South Indians now reverentially speak of him, success on the spiritual path came rapidly. A redoubtable dialectician, he

[1] *Vedānta Keśari*, December 1950. Also published in *A Seminar on Saints*, ed. T.M.P. Mahadevan (Madras: Ganesh, 1960).

used to submit every scholar-visitor to his guru to severe cross-examination. When reports reached the guru of Sadāśivendra's interrogation of scholars, the guru chided him, "when are you going to control your tongue?" From that moment, Sadāśivendra gave up speech and became a silent sage (*mauna-yogi*). Another time, Sadāśivendra was lying down on an open field resting his uplifted head on air as it were; and a farmer passing across the field where Sadāśivendra was lying made a remark against him for demonstrating his yogic power. With this, the lingering infirmities of vanity of scholarship or yogic power were completely removed and his Brahmanhood reached its untainted fullness.

Mad with delight of *Brahman*, native of no roof, eating off his palm whatever fell there by chance, the Brahmendra roamed about, exemplifying the great state of one liberated while alive, *jīvanmukta*, which he himself later sang in the *Ātmavidyā vilāsa*, "The Play of the Knowledge of the Self."

> Verily, the silent sage, ever engaged in inward meditation, takes the alms placed in his hands as food and wanders along the street like an idiot (verse 39).

As the late Nṛisimha Bharati Svāmī of Śrīngeri said in his hymn on Sadāśivendra, the guru of Sadāśivendra—Śrī Paramaśivendra Sarasvatī—heard of his pupil's high *siddhi* and "bemoaned his own failure to reach those heights."

Sadāśiva Brahmendra enjoyed the highest states of consciousness sought by yogis and *sādhakas*, and tasting sublime bliss he was oblivious to the world.

While wandering in this state, he got once buried in the sands of the river near Kodumudi and when four months later the floods subsided a digger's spade found him still in *samādhi*. According to another story, his arm was once severed but he went his way unconcerned! Is not the *ātman*, with which he had become one, incapable of being severed by sword?

His final disappearance was, according to an announcement made by himself, at Nerūr near Karūr, where even now his shrine and festival are kept up by the Pudukoṭṭai State whose then ruler received Sadāśivendra's blessings when the saint was wandering in his dominion. His *mahāsamādhi* was on *Jyestha-suddha-dasami*, coming in the later part of June.

Sadāśiva Brahmendra's Writings

Sadāśiva Brahmendra is an equally distinguished name in the literary history of *advaita.* He has left brief pointed glosses on some of the *Upaniṣads* and the *Brahmā Sūtras.* On the *Yoga Sūtras* of Patāñjali, he commented, and the intricate and ramified material in Appayya Dīkṣita's *Siddhāntalesasaṅgraha* he summarized in his *Siddhānta Kalpavalli.* His guru Paramaśivendra made a valuable compilation of words expressive of *Brahman* found in the *Upaniṣads*, the *Vedānta-nāma-sahāsra-vyakhya.* Sadāśivendra abridged this in 36 verses under the title *Ātmanusandhāna.*[2]

Another interesting work by Sadāśivendra which I have been trying to piece together from scattered manuscript fragments is a compilation of all advaitic passages from the different *Purāṇas.*

Of the other philosophical minor works that he wrote, the most well-known is the *Ātmavidyāvilāsa.*[3] Indeed it is this text to which some historical importance also attaches, as can be gathered from the informing postscript in one of its manuscripts in the Tāñjāvūr Saraswatī Mahal Library. Once when Brahmendra was sojourning in the village of Dipambapura, a *sarvamanya* village (a category of land given by rulers to religious institutions with tax proceeds going to religious leaders) of the Tāñjāvūr Queen Mother, one Malhari Pandita, a friend of King Śāhajī's next brother, Serfojī I, performed three *bhīkṣas* (gifts of food, given to wandering monks) to Sadāśivendra and conveyed the King's request to bless him with progeny; Brahmendra sent to the King a copy of his *Ātmavidyāvilāsa* as his blessings, not long after which Serfojī was blessed with a son.

According to *advaita* on which the *Ātmavidyāvilāsa* is based, the only reality is the *Brahman* sung of in the *Upaniṣads* as being of the nature of *sat-cit-ānanda*, Being, Awareness, and Bliss. The world of name and form, *nāma-rūpa*, is only its appearance, *māyā*, i.e., ultimately unreal but tentatively real; the various individual souls are only the reflections of the one *Brahman.* The perishable phenomenal realities of name and form are mere transfigurations (*vivartas*) of *Brahman*, even as waves are of the water

[2] This, along with a homage to his guru called the *Navamaṇimala* the present speaker [V. Raghavan] had the good fortune to bring to light first.

[3] In fact, the Vani Vilas Press has published in the same booklet two minor works of Sadāśivendra of this name; the second is in 43 *vasantatilaka* verses, more scholastic in style and partly cast as a *Guru-śiṣyasamvada*; the first is in 65 *ārya* verses and is couched in a considerably more felicitous diction and forms a regular poem on *ātman* and *Brahman*-realization. It is this text which is more famous as the *Ātmavidyāvilāsa.* The Kāmakoṭi Kosasthānam Prakāśitam in 1951 published Sadāśiva Brahmendra's *Śivamanasikapūja kīrtanani* and *Ātmavidyāvilāsa*, with translations into Tamil and English by V. Narayanan. The translations in this article follow those renderings.

of the sea. Owing to our ignorance, *avidyā*, we superimpose an erroneous reality, later sublated by correct knowledge, even as we imagine a snake in a rope and run away. The removal of this error (*bhrama*) is achieved by the help of a guru, the cultivation of the four kinds of requisite self-discipline (*sādhana catuṣtaya*), and by listening to, ratiocinating about, and contemplating upon, *śravaṇa*, *manana*, and *nididhyāsana*, *Brahman* and its true nature.

When this knowledge of Brahman dawns, one becomes released though yet embodied and moving amidst us; he becomes *jīvan-mukta*, an ideal as glorious as that of the *bodhisattva* of Buddhism. Texts of the *Upaniṣads* and the *Bhagavad Gītā* glorify this state in which the realized souls, owning to the remnants of the traces of the unburnt karmic legacy that has begun to fructify, still move amidst us and work for our salvation. There is controversy and diversity of opinion on the *jīvan-mukta* doctrine among advaitic writers themselves, but Śaṅkara definitely says in his *Sūtra Bhāṣya* that it is a matter of one's experience and is not to be questioned at all. The life and doings of Sadāśivendra form a further testimony on the *jīvan-mukta*, one who is liberated while still alive. The *Ātmavidyāvilāsa* is a poem on this great state.

After paying obeisance to the divine guru Dākṣinamūrti and his near guru Paramaśivendra, Sadāśivendra opens with a description of the Supreme Soul, pure and always enlightened, incomparable, eternal, and devoid of parts, attributes, or forms:

> The Supreme Soul shines pure and awake and devoid of all mutations (*vikalpas*); It is unique, eternal, and free from passion; It is an indivisible whole untouched by *māyā* (ignorance) and free from the *guṇas* (the three-fold qualities: *sattva*, *rajas*, and *tamas*) (verse 4).

The next two verses show how, involved in its own illusory extension, the soul begins to delude itself and act, but at the end, by the grace of a teacher realizes its delusion and regains its pristine state. Five verses which follow emphasize the important role played by the guru in helping the bound soul to regain its lost freedom. On the attainment of this realization, one is rid of the invidious distinction of you and I, and goes about carefree like a boy, immersed in the ocean of unalloyed bliss.

The *avadhūta* state in which the author himself was roaming is then described:

> Delighted in the *ātman* (the eternal Self which he has realized) and rid of the bondage of *karma* (action), the Prince of *sannyāsins*

> is wandering about in the outskirts of the jungle, like a deaf blind idiot (verse 15).

The four directions are his garments; desirelessness his ornaments; palms, his vessels; the foot of trees his abode; as he lies on the soft sand-dunes of river beds, *vāyu* (the wind) fans him and the full moon holds the lamp.

> The sage shines supreme, silent and placid, with the ground under the tree as his nesting place and with his palm as the begging bowl, wearing no clothes but only the jewel of non-attachment (verse 35).
>
> The great recluse who has awakened to the state of perfect Being-Awareness-Bliss rests in his house, which is the deserted bush on the river-bank, on the rare and very comfortable bed of soft sands (verse 36).
>
> The recluse shines a king of kings, resting serenely on the soft bed of bare ground, with the cool breeze as his unique *cāmara*, the royal whisk, and with the full moon as his lamp in the royal chamber (verse 37).

In a series of poetic fancies, the ecstatic state of *Brahman*-realization is then described, depicting the soul as a lover in spiritual nuptials with the spouse of peace, as the king ruling over the kingdom of *svārajya*, as the intellectual hero who has slain the foes of nescience, as the effulgent sun on the horizon of knowledge, as the cloud raining the nectar of immortality and removing all the heat of inner ills, as the refreshing breeze from the park of bliss, as the swan sporting in the lake of wisdom, as the cuckoo perched on the boughs of the *Upaniṣads* warbling the sweetest notes. He is beyond praise and blame; has transcended learning and left all activity behind; is full and shines like a steady flame:

> The yogi remains in a state of plenitude, like an unruffled lamp, having cast all injunctions (of the *Śāstras*) aside; and having completely rejected (even) acts of duty (verse 42).

Unassailed by any sense-objects, he stands like a log, in his own incomparable plenitude. He makes no distinction between one living being and another, seeing everywhere the full *Brahman*. He rejects none, accepts none; knowing the play of *avidyā*, he is supremely indifferent to everything; in the fullness of his knowledge, there is no retrospection on a past nor a prospecting of the future; a great beggar, yet the king of all the passionless. A rhapsody of four verses on the *Brahman*, which now end the poem, sweeps us off our feet and deposits us on that summit of *sat-cit-ānanda*, infinite Being-Awareness-Bliss, that equanimity which has no limitation and where all fear is completely ended in that unequalled fearless Truth.

Not satisfied with these poems of his on the advaitic *Brahman*, Sadāśivendra, who pursued the time-honored *sādhana* of *nāda-vidyā* (the wisdom of divine sound), also sang musical pieces on the same theme.

As already mentioned, contemporary with Sadāśiva Brahmendra were apostles of the path of adoring the *saguṇa* forms of the Supreme Being through the recital of the Lord's Name, with or without music. Sadāśivendra, who cherished *nāda-upāsana*, devotion through holy sound, as a spiritual discipline, sang several pieces which are even now heard on the music platforms. These songs are on different *saguṇa* forms on the Absolute or *para-Brahman*. Sadāśivendra thus holds a unique place as the bard of *advaita*. Even when he sings of Rāma, he takes the esoteric line and sees in the story the symbolism of the self as Rāma, of the tiny inner ether of the heart, *daharākāśa*, as the City of Ayodhyā, and Sītā as Peace, *śāntiḥ*:

He plays in my heart —
Rāma — he plays in my heart. . . .

He whose consort is Peace,
the daughter of Videha,
(Sītā), and who rejoices
in the city of Ayodhyā ("the Impregnable"),
which is the ethereal center
of the heart (*dahara*) —
He plays in my heart. . . .

The advaitic songs of Sadāśivendra teach the *sādhanas*, the spiritual disciplines. They elucidate the conception of ignorance, *avidyā*, and again and again sing of the advaitic state of realization. The felicity with which this state of realization, this state in which there is no care or thought, and nothing to be said or done and the soul is reveling in the plentitude of its bliss and knowledge, could not have come except from the lips of a *jīvan-mukta*. These songs on the *ātman* in the state of its self-realization read like a musical version of his *Ātmavidyāvilāsa*: When Sadāśivendra sings—

He sports in the material world
of microcosm and macrocosm —
Bhagavan — He
sports in the material world.
He sports, saying "I am that Swan,
I am that Swan,
I am That." He sports. . . .

He sports, saying, "I am the Soul Supreme,
I am all complete, I am
indeed *Brahman*, *Brahman* is my self."

He sports in the form of a Paramahaṃsa,
He who first created
Brahmā, Viṣṇu, Rudra and others.
He sports. . . .

He is singing only in tune with the *śruti*, the revelation which declares that the realized soul is the supreme poet of the Universe and the singer of *Brahman*—

This is the symphony of *Brahman*
that He is singing; Ah!
I am the enjoyed and the enjoyer;
I am the poet-author of
the whole universe; I am elder
to the world, I am earlier
than the very gods; I am the hub
of Immortality.[4]

[4] This verse is cited but not identified in the original article.

7.

Nārāyaṇa Tīrtha: Lyricist of Krishna's Divine Play[1]

Part One

In India there has been a continuous tradition of advaitin *sannyāsins*, renunciate yogis living by the philosophy of monism, cultivating both *bhakti* and *nādopāsana* (devotion through divine sound) as *sādhana* (spiritual exercise). In this line of *sannyāsins* whose names have illumined the pages of Karnāṭaka music history are Nārāyaṇa Tīrtha and Sadāśiva Brahmendra. Of these two, comparatively speaking, the latter is more renowned for his copious philosophical writings, while the former is more famous in music and in literary and devotional writing. From the biographical point of view, we have more abundant and precise data about Brahmendra than about Nārāyaṇa Tīrtha.

Tīrtha Nārāyaṇa Svāmīgal, as he is referred to, is an integral part of the *bhajana sampradāya*, in which he is venerated with invocatory verses and his whole composition is sung in *bhajanas*; but a few of his songs also hold a place in the repertoire of concert musicians. These songs are popularly called *taraṅgas* ("waves") because they are taken from a long Sanskrit poem of his, composed for dance-drama, on the *līlās* (divine sports) of Krishna as a youth, depicting him up to the time of his marriage with Rukmiṇī.

The *Krishna-līlā-taraṅgiṇī* ("Waves of the Sports of Krishna") was

[1] This article was first published in *The Hindu,* Jan. 4, 1970. The earliest publication of the *Krishna-līlā-taraṅgiṇī* was in *grantha* script in the district of its origin; one of these from Kumbakoṇam (1920) was carefully done with brief explanatory notes and variant readings. Two *devanāgarī* editions, including a recent one from Repalle in Andhra have appeared. There is also an incomplete ms. of a commentary on the *Krishna-līlā-taraṅgiṇī*, but a critical annotated edition of it is a desideratum. The Music Academy, Madras, has on hand an edition with notations of select *taraṅgas* by Śrī T.S. Vasudevan, son of the late Sitarama Iyer, Librarian of the Hindu High School, Triplicane, who was a votary of the *bhajana paddhati* and a repository of its authentic and unbroken tradition of songs and their *varṇa mettus*. (Editor's note: Since V. Raghavan wrote this a translation and study of the *Krishna-līlā-taraṅgiṇī* has been published. B. Nataraja (assisted by his brothers, B. Venkataraman and B. Ramachandran), *Sri Krishna Leela Tarangini by Narayana Tirtha*, Vol. I (Madras: Mudgala Trust, 1988). The second volume was published in 1990.)

evidently composed during a period of pilgrimage which extended from Puri in Orissa to Vahahūr in Tāñjāvūr district in Tamil Nadu; for included in the poem are pieces on Jagannāth, Viṣṇu at Śrīkakulam, and Narasimha at Sobhanadri and Vedagiri in Andhra. Evidently, Nārāyaṇa Tīrtha, who attained fame and is cherished and worshipped in Chola Deśa, hailed from Andhra like other celebrities in music and Sanskrit in the Kāverī delta, in the times of the Telugu and Maharatta rulers of Tāñjāvūr. There is a tradition of *Taraṅgiṇī* being sung, sometimes with dance, in Guntur, Krishna, and Godāvari districts of Andhra Pradesh in *bhajana* groups.

There is a legend of how he reached Varahūr. He is said to have been suffering from chronic pain in the stomach and a boar (*varaha*) which appeared before him led him to the village of Varahūr or Varāhapura, previously known as Bhūpatirājapuram. Several legends have naturally grown, some recently, out of the modern pressure to historicize with incidents as against the traditional trend to absorb a personality in the current of the cultural and conceptual universal.

His Masterpiece: The *Taraṅgiṇī*

The *Krishna-līlā-taraṅgiṇī* is dedicated in its opening pieces to Lord Viṣṇu as Śrī Veṅkaṭeśa at Varahūr. There is a continuous *bhajana sampradāya* at Varahūr, initiated by Nārāyaṇa Tīrtha, and his poem is still sung there and all over Tamil Nadu wherever the *bhajana sampradāya* has taken root. At the beginning of the *bhajan*, verses on Nārāyaṇa Tīrtha are sung, as also on Bodhendra, Āyyāvāl and Sadgurusvāmī: these were the four "*ācāryas*" of this tradition which preserved, in the recent centuries, both *bhakti* and music in Tamil Nadu. Nārāyaṇa Tīrtha attained *samādhi* at Tirupponturutti between Tāñjāvūr and Tiruvaiyāru and recently a festival has been growing there in memory of the saint-composer.

In the signature lines of the songs in the *Krishna-līlā-taraṅgiṇī*, the composer calls himself sometimes more fully Śiva Nārāyaṇa Tīrtha and mentions his *Vedānta* teacher as Śiva Rāma or Śiva Rāmānanda Tīrtha. In the fields of *Vedānta*, *saṁkhya*, and *bhakti*, there are some Sanskrit works appearing to be Nārāyaṇa Tīrtha's, but there is no conclusive evidence to identify their authorship with our composer. However, his scholarship and equipment in *Vedānta* and *Śāstras* are fully born out in the *taraṅgiṇī* itself. A slightly greater possibility of authenticity may attach to a sister dance-drama composition in Telugu, found in two manuscripts as the work of Nārāyaṇa Tīrtha, and it is called *Pārijāta haraṇa*. Another work in Sanskrit definitely known as his relates to the *bhakta* tradition and akin in theme in the *taraṅgiṇī*, is the *Hari bhakti sudhārṇava*.

The *Krishna-līlā-taraṅgiṇī* is one of the numerous compositions that arose in the wake and on the model of Jayadeva's *Gītā Govinda* bearing the triune tradition of devotion, music, and dance. Of the numerous compositions of this class, only a few have enjoyed or still enjoy vogue in music and dance, these being the *Krishnagīti* or *Krishnāttam* of Manaveda Zamorin of Calicut, still played at the Guruvayūr temple, the *Śiva gītimālika* of Chandraśekharendra Saraswathī of Kāñcīpuram Kāmakoṭi Pītha, which was being sung as part of the temple routine at Tiruvārūr.

The *Krishna-līlā-taraṅgiṇī* presents Śrī Krishna's *līlās*, his playful pastimes, closely following the *Bhāgavata purāṇa*, sometimes echoing the latter's expressions and going up to Rukmiṇī's marriage, after which it makes a brief reference to Śrī Krishna's other *mahiṣis* (queens) and his stay in all his divine glory in Dwāraka. The text, which is in 12 cantos, comprises narrative verses in diverse meters, *darus*, *gadyas* or prose passages and regular songs of varying length. The song sections are more akin to *Gītā Govinda* and the *padas* of the pre-Trinity (Tyāgarāja-Dīkṣitār-Śyāma Śāstri) period. The *rāgas* and *tāḷas* are given and in some of the songs, *jatis* (a series of rhythmical body movements and hand gestures) are also to be found; for example, *taraṅga* III, Yajñapatnīs' songs, VII *Gopikāgītā*; the long *Rāga-tāḷa-mālika* song describing the *rāsa līlā* and *Gopikā gītā* and is called a *sūlādī prabandha*.

Directions are given about the songs being rendered in gestures (*atha abhimyate*). In fact, each chapter is marked as *abhinaya* of such and such an episode. In the *sūlādī* composition in the seven *sūlādī tāḷas* (cycles of rhythmic patterns in any music composition), the *tāḷas*, the *gatis*, the *abhinaya hastas* and the *aṅga* and *pratyaṅga abhinayas* are mentioned. There are thus over a hundred and fifty songs in the poem. About 40 *rāgas* are used including rare and *rakti rāgas* like *Malavi*, *Ahiri*, *Ghanta*, *Kurañji*, *Dvijavanti*, and *Gaurī*. *Rāgas* which are frequently used are *Mohana*, *Saurāṣṭra*, *Nādanāmakrīya*, *Kedāragauḷa*, *Punnāgavarāḷi*, *Nilambari*, *Mukhāri*, *Bhairavī*, *Kāmbhōji*, *Pantuvarāḷī*, and *Madhyamāvatī*. The work is couched in chaste Sanskrit and classic diction and is rich in poetic quality. For sheer grace and beauty of diction and free and mellifluous flow of words, which do not seem to stand apart from the music, we may note the *Bhairavī* song is *taraṅga* VII. *Govindam iha gopikān-andakandam*. While the style is elegant and generally easy to comprehend, by reason of the theme, it often waxes eloquent with Vedāntin ideas. The author brings out often, by use of double-meaning words, the transcendent and metaphysical aspect of the *para-Brahman* while describing the *līlās* in the Krishna *avatāra*: for instance, the song in *Āva ranam mama dehi* in *taraṅga* V in the *gopī vastrāpakārana* episode in which Krishna steals the milkmaids' clothes, where *avarana* means the clothes as well as the obscuring cover of *māyā*, cosmic illusion. The teachings of Ch. VI of the *Chandogya Upaniṣad* are embodied in the songs of the *rāsa līlā* episode in *taraṅga* VII, in *Nāthanāmakrīya* and *Ghanta rāgas*. The songs of the *yajñapatnīs* in *taraṅga* III may also be mentioned as examples of philosophy turned into lyrics.

Taraṅgiṇī and the *Bhajana Sampradāya*

As the *Krishna-līlā-taraṅgiṇī* was an essential part of the *bhajana* tradition, the ears of Tyāgarāja (who was a flower that bloomed in this same tradition) were naturally filled with the music of the *taraṅgas* and his soul fed with the devotion and ideas of Nārāyaṇa Tīrtha. Upaniṣad Brahmendra of Kāñcīpuram, who invited Tyāgarāja to Kāñcīpuram, composed his *Rāma taraṅgas* under the influence of Nārāyaṇa Tīrtha. There are indeed several echoes of the expressions of the *Taraṅgiṇī* in the *kṛitis* of Tyāgarāja. To give an instance, in *Dhyāname varamaine*, *Gaṅgasnāname* and *Koṭināḍulu*, Tyāgarāja emphasizes that the real *snāna* and *tīrtha* (bath and holy waters of pilgrimage) are to be found in the contemplation of the Lord and in His devotion, and not in Gaṇgā or in other rivers; in the first *taraṅga*, in the song ushering Sānaka and other sages, Nārāyaṇa Tīrtha says: "One should bathe in the super Prayāga (river confluence) of the mingling of the divine names of Rāma, Krishna, and Govinda; *Rāma-nāma* is the Gaṇgā, *Krishna-nāma* the Yamunā, and *Govinda-nāma* the Saraswatī river."[2]

Part Two[3]

Nārāyaṇa Tīrtha is remembered most today by the adherents of the *Bhajana-sampradāya*, and to some extent by Karṇāṭaka musicians who reverentially refer to him as Tīrtha Nārāyaṇa Svāmī or Tīrtha Nārāyaṇa Yati. Indeed a few of his compositions may still be heard in concerts and are mentioned as *Taraṅgas*. The better informed know that his Sanskrit

[2] The passage recommending that devotees bathe in the Name-waters is:
Rāmakrishna Govinda Nāma samprayoge
Kāmamiha snatavyam sarvottama Prayāge.
Rāma Nāma Gaṅgā ya milita Krishna nāma
Yamune Govinda nāma Sarasvatī prathite

[3] First published in a booklet by the Śrī Nārāyaṇa Tīrtha Festival Celebration Committee, Tiruppunturutti, Tāñjāvūr District (Madras: M.W.N. Press, n.d).

songs are taken from a musical poem on Krishna composed by him, called the *Krishna-līlā-taraṅgiṇī* and that the composer was a *sannyāsin* worthy of the highest respect.

Nārāyaṇa Tīrtha, as his suffix Tīrtha shows, was a *sannyāsin;* he was of advaitic persuasion. The use of music as a yogic *sādhana* is known from the times of sage Yajñavalkya, and the singing of God's names, praises, and glory, *bhajana*, as part of devotional exercises is also well-known. There was a line of advaitin *sannyāsins* among whom this tradition of cultivation of music and *bhajana* as a spiritual aid and a devotional adoration of God was prevalent. We have the illustrious example of Sadāśiva Brahman, a great advaitin *siddha*, and author of not only Sanskrit philosophical treatises but also of songs on the supreme *Brahman*, and the various forms of the Godhead. Of equal greatness is Nārāyaṇa Tīrtha, less celebrated as a writer of Sanskrit treatises but occupying a far more important place in the history of Karṇāṭaka music and the *bhajana-sampradāya.* We had also Upaniṣad Brahman of Kāñcīpuram, elder contemporary and inspirer of Muthusvāmī Dīkṣitar and Tyāgarāja and also an incumbent of the Kāñcīpuram *Śaṅkarācārya Pītha* itself who composed a musical poem called *Śivagīti mālika.* It is in conformity with this tradition that the celebrated Tyāgarāja also took to *sannyāsa* towards the end of his career.

Like Sadāsiva Brahman and the later Tyāgarāja, Nārāyaṇa Tīrtha was a Telugu Brahman. When Vijayanagar declined and the kingdom of Tāñjāvūr became, first under the Telugu Nāyaks and then under the Mahrāttas, a center of patronage for art and letters, many families of talent and attainment, authors, poets, musicians, dancers and dance-masters, left the banks of the Krishna and the Godāvarī and sought the banks of the Kāverī. Nārāyaṇa Tīrtha was one of these and it is in the Tāñjāvūr District that he became famous, that he lived and worked and finally attained *samādhi.* The village hallowed by his stay is Varahūr and the village sanctified by his *samādhi* is Tiruppunturutti.

As to how Nārāyaṇa Tīrtha came to the Tāñjāvūr area, we do not have any authentic information. But we have a traditional story told about this. One night, in the village called Nadukkāverī, in an empty *maṇḍapam* (public hall for pilgrims), a *sannyāsin* afflicted with severe stomach ache was undergoing acute pain. As a little drowsiness came on him, he had a dream in which he was told: "Early morning when you wake up, you will see an animal; keep following it and at the place to which it brings you and vanishes, you will be rid of this stomach-ache." When it dawned and the recluse opened his eyes, they fell on a boar which was standing in front of him. The animal began to move and the recluse followed it. They went three miles along the banks of the river *Kodamurutti*, a branch of the Kāverī, and reached the village Varahūr otherwise called Bhūpatirājapuram after a Tāñjāvūr King. In that village was a temple dedicated to Lord Veṅkateśvara and the boar that was leading the *sannyāsin* vanished into that temple. It then struck the recluse that it was the Lord Hari once incarnated as the great boar who had again, out of his compassion for him, showed himself as the boar and brought him to that temple of Veṅkateśvara and that if he stayed on and worshipped Lord Veṅkateśvara in the shrine, he would be rid of his malady. The story is narrated in more or less these details in the opening part (ch. I, verses 70-96) of the poetical work *Śikyotsava Prabandha* by Nārāyaṇa Kavi of Varahūr (1868-1935 A.D.). There is also a Sanskrit *stotra* about Lord Veṅkateśa at Varahūr, available in print, where again the above mentioned episode is touched upon.

The *sannyāsin* was Nārāyaṇa Tīrtha. Because a boar (*varaha*) had brought him there, it is said, the village Bhūpatirājapuram acquired the name Varahūr. Nārāyaṇa Tīrtha stayed on and became freed of his ailment. Consequently, the sanctity of the shrine and the village increased. It was here, as an act of grateful homage to the deity here, that Nārāyaṇa Tīrtha completed and dedicated his musical play on the story of Lord Krishna, from birth up to the marriage of Rukminī, the *Krishna-līlā-taraṅgiṇī* or the "River of the Sports of Lord Krishna." The dedicatory song at the beginning mentions "Śrī Varahapura Veṅkateśa."

That this village of Varahūr was a center of music and dance in the times of the Nāyak Kings of Tāñjāvūr (17th century) is attested by the fact that Kṣetrayya, the celebrated composer of dance-*padas*, visited it and has mentioned it in his *padas*.

In Varahūr, Nārāyaṇa Tīrtha established a *bhajana sampradāya*, of followers of his who sang, danced, and rendered into gesture his musical play on the Lord and celebrated the festival of Krishna every year at the time of *Janmāṣṭami* or *Gokulāṣṭami* as we call it here. The performance of *uriyadi* (the enactment of Krishna stealing butter placed on top of a pole) as part of this festival attracted a large concourse of people. Nārāyaṇa Kavi of this village composed a *campu kāvya* or poem describing this festival.

Thus Nārayaṇa Tīrtha was one of those who augmented the *bhāgavata* tradition in the Tāñjāvūr District and spread the cult of adoring the Lord with song and dance. There are three verses of praise on Nārāyaṇa Tīrtha that are sung at the outset in *bhajanas*. Followers of this *bhajana* tradition would, with *tambura* (stringed drone instrument) and *chiplas* (jingling clappers) in hand and bells (*gajjai*) on ankles, go about singing the Lord's praise and dancing. Of the celebrated *bhāgavatars* of Varahūr were Varahūr Pañju Bhāgavatar and Varahūr Gopāla Bhāgavatar and a portrait of the latter, in typical costume, is still venerated by the votaries of *bhajana*.

In addition to the musical and dramatic treatment of the story of Krishna, Nārāyaṇa Tīrtha, as a Sanskrit writer, has given us a devotional poem on the same theme, *Haribhaktisudhārṇava.* One of the prayer-verses at the opening of this poem forms part of the preliminary songs sung at the beginning of *Harikathās* (musical discourses). As an exponent of the school of *bhakti,* he wrote a commentary also on the *Bhakti mīmāṃsā sūtras* of Sandilya. Both these works are yet in manuscript. On his *Krishna-līlā-taraṅgiṇī* which has so far been printed only in *grantha* and Telugu scripts, there is an unpublished Sanskrit commentary also written by one Veṅkaṭeśa, assisted by a Govinda Dīkṣitā, and recently, I was surprised to find manuscript copies of both the text and the commentary in far away Banāras.

In some of the songs in his *Krishna-līlā-taraṅgiṇī,* the author calls himself also Śiva Nārāyaṇa Tīrtha. His guru was Śiva Rāmānanda Tīrtha.

Nārāyaṇa Tīrtha attained *siddhi* at the village of Tiruppunturutti, seven miles to the east of Varahūr, where at his *Samādhi,* an annual festival is still held.

The same *bhāgavata* tradition was responsible also for the cultivation of a dramatic art, in which devotional stories composed in the form of songs and set to dance were sung and danced and interpreted in gesture by Brahman devotees. This is the tradition maintained in *Kuchupudi* in Andhra and in some of the Brahman villages of Tāñjāvūr, Merattur, and elsewhere. In Merattur and the Saraswatī Mahal Library, Tāñjāvūr, there is a Telugu play intended for such enactment composed by one Nārāyaṇa Tīrtha. This play, called *Parijataharaṇa nāṭaka,* has the *mūdra* or signature of Nārāyaṇa Tīrtha in some of its pieces and from its concluding piece, appears to have been composed at Merattur village and dedicated to Lord Acyuta Varadarāja there.[4]

I started by saying that it was his music that is still best remembered and that of his works, the *Taraṅgiṇī* is most widely known. Under its inspiration Upaniṣad Brahman of Kāñcīpuram, as I have shown in my

[4] V. Raghavan writes: "It was my good fortune to bring to light this composition in the pages of the *Journal of the Madras Music Academy* (Volume XIII, pp. 74-76), but students of Telugu literature who had later occasion to examine this are not unanimous in their opinion about this play being the work of the great Nārāyaṇa Tīrtha himself. If it is a genuine work of his, it would give us some historical data: Merattur was gifted to families of musicians, dancers etc, by King Acyutāppa Nāyak of Tāñjāvūr (A.C. 1561-1614), and renamed after himself as Acyutābdhi. It would show also that Nārāyaṇa Tīrtha had something to do with the dance-drama tradition at Merattur, which is a thing to be expected."

account of his life and works,[5] composed songs on Rāma called *taraṅgas*. It was, as I already said, the example of *sannyāsins* of his type that induced Tyāgarāja also to enter the fourth *aśrama* at the end of his life. The influence of Nārāyaṇa Tīrtha on Tyāgarāja was more than this. The two musical plays of Tyāgarāja (*Prahlāda Bhakti Vijayam* and *Nauka Caritram*) took inspiration from Nārāyaṇa Tīrtha's *taraṅgiṇī*. Also the fact that Nārāyaṇa Tīrtha pieces, from his *Krishna-līlā-taraṅgiṇī*, were widely sung, is borne out by the influence they had on the mind of Tyāgarāja, the great composer, who echoed phrases from Nārāyaṇa Tīrtha's compositions as I have shown.[6]

The *Krishna-līlā-taraṅgiṇī* was evidently composed over a period of time when the composer was on pilgrimages, and finally completed and dedicated at Varahūr. For, included in this composition are songs on Viṣṇu at Śrīkakulam, Narasimha at Sobhanādri and Vedādri, all in Andhra, and one sung at Puri.

The *Krishna-līlā-taraṅgiṇī* is one of the numerous works that rose in the wake of the *Gītāgovinda* of Jayadeva and may be acclaimed as the only one among such works to have gained or maintained a comparable musical status. It is written in perfect literary Sanskrit, a fact to be specially noted because, in the next age, though Sanskrit was handled for music compositions and though even while Telugu was handled, it was a style dominated by Sanskrit; the grammatical and literary equipment of composers became a secondary qualification. The diction in the *taraṅgiṇī* is fine, figures of speech including *śleṣa* (puns) are employed, and the songs are replete with ideas from the *Upaniṣads*. The composition is in twelve *taraṅgas* and the songs are linked with verses and varied by prose passages. It is composed as a regular dance-drama and there are directions that such and such a context is being sung and gesticulated in the coming piece and so on. There are also set rhythm-syllables or *jatis* for dance, fitted to some of the pieces, e.g. the long prayer of the Yajñapatnis in the third *taraṅga*, and the composition on *rāsakriḍa* in *Nāṭa* and *Dhruva tāḷa* in the seventh *taraṅga*. There is also a *suladi* composition.

The rehabilitation of the *bhajana* and *bhāgavata* tradition which put forth these blossoms of the arts of music, dance, and composition would be the renaissance of a cultural heritage whose unity could be seen from the Kāverī to Kāmarūpa.

[5] *Journal of the Music Academy*, Madras, Vol. XXVII, pp. 125-126.

[6] This is discussed in a special article in the Tyāgarāja Centenary volume issued by the Andhra Gana Kala Parishad, Rajahmundry (pp. 84-88).

Part III

CREATIVE EXPONENTS OF THE NAME AND RELATED STUDIES

8.

Vāk Devatā[1]

The *Ṛigveda*[2] says Vāk (Speech) is a divine gift, and in a whole hymn (X.125) of which *Vāk* Herself is the speaker, *ṛiṣi* and deity, She declares that whomsoever She likes, She makes into a Seer and a man of fine intellect. "I make the man I love exceedingly mighty, I make him into a sage, *ṛiṣi*, and a brahman."

Ṛigveda hymn X.71.2 says that the wise ones sift and purify *Vāk* in the sieve of their minds and thereby She becomes auspicious and beautiful. The Seers of the hymns, the *ṛiṣis*, are called *kavis* or men of far-reaching vision (*kranta-darśins*) and later, not only did this word *kavi* become the normal name of the poet but according to the Kashmirian aesthete of the 10th century, Bhaṭṭa Tota, the *ṛiṣi* and the *kavi* were inseparable and represented but the two phases of the same genius, the former signifying the vision and the latter the verbal incarnation of it.[3]

The *Brāhmaṇas* have a high conception of *Vāk* and its role. The *Taittirīya Upaniṣad* says: "Speech, the imperishable, is the first born of Truth, mother of the *Vedas*, the hub of immortality; may She in happiness, come to us, in the sacrifice; our protecting Goddess, may She be easy of invocation for us." (VIII.8.5)

The *Upaniṣads* also assign a high place for *Vāk*. The *Chandogya Upaniṣad* says: "It is *Vāk* which makes us know not only the *Vedas* and the ancillary literature, but also heaven and earth, gods and men, *dharma* and *adharma*, truth and untruth, good and bad; it is *Vāk* that informs us of these; therefore adore *Vāk*" (VII.2.1).

As *Praṇava* or *Oṃkāra*, *Vāk*'s place is close to the Supreme Being, *Brahman* itself, as its nearest symbol (*nedistha-abhidhāna* and *pratika* as Śaṅkara says in his *bhāṣya* on the *Bṛihadaraṇyaka Upaniṣad* (V.i). The whole *Maṇḍukya Upaniṣad* is based on this conception. This Sound (*Om*), the *Śabda Brahman*, and the Supreme One (*para-Brahman*) are the two Brahmans to be known and it is after realizing the former that the man of knowledge passes on to the latter. The philosophy of *Śabda Brahman* in

[1] First published in *Dilip*, May-June, 1975.

[2] *Ṛig Veda*, VIII.100.11.

[3] *nānṛiṣiḥ kavirityuktaḥ ṛiṣiśca kila darśanāt.*

the form of *sphota* lying at the basis of all sounds which grammarians latter evolved and of which Bhartṛihari gave the classic exposition, developed from this Vedic doctrine of *Vāk* and *Praṇava.* The sacred character and the spiritual role of all manifestations of Sound in the form of literature, were stated by the *Bṛihadaraṇyaka Upaniṣad* when it declared that *Ṛik* and other *Vedas,* the Epics and other scriptures were the "breath" of the Supreme Being itself. "Just as smoke and sparks pour out of a fire made of damp wood, the *Atharvāṅgirasa, Itihāsa* narratives, *Purāṇas, Vidyas, Upaniṣads, ślokas, sūtras, Anuvyākhyānas* (explanations of mantras)—all these are the breathing of the Supreme Being" (11.4.10).

And it is this philosophy of literature (as emanation) that the *purāṇas* express and the later votaries of the Muse had before them in their creative work. The *Viṣṇu Purāṇa* says: "Whatever poetry there is, and whatever song there is, all that is an aspect of the all-pervasive Supreme Being in His verbal and sonant form."

The Supreme principle of Speech, in its subtlest form (*para vāk*) was considered as the first *spanda* ("throb" or "heaving") of the Supreme Śiva by the Kashmirian philosophers. The great poet Kalidāsa gave expression to this concept in the opening verse of his long poem the *Raghuvamśa,* thereby giving us his basic faith and inspiration in his approach to the Supreme Spirit through the path and medium of poetry.

It is the marriage of word and meaning that the poet celebrates in his other long poem, the *Kumārasambhava,* where the seven sages who go to Himavan as messengers to ask the hand of Pārvatī for Śiva tell Himavan that he should unite Śiva with Umā, as Meaning with Word.[4]

That Kalidāsa adored the Divine Speech as a blessing and its manifestation in one as being at once the means of sanctity and beauty for one, is seen in his description of Pārvatī's manifestation as the daughter of the Himalayas.[5]

Bhavabhuti, next in rank to Kalidāsa as a poet, was equally an adorer of this *Vāk;* in the concluding verse of his masterpiece, the drama *Uttararāmacarita,* he calls himself not only one of matured intellect but also a knower of the *Śabda-Brahman,* a *kavi* in the true and full sense of the term. And in the opening verse of the same drama, he pays his obeisance

[4] *tāmarthamiva bhāratyā sutayā yoktumarhasi.* Translation: "Śiva, who witnesses all activities in the world and fulfills desires, sending his word through us, requests your daughter's hand; just as if wedding sound and meaning together, please marry him to your dear child" (Kalidāsa, *Kumārasambhava,* VI. 78-79).

[5] *samskāravatyeva girā manīṣī tayā sa pūtaścavibhūṣitaśca.*

to this *Vāk* and describes Her as the immortal digit or sprout of the Self.

The gifted 17th century poet of the Madurai Nāyak court Nilakantha Dīkṣita draws out in fuller form the same idea in the pregnant lines of Kalidāsa, of Śiva as Ardhanarīśvara, the Devī forming the left half of Śiva's form being *Śabda*, and Śiva the right half being *Artha*; and says that it is the blessed ones among men who deserve this Poetry which is thus the embodiment of God.[6] Poetry, the same poet says, is not only the goal but also the path to that goal; a *yoga* not of severe austerities and exacting exercises, but of beauty and bliss.

To compose is to gain composure; to be engrossed in right idea and choice word is to be in concentration on perfect union and harmony; to be thrilled with the fine poetry that is born thus is to be absorbed in the very bliss of *Brahman*, the *rasa*. The aesthetic theory of Indian poetics, in the hands of its best exponents, bases itself on this philosophy of the relish of poetic beauty being of the same category as the relish of spiritual bliss, *Brāhmānanda*; the very word *rasa* goes back to the *Taittirīya Upaniṣad* which states "whatever is done well, that is beauty and bliss."[7]

[6] *Śivalīlārṇava*, I.15.

[7] *yadvai tatsukṛitam/raso vai saḥ.*

9.

Viṣṇu-Sahasra-Nāma: The 1008 Names of Lord Viṣṇu[1]

From the *Mahābhārata*, *Anuśāsana pārvaṇ*, Chapter 254.

Having listened to all the *dharmas*, sanctifying in every way, Yudhishṭhira again addressed Bhīṣma: "Which is the sole divinity in the world? What is the one supreme path? By praising and worshipping Whom will men attain weal? What *dharma*, according to you, is supreme among all *dharmas*? And by reciting which, will a being born here be released from the fetters of birth and rebirth?"

Bhīṣma replied: "If man, with constant endeavor, praises the Lord of the universe, the unlimited Supreme Being, with His Thousand Names, if he worships daily and with devotion the same imperishable Being, meditating on Him, praising Him, bowing to Him, and making offerings to Him, if he sings daily the praise of that Great Lord of the whole universe, Viṣṇu, who has neither beginning nor end and presides over the world, he overcomes all unhappiness. *If man should constantly adore in devotion the lotus-eyed Lord with hymns, that according to me, is supreme over all the dharmas.* The God of gods, He who is the eternal Father of all living beings, from whom all beings proceed on the advent of the primary aeon and into whom they disappear again when the aeon comes to an end, of that Lord of the whole world, the Chief of all beings, hear from me, O King, these Thousand Names which drive away sin and fear! The celebrated names of the great Lord which are based on His qualities, and which the sages have sung, I shall proclaim for the weal (of the world):

"He who is of the form of the Universe and is All-pervasive, who is of the form of Sacrifice, who is the Lord of the past, future, and present, the Creator of all living beings, their Sustainer and their existence, their Indweller and Well-wisher; the Pure and Supreme Being, the highest goal of the liberated, the imperishable Spirit that is the Onlooker and the eternal Knower of the body; who is the Path and the Leader among those that know the path, Himself Matter, Spirit and God, the Supreme Being who took the form of the Man-lion, who has rays of light as hair, and possesses the Goddess of Fortune; the All, the Destroyer, the Beneficent, the

[1] Translated by V. Raghavan. First published in *The Indian Heritage* (Bangalore: Indian Institute of World Culture, 1956), pp. 421-435.

Steadfast, the Prime Source of beings, the Inexhaustible Repository; one who comes into being as He pleases, the Benefactor, the Protector, One whose birth is unique, the Capable, the Master; the Self-born, the Giver of happiness, the Solar deity, the Lotus-eyed, the Speaker of the sublime sound named *Veda*, One without birth or death, the Primary Creator and the Subsidiary Creator (Brahmā) and One beyond even the Primary Creator; the Inscrutable, the Lord of the senses, He who has the Lotus (with Brahmā) in his navel, the God of the gods, the Divine Architect, the Thinker or the Sage-lawgiver Manu, the heavenly Architect Tvaṣṭar, the Huge, the Aged, the Firm; the Incomprehensible, the Permanent, the Attractive Krishna, the bright-eyed, the Destroyer, the Ample; existing above, below and in the middle; the Supreme Sanctifier and Auspiciousness; the Controller, the Life-giver, the Life-breath, the Eldest, the Best, the Lord of beings, the primordial-Creator, He who has the whole Earth within Himself, the Scion of the Medhu race and Killer of the demon Madhu; the Powerful Lord, wielder of the bow; the Intelligent; Power and Order; the Unexcelled, the Unassailable, the Grateful, the Act, the Self-possessed; the God of gods, the Refuge, Happiness, the Author of the universe, the Source of all Beings, the Day, the Year, the Great Serpent (of the form of Time), Understanding, All-seeing; the Unborn, the Lord of all Endowed with miraculous powers, Himself those miraculous powers, the First of all, the Stable, He who took the form of the Boar of Dharma, the Immeasurable, One who has transcended all associations; Wealth, Endowed with an excellent heart, Truth, Serene, Equal, the Unfailing, the Lotus-eyed, the Righteously Active, the Embodiment of Righteousness; the Terrible, the Multi-headed, the Tawny One, the Origin of the universe, of Unstained Fame, Immortal, Eternal, Steadfast, of Excellent limbs and severe penance; Omnipotent, Omniscient, the Shining One whose hosts are everywhere, the chastiser of the erring folk, the *Veda*, the Expounder of the *Veda*, the Full, the Ancillary Lore of the *Veda*, the Inquirer into the *Veda* and One of far-reaching vision; One who presides over the world, the gods and law; the created Effect as well as the uncreated Cause, Who takes four forms for creation, maintenance and dissolution, Who has four tusks (as the Man-lion) and four arms; the Brilliant, the Food as well as the eater, the Forbearing, First-born of the world, the Sinless, the Victory and the Victorious, the Source of the universe and One who repeatedly comes to dwell within beings; Indra's brother and yet above him, the Dwarf as well as the Colossus, the Successful, the Pure, the Strong, the Epitome of (all) Creation, Self-possessed, Regulation and Restraint; the Object of Knowledge, the Learned, ever a Yogin, the Slayer of heroic fighters, the Lord of spiritual learning, the Sweet, One who transcends the senses and is

Dr. V. Raghavan

The Āyyāvāl Maṭh in Tiruviśanallūr

Sadāśiva Brahmendra

Sadāśiva Brahmendra

Nārāyaṇa Tīrtha

Śrī Bhagavannāma Bodhendra

Nārāyaṇa Tīrtha

The well in the Āyyāvāl Maṭh, from which the Goddess Gaṅgā is believed to have manifested herself in response to the prayers of Āyyāvāl.

The lane leading from the Āyyāvāl Maṭh to the Kāverī river, along which Āyyāvāl is said to have encountered a starving *caṇḍāla*, whom he fed.

Veṅkaṭaraman Bhāgavatar of Tiruvidaimarudūr

Bhajana celebrations held in Veṅkaṭaraman Bhāgavatar's home

endowed with mysterious power, of high endeavor and mighty strength; endowed with supreme Intellect, Potency, Power and Luster; of Indescribable Form, the Beautiful, the Vast, the Supporter of the great mountain; the Great Archer, the Lord of Earth, the Abode of Fortune, the Refuge of the good, the Irrepressible, the Delight of the good, the Savior of the earth, the Chief of those that understand Speech; the Ray of Light (or sage Marīchi), the Controller, the Swan of the Spirit, the fleet divine Bird (Garuḍa), the Chief Serpent (Seśa), of golden navel, of excellent austerities, the Lotus on His navel and Brahmā (thereon); Immortal, Spectator of everything, the Fierce, the Link, Linked (with all), the Enduring, the Unborn, the Unbearable, the Ruler, the Celebrated, the Slayer of the enemies of the gods, the Teacher, the Most Weighty One, Light, Truth, One who displays His valor on behalf of Truth, the Moment, the Vigilant, the Garlanded, the Lord of Speech and One of Sublime Intellect; the Foremost, the Chief, the Rich, the Right Path, the Leader, the Inspirer; the Thousand-headed, Thousand-eyed, Thousand-footed, Embodiment of the universe; He who rotates the whole world, yet keeping Himself aloof from it; the Hidden one Overriding all, the Day, the Deluge, Fire, Wind and Mountain; the Supremely Gracious, the Tranquil, the Prop as well as the Consumer of the Universe, the All-pervading; the Bestower of honor, the Honored and the Good: Who draws and hides within Himself the whole Universe, the God who is the Goal of man and the Man himself; the Innumerable, the Unknowable, the Unique, the Patron of disciplined souls, the Spotless, One whose objects and wishes are fulfilled, One who gives success and is also the means of success; One for whom Righteousness constitutes the day, Who showers the desired objects, of giant stride, One who is to be reached by the steps of *dharma* and who is within *dharma*; the Promoter of growth and the Growing, Who is far apart, Who is the ocean of revealed wisdom; of beautiful arms (that protect), whose thought is too difficult to be retained, the Eloquent, the Great Indra, the Bestower of Riches; of manifold and huge form, the Sacrifice and the Revealer; Bearer of Force, Power and Effulgence, Embodiment of Light, the Scorcher, Rich (in everything), the Manifester of syllables and the Sacred Syllables themselves, Moonlike as well as Sunlike in splendor; the Source of ambrosial rays, Himself both the Sun and the Moon, the King of gods, the Medicine, the Protective Embankment of the world, One whose valor is exercised for Truth and Righteousness; the Lord of the past, present, and future, the Wind, the Purifier, the Fire, the Destroyer of lust, the Promoter of noble love, the Loveable, the Lover that gratifies with love; the Promulgator of aeons, the Conductor of aeonic cycles, of manifold mystic powers, that All-devouring, the Unseen, of Unmanifest form, Victor over thousands and the Endlessly Victorious; the Desirable, the Remarkable, Dear to those that conform to His commandments, Krishna who wears the peacock-feather on His crest (or the Śikhāndin who has come as my Death), the Encircler, Dharma, the Destroyer of anger, at the same time its Employer, and the Doer, with a thousand arms, and Bearer of the earth; the Unflinching, the Famous, the Life and Life-giver, Indra's brother, the Ocean, the Substratum, the Vigilant one who is firmly established; the Destroyer (of enemies), the Supporter of such destroyers and Himself the Bearer of the brunt; the Bestower of boons; the Mover of Wind; the Lord in whom all dwell and who dwells in all; the Bigger Sun, the Prime God, and the Destroyer of enemy cities; the Sorrowless, He who helps to cross over, the Crossing over (or the Mystic syllable OM), the Valorous, the Scion of the Sūrasenas (Krishna), the King, the Favorable, Who returns to us innumerable times, the God with the lotus and the lotus-eyes; Who is seated at the center of the lotus, the Lotus-eyed Lord who is within the lotus of one's heart, who takes corporeal forms, the greatly Affluent, the Full, the Old, the Large-eyed, the God with the kite-banner; the Incomparable, the Fierce Being that excels even the lion; the Knower of the esoteric practices (or Knower of propriety), the Offering, the Lord who strips one and tests him, Marked with all features of beauty, Bearing the Goddess of Beauty, the Victor in battles; the Imperishable, He who took the Fish incarnation, the Path, the Cause, One in whom all Names are included, Endowed with endurance, Bearer of earth, of great fortune, the Swift, the limitless Consumer; the Origin, One that stirs up the Creative Activity, the Sportive, Bearer of Prosperity, the Lord Supreme, the Instrument and the Cause, the Doer and the Undoer, the Dense and the Secret; Determination, the Regulator, the End, the Bestower of rank, the Stable, Supreme Prosperity, the Absolutely obvious, the Contented, the Well-nourished, having auspicious looks; the Delighter, the Final end (of all), Free from passion, the Path and the Goal, the Right Policy, and at the same time Himself the Sovereign, not subject to any; the Hero, Best of all the powerful, Dharma, and Foremost of the knowers of *dharma*; the Unimpeded Heavenly State, the Supreme Spirit, Life and Life-giver, the Mystic OM, the Vast, the Creator (Brahmā), Slayer of enemies, the All-pervading, the Wind; He who is realized when the senses are subdued; the Season; Beautiful to look at, Time; the transcendent Lord who yet receives all supplicants, the Severe, He who makes everything abide in Himself, the Capable, Who affords repose to the afflicted, and One who is considerate to the whole world; the Expansive, He who stands stationary, the Measure, the Seed that is not spent, the Purpose (of all endeavor) but Himself devoid of any purpose of His own, the Great Treasury, the Great Enjoyer, the highly wealthy; the Undepressed, the most Expansive, Existence, the Sacrificial Post at which all meritorious acts are offered, the Great Sacrifice, the Hub of the wheel of constellations, the Moon, the Adept, Stripped of all encrustations, of noble aspirations; the Sacrifices of different forms and Himself the minor gods and the Chief God propitiated by sacrifices; the Refuge of the good; One who notes everything, the Liberated Soul, the Omniscient and the Supreme Wisdom; He who takes excellent vows, of beautiful face, the Subtle, the Fine-voiced, the Giver of happiness, the Friend, the Captivating, One who has conquered anger, of heroic arms and One who tears to pieces (the unrighteous); He who makes the unenlightened slumber in His mystic Delusion, Master of Himself, the Ubiquitous, of manifold forms and acts, the Year, the Affectionate, Surrounded by His children, the Source of all precious things, the Lord of riches; the Safeguarder of *dharma*, the Maker of *dharma*, Himself endowed with *dharma*, Himself Good and Bad, the Perishable and the Imperishable, who becomes the unknowing embodied individual Soul; the Thousand-rayed, the Performer of functions, and the Author who has laid down the definitions; Center of an orb of rays, the Spirit that presides over the mind, Lion-like in strength, the great Lord of beings, the First God, the Great God, the God of gods, the Bearer of gods, and the Teacher; the Superior, the Shepherd, the Protector, Realizable by knowledge, the Ancient, the Bearer of the bodies of the beings, the Enjoyer of (everything), the great Boar-incarnation, the profusely Liberal; the Drinker of Soma offering and of nectar, the Soma offering, Victor over many, Foremost among the eminent, Modesty, Victory, the Truthful, Scion of Dasarha race and the Lord of the Sāttvata people (or worshipers); the Individual Soul, the Observer of individuals' humility, Bestower of Release, the immeasurably Powerful, the Reservoir of different orders of beings, the Spirit without any limitation, He who lies on the great Ocean after engulfing the world with it, the Terminator of the world; the Unborn, Fit to be worshiped, Existing in His own innate nature, One who has vanquished his enemies, the Rejoicer, Bliss, the pleasing and Gratifying, Of true virtue, He who measured the universe in three strides; the Great Sage and Teacher (of Saṅkhya) Kapila, the Knower of the created, the King, He who covered the universe in three steps, the Lord of the gods, He who incarnated as the Fish with the huge snout, the Death of the god of Death; the Great Boar-incarnation, Known through the *Upaniṣads*, Possessed of an excellent army, Having golden armlets, Dwelling in the heart, the Deep, the Impenetrable, the Hidden, Bearing the discus and the mace; Brahmā the Creator, Himself His accessory, the Unconquered, Sage Vyāsa, the Strong, One who unfailingly drags beings away at the time of destruction, Varuṇa the Lord of Waters, Sage Vāśiṣṭha, Standing like a tree,

Seen in the lotus of one's heart, Himself of a great mind; Possessed of Lordship, *Dharma*, Renown, Beauty, Dispassion, and Freedom or He who knows the origin and end, the movement and rest of beings, Knowledge and Nescience, He who deprives one also of these excellences; the Joyous, the Wearer of a garland of sylvan flowers, Armed with the plough, the God, the Resplendent Sun-god, the Patient, the Supreme Path to salvation; Possessing an excellent bow, Śiva armed with the axe, the Awful, the Giver of wealth, Heaven-stretching, the codifier of all systems of knowledge, the Self-born Lord of Speech; Lauded by three (special) Sāman hymns, Himself the Sāman chant and its Singer, the Beatific end, the Remedy and the Doctor, the Promulgator of the Path of Renunciation, Quietude and the Quiet, the Final Rest, Peace, the Highest Refuge; of Beautiful form, Bestower of peace, the Creator, He who revels in His creation, Who reposes in the lily of the heart, Benefactor of the world, Lord of the world, He who shrouds Himself in His Mystic Power, Having eyes that rain one's desired objects, Lover of *dharma*; He who does not retreat, Whose mind is turned inwards on the Self, Who gathers up all things at the dissolution, Who brings on welfare, the Beneficent, Bearing the Auspicious mark of *Śrīvatsa* on His chest, the abode of the Goddess of prosperity, Lord of Supreme Energy, Chief of the gods that are endowed with power; Giver, Master, Abode, Repository, Producer, Bearer, Author and Maintainer of Prosperity; the Supreme God and the Prop of the three worlds; of beautiful eyes and limbs, of joys, the Rejoicer, the Lord of the luminaries, of controlled and disciplined Self, of unsullied fame, the Dispeller of doubts; the Excelling, Possessed of eyes all round, He who has no master, Frequently changing and yet stationary, Reposing in earth (Immanent in His creation), the Ornament, Affluence, without Sorrow and the Destroyer of sorrow; having rays of light, Worshipped by all, the Vessel within which everything is, the Pure Soul, the Purifier, the Unobstructed and Unopposed Hero, of superior energy, of unlimited valor; the Killer of the demon Kalanemi, the Heroic, the Scion and chief of the Sura tribe, of the form of the three worlds, Lord of the three worlds, Endowed with power, Slayer of the demon Keśin, the Lord who removes bondage; the Lord of love, the Guardian of love, the Loving, the Lovable, the Promulgator of the spiritual tradition, Of indefinable form, the All-pervading Lord, the Unlimited, the Acquirer of riches; Favorable to the Brāhmanas, the Promulgator of penance and knowledge, the Creator, the Supreme Soul, the Promoter of *Brahman*-knowledge, Knower of *Brahman*, of the form of the Brāhmana, Possessor of the knowledge (*Veda*) and the Beloved of the Brāhmanas; of giant strides and acts, the Superior Light, the Great Serpent, the Great Sacrifice, Sacrificer and Oblation; He who is to be praised, Who loves praises, the Praises, Himself the Praiser, Who loves to fight, the Full, the Filler, the Holy, of virtuous fame; Free from all disease; Fleet as the mind, the Maker of holy places, the Wealth-bearing, the Bestower of the higher wealth of Deliverance, the Son of Vasudeva, the Precious thing, Possessed of precious heart, the Offering; the Meritorious Path, Honour, Existence, Right Being, the Refuge of the good, having heroic hosts, the Chief of the Yadavā, clan, the Abode of the good, He who had beautiful associations on the Yamunā; the dwelling-place of beings, Lord Vasudeva, the Repository of the Breath of all living beings, One for whom there is no sufficiency in anything; Humbler of haughtiness, Bestower of rightful pride, Himself elated in His own bliss, One whom it is difficult to hold within one's heart, the Invincible; Who is of all forms, of huge form, of resplendent form, Devoid of form and at the same time taking manifold forms, the Latent, of a hundred forms and a hundred faces; the One, the Many, the Sacrifice, the Highest import of the words "Who," "What," and "That which"; Father of the world, Besought by the world, Scion of the Madhu race, Affectionate to His devotees; of golden hue and limbs, of excellent limbs, of pleasing ornaments on the arm, the Slayer of warriors, the Difficult, Void of all attributes, One who has quenched desires, the Immobile and the Mobile; without pride or false assumptions, Bestower of honor, the Honored, the Owner of the world, the Bearer of the three worlds, of sublime Intellect, Manifested in the sacrifice, He whose objects are fulfilled, the truly Intelligent, the Support of the earth; the Fountainhead of light, Possessing splendor, Eminent among those bearing arms, the Reins of control, Control, the (always) Preoccupied, of many high reaches (i.e., many exalted aspects), the Elder brother of Gada; of four forms, four arms, four manifestations; the Resort of all the four castes of mankind, the Accomplished, Being in the four states of waking, dreaming, deep sleep, and the fourth beyond them, the Knower of the four *Vedas*, of Whom all that exists is but a fraction; Who returns to the world again and again and thus retires not, the Unconquerable, He who cannot be transgressed, Hard to be attained and known, realized and held in mind with difficulty, the Slayer of the evil-minded foes; of auspicious form, He who takes the essence of things in the world, Who extends Himself gloriously and Himself snaps that extension, doing sovereign and great duty, Who has regulated the acts appropriate to each, the Author of scriptures; of special birth, the Beautiful, of melting heart, the precious Hub which holds together everything, of auspicious thought, the Adored, the Giver of food, the Snouted-Fish-incarnation, He who vanquishes even the most learned; Golden-bodied, the Unperturbed, Lord of all lords of speech, the Deep Lake, the Deep Pit, the Great Being, the Great Treasure; He who gladdens the earth and tears it up as well, (pure and fragrant) like a jasmine, Cloud of coolness and plenty, the Sanctifier, the Breath, Who drinks nectar, Whose body is immortal, All-knowing and All-facing; Easy, of noble Vow, the Realized Soul, the Victor over foes, the Tormenter of foes, the Huge Banyan, the Uḍumbara tree (like unto whose fruit that contains a host of flies inside, Who holds within Himself the whole living world), the Sacred Pīpal, the Slayer of the demons Chanura and Agha; the Thousand-rayed, the Seven-tongued Fire, the State of Sublimity which is fed by the seven fuels, namely, fortitude, forgiveness, mercy, purity, prosperity, soft speech and non-enmity towards beings; Borne on the sacred Vedic hymns in seven meters, Devoid of form, Impeccable, Unimaginable, the Inspirer of fear as well as its destroyer; the Great One who is the Infinitesimal and the Infinite, the Lean and the Stout, the Qualified and the Unqualified, the Unsupported and Self-supported; of a beautiful mouth (wherefrom the *Vedas* issued); Forefather of all families and the multiplier of all families; Bearer of burdens, Proclaimed (in the *Vedas*), who is always engaged in Yoga and is the Lord of those that practice it, the Bestower of all desires, the four stages of life and He who toils therein and is emancipated thereby, the Tree with the rich foliage of all the worlds, Who is borne fleet on the Wind; the Bearer of the bow and the science of archery; the Punishment, the Punisher and the Subjugation; the Unvanquished, the All-enduring, the Controller, the Controlling rule and the Control; Possessed of the luminous quality, the Good, the True, Intent on the True and Righteous, the Object of all seeking, Deserving of all pleasing things, Deserving adoration, the Doer of the pleasant and the Promoter of endearment; Moving in the skies, the Light, Shining beautifully, the Enjoyer of Oblations, the Omnipresent, the Sun that absorbs water, shines in varied hues, urges and produces; and the God who has the Sun as His eye; the Endless, the Enjoyer of oblations, the Enjoyer (of all things), Giver of happiness, Born of many (in his incarnations for the protection of righteousness), Elder to all, He who is never despondent, Ever forbearing, the Foundation of the world, the Wonderful; the Old and Existing from ancient times, the Tawny, the Sun, He into whom creation dissolves at the deluge; Bestower of welfare, Maker of welfare, Welfare, Enjoyer of welfare and Capable Promoter of welfare; Devoid of severity, Adorned with earrings, Bearing the discus, Overpowering, of forceful ordinances, Transcending verbal knowledge and source, (yet) permitting verbal account; the Cool, the Bringer of the Night of Soul; not Cruel, the Delicate, the Capable, the Considerate, the Most Forbearing, the Most Learned, the Fearless, He whose praises it is holy to listen to or sing; He who helps men to cross over transmigratory existence, the Destroyer of evil acts, of the form of Merit, the Destroyer of evil dreams, the Annihilator of warriors, the Protector, of the form of all the good souls, the Life of all beings, Established all round; of endless forms, of endless fortune, One who has conquered anger, the Dispeller of fear, the Perfect, the Profound, the Director, the Commander, the Various Quarters (i.e., of the form of Space); without Beginning, the Imparter of Beauty to the terrestrial and celestial worlds, the Excellent Hero with beautiful armlets, Birth, the Primary source of humanity, the Terrible, of terrible Prowess; the Station of support, Himself unsupported by any, Smiling like a flower, the Ever awake, the Upwardly progressive, the Conduct of the righteous path, Giver of Life, the Lauded, the Guarantee (of fruits of actions); the Authority, the Abode of Life, the Sustainer of Life, Life of Life, the Truth, the Knower of Truth, the sole Soul, He who is beyond birth, death and old age; the Tree that pervades the three worlds of earth, ether and heaven, He who reaches beyond them too, the Father and the Great-grandfather, the Sacrifice, the Lord of the sacrifice, the Sacrificing Priest, the Sacrificial accessories, and Borne by the Sacrifice; the Bearer of the Sacrifice, the Performer of the Sacrifice, the aim of all Sacrifice, the Enjoyer of Sacrifice, the means of Sacrifice, He who brings Sacrifice to an end, the esoteric Sacrifice of Knowledge; the Food and indeed the Consumer of all as food; Himself His source, Voluntarily manifested, Who penetrates (as indweller of all beings or as the Boar-incarnation to salvage the submerged earth), the Singer of Sāman symphonies (in the plentitude of freedom), the son of Devakī, the Creator, the King, the Destroyer of sins; He who holds the Conch, the Sword, the Discus, the Bow and the Mace, the Discus-armed, the Unperturbed, He who can use anything as a weapon for striking.

Thus these Thousand from among the divine Names of the Great Keśava, fit to be sung, have been fully told. He who listens to this or recites it daily shall encounter nothing untoward here or in the hereafter. *In the blessed who are devoted to the Supreme Lord, there will be no anger, no jealousy, no avarice, no evil thought.*

10.

Bhāgavata Purāṇa[1]

> "O ye men of taste in this world! A fruit has dropped from the celestial wish-fulfilling tree of the *Vedas.* The parrot (Sage Suka) has had a peck at it, and found it dripping with the juice of immortality. It is the *Bhāgavata*! Go on drinking its juice till you become liberated completely."
>
> "Unadulterated *Dharma* is its theme; it is for those good souls free from intolerance. What is to be known here is the supreme Truth, the bestower of supreme welfare which is the end of all misery; the Lord is captured immediately in the hearts of those who listen to this *Bhāgavata* composed by the great sage."

Although the latest of the *purāṇas*, the *Bhāgavata* became the greatest, and indeed eclipsed all the other *purāṇas* including the *Viṣṇu Purāṇa* on which it is mostly modeled. A book of devout reading and exposition, *parayaṇa* and *pravacana*, it ranks with and even contends with the *Rāmāyaṇa* in popularity and appeal. Like the works of the three great Ācāryas, the *Bhāgavata*, a product of the South, gained wide sway all over North India where it became the inspiration and the Bible of schools of ecstatic devotion to Krishna, from Maharāshtra and Gujarat, across Mathura, to Bengal and Assam, of the *bhaktimārgas* (devotional paths) of Vallabha, Nimbarka, Śaṅkaradeva and Caitanya. It gave birth to an efflorescence of the music of devotion, in Narasimha Mehtā, Mīrabāi, Surdās and others, and to the birth of a vernacular literature and drama in Assam and a similar literature of Krishna *bhakti* in Sanskrit and the local languages—hymn, song, poem, drama and treatises on the doctrines of devotion in Bengal and Orissa. Several commentaries were written on the *Bhāgavata* to explain its meaning, including the esoteric, adopting the ideologies of the different schools of thought, not excluding the advaitic. In fact, the *advaitins*, who practiced devotion as an accessory to their path of knowledge, contributed perhaps the most important exegesis of the *Bhāgavata*—for example the great commentator Śrīdhara, as also Bopadeva in Maharāshtra, the pioneer to analyze, index, and work out a scheme for understanding the unity,

[1] Originally published in *Vedānta Keśari*, October 1965.

plan, and purpose of the *Bhāgavata*. Bopadeva's *Bhāgavata-mukta phala* is an invaluable aid to the study and enjoyment of this *purāṇa*.

For the *Bhāgavata*, we have a *mahātmya* in 6 chapters given in the *Padma Purāṇa*, which furnishes us with the key to the *purāṇa*. *Bhakti* or devotion is introduced here as a young wandering lady, accompanied by two old sons, *jñāna* and *vairāgya*, knowledge and detachment. She tells Nārada that she was born in Tamil country, grown in Karṇāṭaka, and in a few places in Maharāshtra and became shattered in Gujarat. Unbelievers had attacked her there, but on reaching Brindavana (Mathura), she gained her youth but her two sons continued to be in their shriveled up condition. On behalf of these three, Nārada asks of the four eternally young divine sages, Sanatkumāra and others the way and they assure him: "Let the *Bhāgavata* be read aloud to them; that great book will revive all the three of them." Nārada submits: "But the *Vedas*, the *Vedānta* and the *Bhagavad Gītā* has already been blown loudly to their ears, and all that has not been able to rouse them from their prostrate condition." The four Kumaras explain: "Well, the *Bhāgavata* is born of the essence of the *Vedas* and *Upaniṣads*. In a tree, no doubt, the juice is present all over, but cannot be relished; when it gets concentrated into the fruit, it is enjoyed. It is even as butter which has to be churned out of milk and sugar from the cane. Such is the *Bhāgavata*, composed by Vyāsa, especially for the resuscitation of *bhakti*, *jñāna*, and *vairāgya*."

In the opening chapters of the *Bhāgavata*, we are told of how Vyāsa came to compose this *purāṇa*, par excellence, of the Lord, as it is called. Vyāsa had already codified the *Veda*'s, distilled the *Upaniṣads* into the *Vedānta Sutras*, composed the *Mahābhārata* together with the *Bhagavad Gītā*, and several other treatises including all the other *purāṇas*. Yet in his inner heart there was a dejection and an emptiness and when none could give him any consolation and explanation, Nārada came and enlightened him. This initial chapter of the *Bhāgavata*, forming an exordium, is also an essay in criticism and a comparative estimate of the great sacred books, the *Vedas* and *Vedānta* and the *Mahābhārata*. "The impersonal principles of *dharma* and *Brahman* have been presented in the former; but for attracting and holding the human heart, the emphasis should be on the personality, particularly in the present age. You no doubt shifted to the personality in the epic, but you lost yourself in the fineries of poetry and expression and in the passions and violence of unseemly story and mess of episodes. Indeed, the people missed your message in it. Do not hide your mission; let not expression nor interesting story divert your attention or that of the readers. Declare your subject, the Lord and the singing of His Name and Glory, as your sole objective and compose a new *purāṇa* to this end."

Vyāsa obeyed, sang this *purāṇa* of Bhagavan, the *Bhāgavata*, and found his complete satisfaction.

The *Bhāgavata* achieved the above purpose by its own reorientation of the conception of *purāṇa. The purāṇa* is defined by five topics, *Pañcalakṣaṇas*, comprising the following: primary and secondary creations, the genealogies of gods and sages, periods of time and the dynasties of kings. Through these, it was intended to reinforce the supremacy of the Lord and *dharma*. This again, the *Bhāgavata* felt was overlaying the essential teaching with too much of other material and in a scheme in which it obviously doubled the topics to ten, *dāsalakṣanas*, it yet unmistakably declared that the tenth is the highest, viz. the Lord Himself, and that it is to clarify the tenth that the other nine were used (*daśamasya viśuddhyartham navamam iha lakṣaṇam*). And it also declares in the beginning that this tenth subject, the Lord, is brought out in a most emphatic manner in the tenth of the twelve books of the *purāṇa*, by which it means that although the pronounced theme of the *purāṇa* is to speak of all the major incarnations and the partial manifestations of the Lord for the redress of the imbalance in the reign of *dharma*, the appearance as Krishna is the greatest, the crown and culmination.

The accounts of creation, of deluge, of the different *yugas* and *manvantaras* are all here, but the treatment is such that in every narrative it is the greatness of the Supreme Being that is again and again brought home to us. As part of this endeavor, the *Bhāgavata* gives in abundance *stotras*, hymns to the Lord, strewn all over the work, embodying Upaniṣadic ideas and feelings of devotion. If one should attempt the difficult task of choosing among these, one many mention the hymns of Kuntī, Parikṣit, Bhīṣma, Dhruva, Vṛitra, Prahlāda, Gajendra, Brahmā, Vasudeva, and Devakī, Akrura and the Veda-stuti. To the same end are addressed the several exalted discourses in the *Bhāgavata* of which again mention may be made of those of the Lord to Brahmā (II), Kapila's to Devahūti (III), the Lord's to King Pṛithu (IV), those in the story of Pracinabarhis (IV), Brahmā's to Priyavrata (V), Ṛiṣabha's (V), Jaḍabharata's to King Rahūgaṇa (V), to Citraketu (VI), Prahlāda's to his classmates and his father (VII), Ajagara's (VII), Krishna's to the *gopīs* (X) and above all Krishna's discourses to his friend Uddhava in Book XI which form a veritable *Bhagavad Gītā* in themselves.

The *Bhāgavata*'s exhortation is for *bhakti*. In fact, what it has said on *bhakti* and its forms and phases, on the recital of the Lord's Name, *nāmam*, all this has become the basic tenets of the *bhakti* school expounded in many later treatises. The adoration of Krishna, especially as the child, and the love of the *gopīs* as the prototype of *bhakti* at its height, all this again we owe to the *Bhāgavata*. But the *Bhāgavata* deals with all the three *yogas*—*jñāna*, *karma*, and *bhakti*, and the *bhakti* that it emphasizes is a synthesis of all the three *yogas*, as the one naturally involves the other. To love God is to know and realize His true nature, as also to serve Him in all manner possible. Hence it is said in a verse setting forth the theme of the *Bhāgavata* that it expounds *naiṣkarmya*, cessation from all mundane activity, informed by knowledge, detachment, and devotion: *jñāna*, *viraga*, and *bhakti*: *yatra jñāna-virāga-bhakti-sahitam naiskarmyam āviṣkṛitam*. Kapila, who teaches the *samkhya* path of knowledge, calls it *bhakti yoga*; and explains highest *bhakti* as the realization of oneself and the Lord in every being around one. The *mukta*, the *bhakta*, the *sādhu*, the *bhāgavata*, the *jñānin*, and the *muni* are all described in different contexts but their characteristics are mostly in identical terms. In his summing up to Uddhava, the Lord says: "Of the three *yogas*, those who have desires and projects and programs in the world should take to *karma yoga*; those who can detach themselves and are given to stoic nature, may take to *jñāna yoga*; but those who are in the middle, who have desires and yet can think of the Lord, let them cultivate the path of devotion to Me, surrender unto Me themselves and the fruits of their acts, and do their appointed duties as an adoration and offering to Me."

From what was said at the beginning, it should not be supposed that the *Bhāgavata* has no appeal of language. It no doubt rides roughshod over classical grammar and lexicon but only as a master of both; this it does consciously, to elevate its diction to the Vedic plane. It can pour forth exquisite poetry as in the description of the seasons and of moonlight and the *rāsa-līlā* dance of the *gopīs* with Krishna in Book X. By its compounds it imparts a vigor and rhythm to its *anushtubh* and *upajati* verses which make it a delight to read them aloud and get them by heart.

In putting across ideas, in denunciation of the small things of material life, the *Bhāgavata* does not mince matters; it speaks forthright and as the Tamil saying goes, drives in its ideas like nails into green wood. It rises to heights sometimes and expresses its ideas in an astounding manner, with an intellectual and modern ring. "He who wants more for himself and accumulates is a thief, he is to be punished," it declares in one place. "Let us have adversities more often, so that we may remember the Lord more incessantly," prays Kuntī. "The Lord is in the form of Dharma which is a means to self-purification." The Lord says through Kapila: "I am not pleased with all the pomp of worship if one insults the living beings in whom I am immanent." "Leave off pride and shame and prostrate before all creatures, including the dog and the ass," says Krishna to Uddhava. Prahlāda says out of compassion for the suffering beings: "There are sages retired in forests striving for their own lonely salvation; but I do not want to leave behind these wretched folk in suffering and seek salvation, for myself alone." King Rantideva prays: "I do not aspire for divine status or miraculous powers; no, not even salvation; I want to enter into fellow beings in suffering and see that they are rid of their misery." In another place, Manu defines the Lord "as the exemplar of Man, one who works but is selfless; being full, wishes for nothing; acts without being urged by anybody; and teaches, by himself following the proper path and thus promulgates all *dharmas*." Lastly, listen to the universal prayer in the *Bhāgavata*'s own characteristic language: "May there be welfare for the world; may the wicked become tranquil; may beings contemplate each other's good; may the mind take to the good; and our thought become naturally possessed of the Lord."

11.

Encountering Tulasidās: The Rāma Story in Translation[1]

In 1948, I was traveling by rail to Darbhanga for the 14th session of the All-India Oriental Conference. On the platform of one of the larger stations, where the train stopped at daybreak, I suddenly heard some song on Rāma that set a thrill through my whole body. I looked out and saw a poor man in a rag of a cloth, just bathed at the water-tap on the platform and with his bare frail frame walking in the cold with a bucket of water in hand. He continued to sing and I to listen; and in a short while, I realized that it was from Tulasi's *Rāmāyaṇa* that he was singing. The impression has remained indelible; it was not only the magic of Tulasi's words but also the miracle of how all this heritage has had its hold over the people, even the very humblest of them.

The *Rāmāyaṇa* (*Rāmacarita mānasa*) of Tulasidās (1532-1574 A.D.) is, in the words of Sir George Grierson, the great linguist, the universally accepted Bible of all classes from the Himalayas to the Narmada, "the perfect example of a perfect book," exercising its spell over the unlettered millions to whom it brought in their language the entrancing and elevating personality of Vālmīki's Rāmacandra, the incarnation of *Satya* and *Dharma*, the saving grace of *Rāma-nāma*, and the ideal of Rāma *rājya* as the kingdom of God on earth. The Muslim-Hindi poets Abdur Rahim Khani Khan and Raskhan adored it as the "very life-breath of saints" and "endearing as the stream of milk flowing from the udders of the celestial cow." Grierson hails Tulasidās as "one of the half-dozen great writers that Asia has produced" and "a savior of Hindustan."

It is through Tulasi that Rāma *bhakti* and *Rāma-nāma* gained their sovereign sway over the whole of North India. It is through Tulasi that Gandhiji came to prize *Rāma-nāma* as the most potent medicine and cherish Rāma *rājya* as his ideal of *svarāj*—spiritually empowered self-rule.

Long before any of the recent organizations or movements started their efforts to make the literary treasures in one Indian language known to the people of other languages, the name and work of Tulasi had spread to South India. The tradition of the Saint-singers, the *Bhāgavata* and *Bhajana-kīrtana sampradāya* and the movement of the votaries of this tradition

[1] Originally published as a foreward to S. Jagannarayan's Tamil translation of the *Rāmacaritamānasa* of Tulasidās.

from one part of the country to the other had brought the life story of Tulasidās and his songs and his *Rāmāyaṇa* to the devout Tamil people. To the Tamils who get so deeply involved in music and devotion, the *Mahātmas* of Mahārāṣṭra, of the Hindi areas and of Bengal are all objects of veneration and their *abhangs*, *chaupais*, and *padas* are part of the repertoire of Tamil *Harikathā* performers. Our great singer of Rāma-songs, Tyāgarāja, pays his homage to Tulasi as one of those who had blazed the path of Rāma *bhakti* and Rāma *kīrtana* before him.

Outside of this religious milieu, it is but proper that an outstanding classic of the kind of the *Rāmacaritamānasa* should be made available to the literary world of Tamil Nadu. This service, Śrī S. Jagannarayanan has done in his Tamil rendering which he did together with comparative notes from Vālmīki, the Tamil *Rāmāyaṇa* of Kambar and the songs of Tyāgarāja. The translator, along with his late talented wife, has been for long a worshiper at the altar of music and devotion and has naturally brought to his translation his dedicated spirit. This is seen prominently in the *dhyānas* or preludes for helping contemplation of Rāma that he has put in all through the narrative. The knowledge of the Hindi that he had gained through his long stay in the north has had its best fruit in this sacred task he had set for himself and has accomplished.

Although each of the books of the *Rāmāyaṇa* has its own importance and projects a prominent phase of the scintillating prismatic personality of Rāma, it is the *Ayodhyā Kāṇḍa* that narrates the great giving up of the kingdom and the greater thing, namely Rāma not being affected in the least by this apparently serious loss and continuing to have the wonted and excelling cheer on his face, and in the midst of everyone else in a disturbed state at the sudden turn of events, he alone, standing like a rock of *Dharma* and *Satya*, as one towering above all others, the veritable God among men that indeed he was. In his memorable lines on this, Vālmīki said: "Losing his kingship diminished his great majesty no more than night lessens the radiance of the moon's cool light, which charms the world. Although Rāma was about to leave his own land and journey in the forest, his composure was that of a man who has transcended all worldly things."

It is this idea that Tulasi seizes as most significant and embodies in one of the three opening Sanskrit verses of his *Ayodhyā Kāṇḍa*: "That which did not wax more gracious because of the (proposed) coronation nor wane because of the (impending) difficulties of forest life, may that charm of the lotus-face of Rāma be for all time the bestower on me of things pleasing and auspicious." No image of Rāma in the epic could be more inspiring and thrilling than the one at this moment as he strode out of the chamber of Kaikeyī, having promised her that he was going to the forest and with the charm of his face not diminishing even by the slightest shade!

12.
The *Bhakti* of Guru Nānak[1]

Motto: Let me be a sacrifice unto that song
By which we attain immortality.—Guru Nānak

Guru Nānak, Singer-Saint

Guru Nānak appeared as one of the high billows in the great popular upsurges of religion and devotion, which began in the 7th century with the Tamil Śaiva and Vaiṣṇava saints, *nāyanmārs* and *āḷvārs*, and spread all over the country, a movement which had been active till very recently. This was, so far as this country was concerned, universal and comprehensive of all the faiths and sects and schools of thought, orthodox and heterodox, the Jain and Buddhist mystics having also participated in this movement with their own output, in verse and song, of religious and devotional mysticism. The adoption of the popular languages as the medium of expression and the harnessing of the art of music as effective means of reaching the masses, the compositions being mostly of the form of songs, the employment of homely diction, telling parables and suggestive similes and analogies—all these form on the external side common features of this vast literature of the popular saints, which forms in the history of almost all the regional languages the foremost if not the first creative work. On the more substantial side, leaning towards the practical aspects of the spiritual and religious pursuit, there were ideas which were common to all these saint-singers, the most prominent of which are the emphasis on the *name* of the Lord and its recitation and contemplation, and the *guru*, and its extension the *satsang*.[2] While all these common features were there, it

[1] First published in *Guru Nanak—A Homage*, ed. K.R. Srinivasa Iyengar (New Delhi: Sahitya Akademi, 1973). I have left the information in the footnotes as they are found in the text, when unable to add further information to them. See also V. Raghavan's Patel Memorial Lectures of 1964, published as *The Great Integrators—The Saint Singers of India* (New Delhi: Publications Division, 1966; 1979, 4th ed.).

[2] Maṅgala Śloka: Raghavan's Sanskrit version of the Mūlmantra was placed next to the motto in the original publication: *Eka Omkāra-San-Nāmā kartā Nirbhyapūruṣaḥ/ Nirvairo'kāla-mūrtaś ca'pyayoniśca svaykamprabhaḥ / Guruprasādo jayati yenaivam jñāyate Prabhuḥ*

should not be forgotten that those who participated in this great religious creative activity belonged to different traditions and schools of thought and their ultimate literary and philosophical background or affiliation varied. There is, no doubt, a large part of their musical, religious, and devotional outpourings which disclose universality and a synthetic trend but behind this patent unity there are the basic ideas of the schools of thought or tradition from which each one of them emerged. While it is useful to emphasize the great integrating role which they played, it is also necessary, in the interests of complete and scholarly understanding of the thought-content of this song literature to examine the underlying philosophical ideas which have gone into the making of the songs of each school or succession of these saint-singers.

Ideas Symbolized in Lyrics

Among these saint-singers there are those who sought the Personal God, the *saguṇa Brahman*, God with form; among these again, those who sang of one form or the other, Śaiva or Vaiṣṇava; of these last again, those who loved Rāma or Krishna, the latter in larger number. On the other hand, there were those who sought the Impersonal, the *nirguṇa Brahman*, God without form. Looking at them from the standpoint of philosophies, we had dualists, monotheists, qualified monists, and monists. These affiliations are known from history more than from views expressly or clearly found in the songs. The saints had intuitions and mystic experiences and ecstatic communions and trances and what flowed out of them in songs and through parables, analogies, and metaphors is too artistic a medium to allow of systematic analysis and tracing of self-contained logical systems of thought. But many schools and sects have grown, developed theologies and metaphysical systems just from out of these songs. The Ṛig Vedic hymns themselves form the foremost and earliest examples in this respect. We may therefore legitimately study in depth the songs and trace the thought-pattern as closely as possible.

That song-poetry could be interpreted so as to yield phases of thought may be illustrated from one of Nānak's compositions, in *Śrī rāga*: *Re mann aisi har sio prīt kar*,[3] in which Nānak uses a series of five similes for the love of man for God; the love of the lotus for the water, that of the fish

[3] *Japji* (UNESCO edition) entitled *The Sacred Writings of the Sikhs*, translated by T. Singh and others (India: National Academy of Representative Works of India Series, 1960), pp. 71-73.

for water, that of the *cātaka* bird for water—these three in one set, and two more, that of the water for the milk with which it is mixed and that of the *cakravaka* bird for the sun and its beloved one. The first series of three illumines three stages of the condition of the devotee: In the first the lotus is tossed and tormented by the waves of the water, bears all the trials and tribulations to which it is submitted and without getting uprooted, sticks on to the water in which it is born and has its being. In the second, whatever the flow and surge and depth of the water, the fish buoys itself up and swims through; this is a higher stage in which the devotee has achieved an inner capacity and poise and can never get sunk. The third is a still higher stage in which, although there is a flood of water all round, the *cātaka* thirsts only for the drop of water from the cloud above; that is, the devotee, a master of the situation around, is not satisfied with any affluence, power, or plenitude here, unless he has at least a drop of divine grace, which outweighs all else. The next two similes, the fourth and fifth, refer to conditions of union and separation; man and God are united like water and milk; the comparative nature and position of the two are no doubt clearly brought out by the two subjects chosen, but what is more significant is the idea that for the sake of the latter, the Lord (the milk), the former (water), the self of man, has to efface or annihilate itself completely. The last simile of the *cakravaka* bird and its beloved partner and the sun brings out effectively the ideas of how the beloved partner is all the time near at hand, but because of the darkness of ignorance, it is not able to see the beloved, and pines and pines, till on the rise of the sun and knowledge in the morning, the discovery and union take place automatically.

Following this method of intensive study of the songs, we can cull together the ideas which could build up to a thought-pattern with contours more or less clear. The first question will of course be: What is the nature of the God or Godhead adored by Nānak?

The Nature of God

Bhakti is advocated at every step in the songs of Nānak. There is reference to God as a storehouse of qualities, *Guṇa nidhāna*[4] and an ocean of virtues.[5] Stress is laid on the Lord's grace as necessary for release. "By God's

[4] *The Sacred Writings of the Sikhs*, p. 31.

[5] Ibid., p. 52.

Grace alone," says Nānak, "is God to be grasped" says *Japji*[6] echoing the *Upaniṣad*'s *Yam evaiṣa vṛinute tena labhyaḥ* ("The supreme Self reveals itself only to the soul who embraces the Self as the Master within the heart"). Again, "In the realm of Grace, spiritual power is supreme, nothing else avails."[7] In a *Śrīrāga* song, we find: "Those on whom descends the Grace of God are his favorites."[8] Nānak points out that the law of karma, of one reaping the fruits of one's action, as inexorable, but observes that the Lord can always forgive and save: "When the balance of deeds is struck, Yāma strikes us on our head. Then we have to render the account when he asks for it. It is on the mediation of the True One (i.e. the Lord) that we are all saved and the Lord forgives us."

This Being of grace, whom one must adore with love and devotion, is however not any *avatāra* like Rāma or Krishna, nor any of the three Gods: Brahmā, Viṣṇu or Hari, and Śiva. Nānak may refer to Harinām but Hari of Nānak is just God, like Rām of Kabīr. For according to *Japji* 30[9] the *Trimūrtis* (three forms of God) are just three acceptable disciples brought forth from the one God, by *māyā*. In the same text[10] in which God is mentioned as "treasury of qualities," he is also called *Nirañjana* (pure, free from passion) and it is said that he cannot be installed anywhere nor is He in a form that could be installed. The *Japji* adds: "If anyone thinks he knows Him (that Lord), one does not speak the truth, as such an utterance is not possible," recalling the *Kena Upaniṣad*:

> *Yasyāmatam tasya matam matam yasya na veda saḥ*
> *Avijñātam vijñānatām vijñātam avijānatām*
> "He has neither form (*rūpa*) nor material sign."[11]

In a *Rāmakali* song, he says: "Our creator the Lord Himself creates all; Brahmā, Viṣṇu, Śiva too are contained in Him, the One Alone." The *Mūla mantra* itself declares the Lord as the One, the True, Timeless, Formless, Unborn, Self-luminous *sat* (eternal being), *akāla* (beyond time), *amūrta*

[6] Ibid., p. 32.

[7] Ibid., p. 37.

[8] Ibid., p. 68.

[9] Ibid., p. 46.

[10] Ibid., p. 5.

[11] *Kena Upaniṣad, Suhi Ast.*, 1.3.

(formless), *ayoni* (without womb), *svayambhu* (self-dependent). In *Japji* 4, he is called the Lord who is Truth, having Truth as his Name. In *Japji* 29, the following terms are used to designate Him: the beginning, colorless, the beginningless, the subtle Sound: *ādi, anīla, anādi, anāhata.*

All the forms into which It spreads out, all the diverse forms which different schools speak of, are only the many aspects of the one Lord. Says Nānak with a telling simile:

> Six the systems, six their teachers,
> And six their different teachings,
> The Lord of them all is the One Lord
> However various His aspects are:
> O, brother, follow that system
> That sings the Lord's praises:
> There thy true glory lies.
>
> Seconds, minutes, hours, quarters of a day;
> Lunar and solar days make up a month.
> Yet there are many times and many seasons;
> One single sun runs through them all.
> O Nānak, Thy Lord is likewise One,
> However various His aspects are.

The One Lord is not only of the form of the many but He is also above all forms. In a *Dhansari rāga* song, Nānak says: "Thou hast a thousand forms and yet not one form," and in a *Pauri rāga* song, "Thy Name is Formless."

Contrary to some opinions held,[12] it is only on the basis of the *advaita* of the *Upaniṣads* and Śaṅkara that we can explain the above statements of Nānak. The *nirguṇa sampradāya* (or tradition of the Supreme as formless) in which Nānak emerged and the well-known epithet *Nānak Nirankār* cannot be explained otherwise. The ultimate disappearance of duality and realization of unity are both voiced forth in the songs. "Then the *ātman* becomes one with the *parāmātman* and duality is destroyed."[13]

In a *Bhairava rāga* song: "Without the Name the disease of duality

[12] See *Guru Nānak and the Sikh Tradition*, W.H. Mcleod (London: Oxford, 1968), pp. 165, 185.

[13] Jogendra Singh, *Thus Spoke Guru Nānak* (London: Oxford University Press, 1934), p. 61.

has spread throughout the world." Elsewhere, "Thou the Formless One, beyond fear and enmity, I blend in Thy pure light."[14] In a song in *Śrī rāga*, Nānak says: "Through the guru's words alone there comes the moment of knowing 'Myself is that Self.'"[15] And in another in *Maru rāga*, "I am that, that is I; the three worlds are included in that formula."[16] Thus, in the words of a recent Sikh writer on this subject,[17] "*Bhakti* of the Guru-poets is of absolute monistic nature and of the formless and ever-living God."

The Self and the Infinite

In an advaitic poem called *Prabodhasudhākāra*, the aspirant after union with the supreme exclaims to the Lord: "Even if our difference ends, I am yours, not you, mine; the wave is the ocean, not vice versa."

On this question of the relationship between the supreme Self and the finite self, Nānak has a riddle, in a song of riddles in *Rāmakali rāga*. The intriguing nature of the question is well answered by propounding the things as a riddle, the secret of which, is, Nānak says, known only to the Lord; but his answer is clear, viz., the unity of the two. Using almost the same analogy of the sea and a part of it, Nānak asks:

> The drop of water is in the sea,
> And the sea is in the drop of water;
> Who shall solve this riddle?
> Who knoweth the secret?
> He from whom all creation came,
> He surveyeth that which He hath created,
> He, the Lord, is the One knower of the secret;
> And the man who understandeth this in his heart
> Is freed from human bondage,
> Is made at one with the Lord.

Māyā

For the process of the One Absolute becoming diversified and dynamic and creative, Nānak uses the Vedāntic concept of *māyā*, the primal potency

[14] *Asa Ast.*, 8.7.

[15] *The Sacred Writings of the Sikhs*, p. 73.

[16] Ibid., p. 106.

[17] *Bhakti of the Sikh Guru*, Dr. Darshan Singh, *Parkh*, A Research Bulletin in Punjabi Language and Literature, Chandigarh, II, 1967, p. 105.

conceived as the Goddess and Mother of all creation. The *Japji* (30) states: "The Lord of *Māyā*, through Her union becomes manifold into the Creator, Sustainer, and Destroyer; and as He directs they obey and do their duties." In a song in *Maru rāga*, it is stated that *Māyā*, the Goddess is the veil of illusion which obscures the Truth and increases worldly attachment. It is the cause of duality, falsity, ignorance, attachments to mundane things and eventual transmigration and bondage. In these roles it is repeatedly denounced: "*Māyā*'s disciple is false; he abhors truth. Bound up in duality, he transmigrates,"[18] "the fool is entangled in duality and forgets the divine Name."[19]

All this is quite in conformity with the Vedāntic ontology and creative process. If the one timeless absolute alone is truth, it follows that the manifold that has arisen therefrom is the opposite of truth. It may, for the time being and for practical purposes, be real but is not really real. It has been accepted in the monistic tradition that all teachings and endeavors on the spiritual path are only the means to reach the goal, effective for the duration of their agency, and transcended or sublated when the Truth is reached. It is this ultimate falsity that Nānak speaks of:

> False is the king, false are the subjects, false is the whole world.
> False is the palace, false are the skyscrapers, false the indwellers.
> False is gold, false is silver, false is the wearer.
> False is the body, false the garments, false the infinite beauty.
> False is the groom, false the bride, they are wasted away. . . .
> O Lord, without Thee all is false.

Nānak and the Name

Like the other members of the galaxy of Saint-Singers of India, Nānak also assigns a high place to the Lord's Name, *nāma*, and gives the three requisites or *sādhanas* of *śravaṇa*, *kīrtana*, and *smaraṇa*, listening to the Name, its recitation, and its uninterrupted remembrance. The lines referring to these ideas are too numerous and too well-known to need any quotation. We should rather linger to consider what this Name is. *Nāma* occurs along with the related concept of *śabda* which we are coming to shortly. It is not the Name like Rāma, Krishna etc. which are well-known to adherents of other paths of devotion centering round particular personal

[18] *Majh Ast.*, I. 5.

[19] *Asa Ast.*, 9 (2).

deities; they are rather on a par with the attributes or terms applied to the Supreme Being in the *Upaniṣads*, in its *nirguṇa* aspect, as also in its primary *saguṇa* aspect; *akāla*, *nirañjana*, and so on, in the *nirguṇa*; and *karta*, *puruṣa*, and so on in the latter primary *saguṇa* aspect as Creator, Sustainer, Destroyer, the immanent indwelling Self (*antaryāmī*), and so on. A *Rāmakali rāga* song says: "From the Absolute He of Himself became manifest the Pure One; from being attributeless (*nirguṇa*), He was endowed with attributes (*saguṇa*)." Again, "He the Lord Himself created Himself and assumed Himself the Name and then He created Nature, and abiding within it, He reveled in His wonder." In a song in *Sorath rāga*, "In all hearts is hid the Lord, all hearts are illumined by the light of the Lord." It is these terms by which the Supreme Being is characterized in its absolute aspect or its creative and primary *saguṇa* aspect that constitute the Names to be meditated upon constantly. This is quite germane to the advaitic tradition and indeed there is a collection and exposition by a South Indian *sannyāsin* scholar, Paramaśivendra Sarasvatī, of these epithets of the *nirguṇa* and *saguṇa Brahman* as the "One thousand Names of the Supreme from the *Upaniṣads*"—*Upaniṣan-nāma-sahasra-vyākhyā*. It is in this sense again that Islam also cherishes the Names of the Lord: "The Divine Names are either names of the Essence e.g. the One, or names of attributes, e.g. the Merciful, the Knowing"[20] and so on.

Śabda

One with the idea of *Nāma* is that of Word, *Śabda*. As often as *Nāma*, *Śabda* also occurs in the songs. It is also one of the concepts whose correct understanding and identification are not easy. It is used both as being one with God and also as a means of gaining that state. On the other side, it occurs as a compound with *Guru*, *Guru-Śabda*, and sometimes as Guru's *Śabda*, the former signifying an identity. In answer to the question of a yogi, as to who his guru was, Nānak replied: "The true Guru is the Word."[21] Thus *Śabda* is something which is almost identical with the highest, the highest means of attaining that, and the words of Teacher, e.g. the scriptures and the songs themselves. It has been recorded by Nānak that whenever he heard the "Word," he immediately sang,[22] and that he once

[20] R.N. Nicholson, *Studies in Islamic Mysticism*, p. 93.

[21] *The Sacred Writings of the Sikhs*, p. 102.

[22] Cf. song in *Tilang rāga*, *The Sacred Writings of the Sikhs*, p. 69.

exclaimed when he was in meditation: "Mardan! Touch the chords, the Word is descending," but Mardana who played the rabab for him replied: "But, Master, the horse is grazing and my hands are occupied holding the reins, lest the animal run away." Nānak said: "Let go the horse." As already mentioned Nānak was asked by the yogis and *siddhas* as to who his Guru was and Nānak replied that *Śabda* was his Guru; "The Word is the Guru and the mind attuned to the Word is the disciple."[23]

In *Var-malar*, he says: "He who meditates on Thy true *Śabda* is joined in union with Thee. . . . The Guru's *Śabda* is like a gem which reveals Thee by its light." In a song of his in *Sorathi rāga*, we read: "God has neither form nor color nor material sign but he is revealed through true *Śabda*." In another in *Gowri rāga*: "Meditating on *Śabda* and repeating the Name of the Lord, man is released." In a third in *Śrī rāga*: "Without the *Śabda* one is condemned to wander." In a further one in *Śrī rāga*, we read: "In the contemplation of the Word is bliss" and ". . . release from bondage comes from contemplating the Word."[24]

From some other utterances, *Śabda* is seen to be all-comprehensive. "The Word is my meditation, divine instruction, the music of my horn for me to hear."[25] "All acts of purification, austerities, devotion, penance, and pilgrimages abide in the Word." A piece in the *Japji* describes *Śabda* as something to be realized through the virtues of chastity, patience, understanding, knowledge, austerity, fear and devotion.[26]

In the forge of continence,
Let patience be the goldsmith,
On the anvil of understanding
Let him strike with the hammer of knowledge:
Let the fear of God be the bellows,
Let austerities be the fire,
Let the love of God be the crucible,
Let the nectar of life be melted in it;
Thus in the mint of Truth,
A man may coin the *Word*.

[23] Song in *Rāmakali rāga.*

[24] *The Sacred Writings of the Sikhs*, pp. 74-75.

[25] M.A. Macauliffe, *The Sikh Religion, Its Gurus, Sacred Writings, and Authors* (London: Oxford, 1909), p. 172.

[26] Ibid., p. 378.

A song in *Bilaval rāga* says: "The Lord himself is the Word; Himself stamps it with his approval."

From all this it is clear that the concept of *Śabda* is both intriguing and interesting and deserves some examination, particularly because it has a fundamental place in Nānak's thought. It is well-known that part of the heritage of Nānak lay in the tradition of the *nāth yogis* and according to the tradition of the yoga, a stage is reached at the heights of perfection when the yogin is able to hear the subtle Sound pervading the universe. This is the unmanifest or unstruck Sound, *avyakta, anāhata nāda*. Nānak has of course denounced the mere physical practice of the yogic exercises, without real spiritual attunement, but it is clear that he had some esoteric practices of his own. When he was asked by the yogi Loharipa to adopt his system, Nānak replied, "My own system is the constant contemplation of the Word,"[27] and we find references to the *anāhata nāda* in the *Japji*[28] and his songs.

In a piece in *Asa rāga* we find the following: "One loves one's Lord, ever attuned to him, imbibes the *unstruck music of the Word* in the mind." In *Japji* 29 the Lord is described as the Primary Being, one devoid of all color, beginningless, and *Anāhata*. In the beautiful cosmic *Ārati* song, the first part ends: "Unstruck music is the sound of Thy temple drums."[29] Elsewhere[30] I have drawn attention to the text *Haṭhayogapradīpikā* and what it says about this subtle inner *Nāda* in which the mind gets dissolved and beyond the state of *Manolaya* is the soundless state of the Supreme Being. This *anāhata śabda* or *nāda* has unfortunately not come out in its correct form in the translations of or commentaries on the songs that we have. There is however no doubt about this *śabda* being, in its ultimate sense, the *anāhata nāda*. This will be clear from the universality of the concept of the Primordial Sound which all the scriptures of the world mention: for example, in the Bible, John: "In the beginning was the *Word* and the *Word* was with God and the *Word* was God." In the further interpretation of this word the philosophy of the *Logos* developed and

[27] *The Sacred Writings of the Sikhs*, p. 101.

[28] In a learned Sanskrit commentary on the *Japji*, this is rendered as *avrara*, uninjured, according to a description in the *Upaniṣad*. In a well-known English translation, it is just rendered as "changeless."

[29] *The Sacred Writings of the Sikhs*, p. 61.

[30] In the article, V. Raghavan, "Nānak—Tradition and Thought" in the volume *Guru Nānak* (New Delhi: Publications Division, 1969), pp. 18-32.

the *Logos* was identified with Sophia, Thought and Idea. The Hermetic tradition of the Hellenized cities of Egypt identified that the Logos was first-born of the Lord: "With Logos, not with hands, did the Creator make Universal cosmos." It would not be difficult to see the parallel in the *Upaniṣads* where the one *Brahman*, which becomes two and creates the Universe, is said to be in *tapas* or in brooking, contemplation or thought, *ālochana*. In other schools of thought, this is termed *vimarśa* and identified with *Devī* or *Śakti* and *Śabda*. We see this also in the Islamic and Sufic background which was the part of the heritage of Nānak. We can go to no better authority for this than the pioneer student of comparative religion, Prince Dara Shikoh and his work *Majma-ul-Bahrain* or "The Mingling of the Two Oceans (of Islam and Hinduism)" where he says in section 8 on Sound:

> Sound emanates from the same breath of the Merciful which came out with the word *Kun,* at the time of the creation. The Indian divines call that Sound *Sarasvatī*, which they say is the source of all sounds, voices, and vibrations. According to the Indian monotheists, this Sound, which is called *Nāda* is of three kinds. First *Anāhata*, which has been in Eternity Past, is so at Present, and will be so in Future. The Sufis name this sound *Swaz-i-Mutlak* (The sound of the Absolute) or *Sultan-ul-Adhkar* (king of all devotional exercises). This sound is eternal and is the source of the perception of *mahākāśa*; but this Sound is inaudible to all except the great saints of both the communities. Secondly *Āhata*. . . . Thirdly *Śabda*. . . . *Śabda* possesses an affinity with *Sarasvatī* and is the source of *Ism-i-Azam* (the Great Name) of the Musalmans and the *Veda-mukha* or OM of the Hindu divines. *Ism-i-Azam* means that He is the possessor of the three attributes of Creation, Preservation, and Destruction; and *Fatha*, *Dhamma*, and *Kasra* which correspond with *a-kāra*, *u-kāra*, and *ma-kāra* have also originated from this. They (the Indian divines) assign a special symbol to this Sound which bears a close resemblance to our *Ism-i-Azam* and in which traces of the elements of water, fire, air, dust and of the Pure Self are manifest.

As in the philosophical interpretation of the Biblical concept of the Word, in respect of this Word *Kun* it has been said: "According to Muhammadan belief the word owes its origin to the Will of God which was expressed by the word *Kun* or 'Be.'"[31] In his *Studies in Islamic Mysticism*,[32] R.N. Nicholson says, "Mohammed is the Logos who unites the Essence, the Attributes, and the Names in a single nature. The Perfect Man is neither Absolute Being nor contingent Being, but the third metaphysical entity i.e. the Logos." The relation of the will of God to create and the Word is seen in a long song on creation in *Maru rāga*, where Nānak says: "When He so *Willed*, He shaped the Universe. . . . To some, chosen few, the Guru revealeth the Lord's Word."[33] The will of the Lord such as that "Let the worlds be" is also called the *saṅkalpa* of Īśvara. Nānak calls it the *hukam* or *ājñā* or Order in *Japji* 2: "Through His Will He creates all the forms of things" and adds that this will of the Lord is inscrutable.

Śabda is therefore the same highest symbol of the Supreme Being that the *Upaniṣads* speak of as *Om* or *praṇava*. That this is so is borne out by a song in *Rāmakali*:[34]

> Oṃkār is He who created Brahmā,
> Brahmā who treasured God in his mind.
> Oṃkār is He who created the mountains and the *yugas*.
> Oṃkār is He who created the *Vedas*.
> Oṃkār is He who, through the Word, emancipated all.
> Oṃkār is He through whom the God-conscious beings were saved.
> Hear ye, the meaning of the Word OM,
> Which indeed is the essence of the three worlds.

In fact, at the very opening, the *Mūla mantra* begins with this highest mystic syllable. *Oṃkār Sat-Nām kartā puruṣa* and so on.

Nānak's Ideal Way of Life

The monistic view is not inconsistent on the empirical plane where ethics based on duality has its fruitful role to play. *Jñāna* and *dhyāna yogas*, rarefied *bhakti yoga*, and *karma yoga*, as taught by the *Bhagavad Gītā* as submission to the will of God and discharging one's duty with detachment—all these

[31] M.M. Huq, in his translation of *Majma*.

[32] R.N. Nicholson, *Studies in Islamic Mysticism*, p, 157.

[33] *The Sacred Writings of the Sikhs*, p. 105.

[34] *The Sacred Writings of the Sikhs*, p. 93.

form an amalgam in the approach of the mystic, such as Nānak was. "True yoga," says Nānak, "lies in living a detached life amidst attachments."[35] "One liveth detached, enshrining the One Lord in the mind. . . ."[36] The ideal of such a God-centered life of contentment, dedicated work, and service is the message that Nānak gives all men, whatever their walk of life or opportunity to play their part: "Serve others and dwell on the Word; practice contemplation and self-control and overcome the ego."[37] "Dedicate thyself to service in the world and thou gettest a seat in the Lord's Court."[38] "The man who earns his bread by sweat of his brow and gives some of his gains in charity knows, Nānak, the true way of life."[39]

> Man set in authority,
> Let devotion to God be thy service,
> Let thy toil be faith in the Name.
> Check thy mind from wandering after temptation
> Stand alert on guard against all evil,
> So from all men thou shalt earn the praise,
> And the Lord, thy Kind, will delight in thee
> With a four-fold increase of His Love.[40]

The following universal message of his may be the fitting finale to his homage to the Guru: "Let there be brotherhood with all men. To subdue the mind is to subdue the world."[41]

[35] Suhi, M.1.

[36] *Rāmkali.*

[37] Pārbhatī, M.1.

[38] *Śrī rāga*, M.1.

[39] Var Sarang, *The Sacred Writings of the Sikhs*, p. 116.

[40] *The Sacred Writings of the Sikhs*, p. 116.

[41] *Japji* 28.

13.

Bhadrācalam Rāmadās: The Singer-Saint Whom Rāma Sprang from Jail[1]

The Era in Which Rāmadās Lived

It was the time when the Qutub Shāhis were ruling in Golconda. Although these rulers were Muslims, they were great patrons of the local language, Telugu, and the local arts of music and dance. The best of them, Malik Ibrahim patronized Telugu writers and the "Iburanu" figuring in many Telugu songs is this Malik Ibrahim. His son Muhammad Quli Qutub Shāh became attracted to a temple dancer, a *devadāsī* proficient in music and dance, named Bhāgamatī, and named the city Bhāgnagar after her; the city later came to be known as Hyderabad.

Later, Kṣetrayya, a devotee of Krishna as Muvva Gopāla, came to the court of Abdulla Qutub Shāh. Kṣetrayya, a Telugu poet, music-composer, and authority on *rasa* and *Alaṁkāra śāstra* had a contest in the Golconda court on the subject of *nāyika-nāyaka-bhāva* with another scholar Tulasimūrti and in this connection composed under the patronage of the Padshāh and by the grace of Krishna in the form of Muvva Gopāla, 1100 *padas*. Evidently at this time the *nāyaka-bhāva* (the mood of longing for the beloved which had also much to do with the phase of devotion called *madhura-bhakti* ("the sweetness of spiritual love") and music compositions based on it inspired much interest. One of the divines, connected with the court as preceptors, at the royal school or *dargah* at Gulbarga of Gezu Daraz, Shāhrāja or Bada Akbar Shāh, also evinced keen interest in the subject and a text entitled *Śṛingarāmañjari* in Telugu and Sanskrit versions was produced on this subject.[2]

In the time of the successor to these rulers, Abul Hasan known as Tani Shāh, Hindu-Muslim unity had grown further. Not only were his ministers,

[1] This piece was first published in *Devotional Poets and Mystics, Part II* (New Delhi: Pub. Div. Ministry of Information and Broadcasting, Government of India, 1978).

[2] This very erudite work on *nāyika-nāyaka-bhāva*, in its Sanskrit version, was discovered and edited by V. Raghavan for the Archaeological Department of Andhra Pradesh, 1951. See also V. Raghavan's article, "Hyderabad as Center of Sangita," *Journal of the Music Academy*, Madras, XVI, 1945, pp. 116-20.

the two brothers Akkanna and Madanna, Hindu, but many Muslim officials freely participated in Hindu festival.

It is this Muslim ruler Abul Hasan Tani Shāh who figures in the story of Śrī Bhadrācalam Rāmadās. It is necessary to know something about the history of Abul Hasan to understand the background of this ruler in proper perspective.

Abdulla Qutab Shāh was thinking of giving his daughter in marriage and naturally his thoughts went to the *dargah* (royal school) of Gezu Daraz at Gulbarga whose divines had always advised the rulers. Shārāja or Bade Akbar Shāh was in charge of the *dargah* at that time. Abul Hasan, a young boy, who descended on the side of the mother of Abdulla, was studying at the royal school. The boy had been under Shārāja's tuition for twelve years. Abdulla took a sudden decision to give his daughter to him and later to give him the kingdom as well.

Abul Hasan was more popularly known as Tani Shāh, which means "jovial king." But deep below his gaiety, there was all that he had imbibed during his youthful stay in the religious atmosphere of Gulbarga. His maturity of spirit was due also to the rare experience he had in his contact with Rāmadās, in the sight of Śrī Rāmacandra with which he was blessed. It is not a matter of wonder that through his *bhakti* to Rāma, Rāmadās attained salvation. The wonder is that Rāmadās took with him the Muslim ruler.

> "O you are a more fortunate man than I am—
> You saw with your own eyes the feet of Rāma my father!"[3]

Thus did Rāmadās himself exclaim and felicitate Tani Shāh on the divine *darśan*, the vision of Rāma, with which he was blessed.

The time of Tani Shāh is 1674-1699 A.D. Traditionally Kabīrdās of Banāras is said, by Harikatha performers, to have been the guru of Rāmadās but this is not possible as Kabīr, a disciple of Rāmānanda, flourished between 1440 and 1518 A.D.; further there is nothing hazy about the figure of Rāmadās who is a well known name in Telugu history and literature. All that he wrote, his time, his life, —all these are known to us authoritatively, more authoritatively than the life and career of Tyāgarāja who lived much nearer our time. We can visit Golconda and see the hill and the place where Rāmadās was imprisoned and the hole through which food is said to have been dropped for him.

[3] *Dhanyuḍavu Tanīsā nīvu/nannu kannayya padamulu kanula/kannāvu.*

In 1832 A.D. one Varada Rāmadās who described himself as a descendant of Bhadrācalam Rāmadās, made a representation to Chandulal, Dewan of the Nizam of Hyderabad, that he should be appointed to look after the Rāma temple at Bhadrācalam, and got his request granted. In confirmation of the historicity of the whole story of Rāmadās and the Muslim ruler, we have had the continuing practice of the Nizam of Hyderabad making a grant for the conduct of the festival of the temple of Rāma at Bhadrācalam. It was reported in the papers that during the anti-Hindu agitations and activities of Razakars and their leader Kasim Rizvi, the Nizam stopped the grant to the Bhadrācalam temple, but soon realized that this was a wrong action and restored the grant.

Biographical Background

Tani Shāh had a Brahman Minister named Madanna. Madanna had a sister Kāmāmbā who was given in marriage to Liṅganna Mantri. Rāmadās was the son of Liṅganna. His real name was Gopanna. They belonged to the family surnamed Kañcharla whose members were spread all over South India. One of the *stotras* or (hymns) written by Rāmadās is the *Bhadrācala Daśarathī Śatakam* and in this Rāmadās gives at the beginning biographical details about himself. They belonged to the place called Nelakondapalli in the former Nizam's dominions. His gotra (lineage of male descendants from a sage ancestor) was Atri, his Veda *Śuklayajus* (each family of *brahmans* being associated with a *Veda*, which they were to learn and transmit to future generations) and as stated above, his house-name was Kañcharla.

> His father was Allana Liṅga Mantri
> He belonged to Atrigotra Adi-sakha
> His family name was Kañcharla
> The family composed songs in praise of Bhagavan
> And I myself composed one hundred verses
> on Rāma who is the ocean of mercy.[4]

In this same text, the *Daśarathi Śatakam*, he mentions his guru, Raghunātha Bhattāchārya:

[4] *Allana Liṅga mantri sutuda/Atrigotrajuda Ādi-sākha/Kañcharla Kulodbhavundanu*
Prasiddhudanai Bhavamdankitamuga/yella kavul nutiyimpa rachiyiñchithi
Gopa-Kavinḍrudan Jagadvallabha/nīku dāsuḍanu Daśarthi Karunāpayonidhi.

With body bent I bow to all gurus
I bow to my guru Raghunātha Bhattar Añjaletti.[5]

This guru was a Śrīvaiṣṇava who belonged to the "Śeṣa" family.

Because of his *Rāma-bhakti*, the boy named Gopanna came to be known as Rāmadās, "the servant of Rāma." The whole family was devoted to *bhakti* and its propagation. According to an unpublished document, his uncle the Minister Madanna arranged for a *yakṣagāna* or musical dance-drama troupe to tour from village to village, enacting purāṇic stories and spreading *bhakti*. Rāmadās continued this tradition, courting the company of *bhaktas*, and arranging for *bhajanas* and festivals. Rāmadās must have had initiation and *mantropadeśa* (instruction in the mantra) from some great soul and progressed in the spiritual path to such an extent that he saw Rāma in all beings and things, a state which he himself expressed in one of his songs: "The whole universe of full of Rāma."[6]

By constantly inviting *bhāgavatas*, devoted singers and expounders, to his home, and entertaining and attending upon them, Rāmadās spent much wealth and gradually became reduced to poverty. Thereupon, through the good offices of his uncle Madanna, he got from the Nawab the Tahsildarship (the position of revenue officer) of the *firka* or area of Bhadrācalam. He was discharging his duties well in this office for some time.

The Story of Rāmadās' Imprisonment

The Rāma shrine for which Bhadrācalam was well known was in a damaged state. Rāmadās felt that he should repair the temple and provide the Rāma image there with new jewels. Until that time Rāmadās, responsible for revenue collection, was prompt in remitting the revenues of his division to the Central Treasury but after his mind turned to the renovation of the Rāma shrine, the collections came to be directed towards the Rāma shrine and not to the Padshāh's exchequer. In one of his songs on Bhadrācalam, Rāma and His temple there, Rāmadās describes the golden pinnacles of the towers of this temple, the bejeweled flagstaff, the tank, the garden, the surrounding shrines, the Brahman neighborhood, and so on. From this song which refers to Bhadrācalam as "Vaikuntha, Viṣṇu's heaven on earth in this Kali age," we may see the nature and extent of improvement that Rāmadās

[5] *Ācāryula kella mrokki vinatāngudanai/Raghunāthabhattārācāryulaku añjaletti.*

[6] *Anta Rāmamayam, ī jagad anta Rāmamayam.*

had effected in the temple. In a further song of lament which he sang in prison (*Sītā Rāmasvāmī nā jesina neramuleni*), he asks "What wrong did I do? did I make the earrings, the rings for all the ten fingers, the diadem, for myself? It is to give honor to you, Oh Sītā-Rāma, that I did all this!" From this again we see that he spent large sums of money on the decorations of the image of Rāma at Bhadrācalam.

The revenues had not been remitted for a long time and notices sent from time to time produced no response. Then the State officials had Rāmadās arrested and thrown into the prison in Golconda. That he suffered in the prison for twelve years is mentioned by him in a song of his:

> Why has your compassion not come, O Rāma,
> Why are you not saving me?
> I shall not request any other deity's help
> I am forever attached to you
> I have been languishing in this jail
> twelve years now.[7]

It was during this twelve years of prison-life to which he had been condemned by the Padshāh that Rāmadās sang most of his moving songs. Why had Rāmadās to suffer so long in this manner, when his own uncle was Minister? Firstly, Minister Madanna could not go out of the way and do anything to save his nephew who had spent state money excessively on the temple; nor could the uncle have had that large amount of money that his nephew had spent, to be paid to the State and release his nephew.

Songs Reflecting Rāmadās' Sufferings

The State officials must have from time to time beaten Rāmadās for the payment of dues. This is clear from the cries of pain that we hear in the *Asāveri rāga* song:

> O my father,
> I cannot bear
> these beatings —
> They are lashing me with whips,

[7] *Emitiki dayarādu Śrī Rāmulu nannu./Emiṭiki rakṣimpavu Śrī Rāmulu/Parulanu ne védabonu Śrī Rāmulu/nike karamula sāchi yunnanu/pannendenḍlu āye nedu/bandikhānalona yundinānu.*

So please
come and save me![8]

Gopanna believed that whatever the treatment he received, Rāma always stood by his side armed with the discus of Viṣṇu, and therefore that he had nothing to be afraid of: "There is no lack of anything as long as my Rāma is there with me, standing at my side like a friend, *cakra* in hand."[9]

Rāma alone constituted Rāmadās' wealth and strength; in happiness or misery he was always with Rāma. "As long as I have no famine, as long as I surrender to you, you may drown me in milk or in water, and now it's left to you to drown me or save me, so don't try to cheat me."[10]

Recalling how, in their times of distress, He appeared before Gajendra and Pañchali, he asks Rāma in a song in *Natakurañji rāga* where He was and why He was not coming to him when he was suffering like that:

Where is my Lord
the one who dwells
in Bhadrādri?
Where is my Rāma,
Protector,
and Shelter?[11]

In another song he asks what he will do if Rāma does not protect him:

To people who have said "O Lord protect me!"
You are the refuge, you have been saving them all along.
You have the reputation of sheltering all souls
who take refuge in you, but when I keep shouting
now, and crying in different ways
you do not show your mercy, so how shall I call you?[12]

[8] *Abbabbā debbalaku tālalera/Rāmappa Gobbuna nannādukōra.*

[9] *Takku vemi manaku Rāmuḍu Okkadu undvaraku/Prakka toduga Bhagavantuḍu munu/Chakradhāriyai sagucu nunḍaga* (*Nādanāmakriya*).

[10] *Kalimi balami nāku ilalō nī vani . . . variñchiti nī/pālamunchinanu nīlamuñchinna nī/Pāla paditi-nika jalamu cheyaka.*

[11] *Edannāḍo Bhadrādrivāsuḍu/éḍannāḍo nāpāli Rāmuḍu éḍannado.*

[12] *Sarananna janamula birabira brōcheḍu/Birudu galgina dorave ō Rāma Paripari vidhamula moralida vinaka Nannaramarachésina Harininné mandu.*

At one moment he lays all his burden on Rāma, declaring in a mood of strength, "I belong to Rāma, why should I be afraid? All my burden is His."[13] Elsewhere he remarks,

> Although we suffer at this point
>   in the turn of fortune's wheel
> we always have faith in Rāma;
>   why should we ever
> resort to anyone else
>   for any reason?[14]

And: "Rāma, why do you not speak? Are words pieces of gold? Would you be casting away pearls by uttering a few words? I have never lost the thought of your Name—not even when I am dreaming."[15]

Finding Rāma silent, he calls upon Sītā to speak to Rāma on his behalf, in *Nannu brova* and *Rāmacandrulu.* In the latter he pleads: "O Sītā, Rāma is angry with me—please put in a good word for me."[16]

Finding no improvement in his situation, for a moment he appears in his wailings as if his faith was slipping, as he demands to know if Rāma cannot respond with pity why then should devotees pray: "Are you so devoid of grace? Why is Goddess Pārvatī doing *japa* of your Name? Why do Prahlāda and other devotees have faith in you?"[17]

In another mood, he regrets that, being in prison, he is not able to perform the worship of Rāma in proper form and goes through its required details mentally instead, doing what is called *manāsika pūjā*, in his song beginning *Rāma Rāma manasā.*

The Story of Rāmadās' Rescue

The moment of succor from Rāma finally arrives when Rāma and Lakṣmana

[13] *Rāmuni vāramu mākemi vichāramu/Svāmī nīdé bhāramu Dāśarathe jīvādharamu.*

[14] *Rāmuni vāramaināmu/Itarādryula ganana chéyamu Graha / gatulaku verava bōmu Maku kaladu Daivānugrahamu.*

[15] *Paluké bangāra māyena kodaṇḍapāūni/Kalalō nī nālnasmarana maravā chakkani Tandri.*

[16] *Rāmacandrulu nāpai calamu/Cesinaru Sītāmmā ceppavammā.*

[17] *Ādaraṇaleni nī Nāma-mantra japam/Adrija emani jesera Rāma?*

put on the guise of two employees of Rāmadās, enter one night the apartment of Tani Shāh, pay him the entire dues that Rāmadās owed and ask for a receipt. Tani Shāh is stunned. The extraordinary effulgence and charm of the two servants overpower Tani Shāh. All of a sudden, the dues of several years being paid together, all in gold, at that time of night, the appearance of the two who brought the money, and their disappearance, —all these revolve in Tani Shāh's mind and make him decide that the servants are none else than Rāma and Lakṣmana whom Rāmadās had been worshipping. Tani Shāh then ran to where Rāmadās was imprisoned and reported to him the miraculous *darśan* he had. Rāmadās congratulated the King: "Tani Shāh! You are blessed, you have seen face to face Rāma whom I am yet to see."[18]

Tani Shāh, for his part, expressed his gratitude to Rāmadās, loaded him up with an enormous amount of money, put him on a palanquin and sent him to Bhadrācalam to continue his devotion and service to Rāma. To keep guard over his devotee and the riches he was taking, Rāma and Lakṣmana walked, bows in hands, on either side of the palanquin. So says Rāmadās in his song *Rāmuḍu galadu.*

Rāmadās' Vision and Lyrics

Rāma blessed Rāmadās too with *darśan* for which Rāmadās had been yearning: "Rāma, your sweet face I have seen!" (*Rāma nī muddu momu jupara*). In the ecstasy of the sight of Rāma, Rāmadās sang, "O Rāma I gaze upon your lustrous face!" (*Kanti nīḍu Rāmula kanukoṇṭi nīḍu*). Taking humiliation and honor as equal, deeming as friends even those who subjected him to suffering, Rāmadās, exemplifying the Gītā-ideal of equanimity—being alike in praise and blame, and being serene under all conditions, treating friends and foes the same (*Tulya-ninda stutiḥ, Talyo manapamanayoḥ . . . Tulyo mitraripakṣayoḥ*), he became the recipient of the grace of the Lord in full.

What does it matter
    if someone abuses me?
What does it matter
    if someone praises me?

[18] *Dhanyuḍavu Tānīśa nīvu nannu/Kannayya padamulu kanula/Kannāvu.*

Probably those who want to harm me
are really doing me some good.[19]

In addition to these songs, as already noted, Rāmadās wrote on Śrī Rāma at Bhadrācala. His Śataka *stotra* in Telugu, entitled *Daśarathī Śataka*, is considered as one of the best compositions in this class. Rāmadās has shown his literary gifts here and worked in many sound effects. "To me Rāma alone is God; there is none to equal Him—this I can proclaim by beating the drum placed on the back of the elephant." When he says this in one of the verses here, Rāmadās produces the verbal sound effect of a tom-tom by repetition of the syllables "*ndu*" and "*du*":

Pa*nda*na bhimu*ḍu* artajana ba*ndhavuḍu*
Ujjavala-bana-tuna Koda*nda*kalaprachan*da* . . .
Kadakatti bherika *tanta-tatanta tanta*

"My poetry is fit for dedication to God alone, I will not let myself down by employing it for the flattering of man." He says in another verse of the *Daśarathi Śataka* that his lyrics are not composed with human listeners in mind: "How can I throw pearls before swine? I suffered and offered my poetry to evil men and I was cheated in doing that. My poetry is fit for dedication to God alone. I will not let myself down by employing it for the flattery of men. So, O Rāma, ocean of mercy, please listen to my lyrics and respond accordingly."

Rāmadās and Tyāgarāja

Rāmadās was well versed in Sanskrit also and using twenty-four names of the Lord Keśava, Nārāyaṇa etc., he has summarily set forth the whole *Rāmāyaṇa* story in the form of a prose-poem, a *churṇika*.

Rāmadās gained a noteworthy place in the tradition of the galaxy of *Rāma-bhaktas*. His songs on Rāma spread all over the country. His life, his sufferings and his obtaining in the end the blessing of Rāma became a common story among the people. His songs on Rāma showed the way to the other great Telugu *Rāma-bhakta* who was born in the South land, in Tamil Nadu—Śrī Tyāgarāja. Tyāgarāja salutes Rāmadās at the very outset of his long narrative with songs entitled the *Prahlāda bhakti-vijaya*. In two of his pieces Tyāgarāja has made a special reference to Rāmadās, his

[19] *Evaru dūshiñchinanémi, mecchi / Evaru bhūsiñchinanemi. . . .*
Aparādha mula neñchuvāru māku / upakārulai yunnavāru (*Bilahari rāga*).

sufferings and the blessings of Rāma that he eventually received. In the song *Kṣirasāgara sayana* in *Devagandhāri rāga*, Tyāgarāja says: "I have heard you saved the brave Rāmadās from the prison."

In the song *Emitova* Tyāgarāja says, "Had I been Rāmadās, Sītā would have come forward to speak to you on my behalf." The ideas and expressions in Rāmadās' songs are echoed by Tyāgarāja in several songs. It is to be noted that, apart from the vogue the songs of Rāmadās enjoy in devotional congregations where *bhajans* are sung, some of them continue to be sung in Karṇāṭaka music recitals. Portions from several of his songs have already been quoted above.

A Song by Rāmadās on the Power of the Name

The following song shows the style of Rāmadās and his treatment of the subject of devotion to Rāma.

> Oh all you people of the world!
> Why not buy the Rāma *jogi*'s medicine?[20]
>
> When, with love, you take this remedy
> of the Rāma-mendicant,
> it completely destroys pride, jealousy, avarice,
> and the accumulation of *karmas*.
>
> The remedy of Rāma *jogi*,
> which is unequalled in the world
> and destroys the formidable fetters of life,
> the remedy which cannot be obtained
> even by spending crores of rupees
> and is always remembered
> by the unequalled devotees of the Lord;
> it is the remedy at Bhadrādri[21]
> which helps attainment of salvation
> and which is ever worshipped
> with devotion by Rāmadāsa.

[20] The "Rāma *jogi*" mentioned is the mendicant from whom medicines and antidotes could be had; the prescription meant here, as given by God Rāma is himself, His name and worship.

[21] Bhadrādri is the shrine in Andhra. For renovating this temple with state funds, the saint was imprisoned.

14.
Upanisad Brahmayogin: *Maṭha*-Founder, Commentator, Composer[1]

Upaniṣad Brahman's Contributions

Upaniṣad Brahmayogin occupies a noteworthy place in the school of *advaita-vedānta* as well as in that of *nāma-bhajana*, the tradition of *bhakti* in which the Lord's Name is recited and adored with the aid of the art of music. With his *maṭha* (monastery) at Kāñcīpuram, his works, long and short, with which he was ceaselessly engaged, and his *bhajanas*, he played a dominant part in molding the devotional spirit and musical activity of the Tamil country in the middle of the eighteenth century.

The author was first known, after taking *sannyāsa* vows, as Rāmacandrendra, but because of the special efforts made by him to collect together and present all the major and minor *Upaniṣads* with his own commentaries, he came to be called Upaniṣad Brahmendra, which became his more popular name.[2]

So far as his contribution to *advaita* is concerned, it suffices for the present to mention that although a follower of classical *advaita*, he made several innovations in minutiae and introduced a fresh orientation, classification, and terminology in which he seems to have reveled. This last-mentioned aspect remains to be studied fully and presented to the world of scholars.

His *Upeya-nāma-viveka* ("Discernment of the Name as the Goal") appertains to the other side of his personality and activity, the *bhakti*

[1] From V. Raghavan's Introduction to *Upeya-nāma-viveka*. The *Upeya-nāma-viveka* was first edited and published with a more complete version of this introduction by V. Raghavan in *The Adyar Library Bulletin*, vol. XXIX, parts 1-4, 1967. For the sake of easier reading I have placed some parts of the text in footnotes and omitted other parts because of considerations of space. I have also added subheadings.

[2] These commentaries of his on the *Upaniṣads*, and his gloss on the *Bhagavad Gītā*, as also his short treatise on the *Brahmā sūtras* and some other minor Vedāntic tracts have been published by the Adyar Library, as independent works or as reprints from *The Adyar Library Bulletin*.

tradition based on the recital of the Lord's Name and its glory and efficacy, *nāma-mahātmya.*[3]

Nāmasiddhānta Leaders in the Kāverī Delta

It was, as we have seen, the two contemporaries, Śrīdhara Veṅkaṭeśa Āyyāvāl and Bodhendra, who gave a great stimulus to this devotional movement of repeating and chanting the Lord's Name, particularly in the Cola regions, at the end of the seventeenth and the beginning of the eighteenth centuries. The latter founded a *maṭha* at Govindapuram in Tāñjāvūr District with a succession of teachers of that *maṭha* to carry on the teachings of the *Nāmasiddhānta* school and propagate the *bhajana paddhati.* Even now in numerous *bhajana-maṭhas* all over Tamil Nadu devotees venerate portraits of Śrīdhara Veṅkaṭeśa Āyyāvāl, Bodhendra and another saint, Sadgurusvāmī, and in all *bhajana* recitals which have been codified, songs and verses paying homage to these pioneer gurus of this school are sung at the outset.

The school of thought referred to as *Nāmasiddhānta,* according to which the repetition or singing of the Lord's Name, *nāma-japa* or *nāma-kīrtana,* is the easiest and most efficacious path for liberation in the present age, has a great bearing on the art of South Indian music. The greatest South Indian music composer, Tyāgarāja (A.D. 1767-1847), was a follower of this tradition and it is believed that he recited the *Rāma-nāma* nine hundred and sixty million times as enjoined by the scriptures and thereby attained his great creative powers. In the large corpus of his songs are some on the greatness of the Lord's Name, and the doctrines relating to it and its recitation. A proper understanding of the import of these musical compositions requires an adequate knowledge of the tenets of the *Nāmasiddhānta* school of thought. Tyāgarāja appeared in an area and at a time surcharged with the fervor of these religious movements, and for his inspiration and background he had the tradition handed down not

[3] The *Nāmārtha-viveka* with the gloss *Upeya-nāma-viveka* of Upaniṣad Brahmendra falls in line with works like the *Bhagavannāma-kaumudi* of Laksmīdhara, the *Bhagavannāma-māhātmya* of Puruṣottāma, the *Bhagavannāma-mahātmya of* Raghunāthendra Yati, and the *Bhagavannāma-darpaṇa* and the *Bhagavannāma-vaibhava* of Muralīdharadāsa written in the North; and in the South, the *Bhagavannāma-bhūṣana* of Śrīdhara Veṅkaṭeśa Āyyāvāl, the *Nāmāmṛitarṇava,* the *Nāmāmṛita-rasāyana,* the *Nāmāmṛita-sūryoḍaya* and the *Nāmamṛita-rasodaya* of Bodhendra Yati, the *Nāmātaraṅga* in the *Puruṣārtha-ratnākara* of Bālakrishnānanda, and the *Bhagavan-nāma-cintāmani* of Veṅkaṭakrishna.

only from Śrīdhara Veṅkaṭeśa Āyyāvāl and Bodhendra, but also from one who was an older contemporary of his and most active at that time in this devotional movement, namely Upaniṣad Brahmendra. Although according to a basic tenet of this school, no distinction is to be made between one kind of divine Name and another, e.g. Śiva, Hari, or Rāma, the cultivation of any one Name as the favorite of the devotee is permitted, according to the doctrine of *iṣṭadevatā*; and in respect of the *iṣṭadevatā*, again Tyāgarāja and Upaniṣad Brahman had a special bond as co-worshippers of *Rāma-nāma.* Indeed there is a *śrīmukha* (letter) from our author to Tyāgarāja, asking the latter to visit Kāñcīpuram which has been preserved by the latter's pupils.

Having considered these aspects of Upaniṣad Brahmayogin's background we may now devote some attention to the ideas expounded by him and discuss them in relation to earlier literature and thought which might be taken to have some significance in the growth of the ideas on *nāma* and in our attempt to understand the views of our author on that subject.

The Nature of the Name and *Advaita* Oneness Via *Nāma*

The special feature of the *advaitin*'s adoration of the Lord's Name, whichever name it is, is the contemplation of that Name and the deity for whom it stands as being the *Brahman* which is identical with one's self, i.e. the *advaita bhāvanā*, or contemplation of oneness, in which *bhakti* is cultivated.

This realization of oneness is declared as the main theme of the present work. The idea is first reinforced by the author with quotations from the *Rāmatāpinī Upaniṣad.* In the lower rungs of spiritual effort, the recitation of the *nāma* functions as a means, *upāya,* for attaining the Ultimate, the non-differentiated Bliss of *Brahman;* but the same *nāma*, as meaning the supreme *Brahman* itself, becomes the ultimate Reality gained, i.e. it is itself the end, the *upeya.* In the latter aspect, it is not the name of something, a deity, but it is itself the supreme Being, Knowledge, and Effulgence.

Rāma is no longer a *nāma* of a *rūpa* (form), but the *rūpa* itself. Quoting Śaṅkara's words, when he elucidates at the beginning of the commentary on the *Maṇḍukya Upaniṣad* the nature of OM as a symbol of *Brahman*, our author affirms the identity of the *abhidhāna* and the *abhidheya.*

The two-fold nature of *nāma* or *nāma-cit, nirviśeṣa* and *saviśeṣa*, the Absolute Being and the Name of a personal form of that Being, *upeya* and *upāya*, is then set forth in clear terms in verses 12-15 and the gloss thereon: *nāma* is the *upāya* when it is cultivated as the means to attain the possessor of the *nāma*, the *nāmin* or deity; although fundamentally, owing to their interdependence, the two do not differ, the notion of duality, in the earlier stages, makes the *nāma, upāya.* By constant cultivation on this plane, a stage is reached when in the final birth or the last embodied state, the soul knows the *nāma* as none else than the Supreme Being itself.

The *nāma*, in its *upāya* stage is of four forms, each one higher and more refined and subtle than the previous. By contemplation of it in its *sthūlāṃśa*, the annihilation of sins caused by bad deeds is achieved; by contemplation of its *sūkṣmāṃśa* (subtle aspect), one is freed of the effects of the good deeds done; through its *bījāṃśa* (seed aspect), the four kinds of liberation, *sālokya* (residing in the same heaven or world), *sāmīpya* (being near to the deity), *sārūpya* (being assimilated to the deity), and *sāyujya* (being absorbed into the divine essence), are gained; as a result of the meditation of its *turīya*, fourth or transcendent aspect, union with the *Brahman* is attained. These four aspects of the *upāya-nāman* are further elucidated with reference to the specific ends gained from the cultivation of each and the four ascending grades of aspirants who are fit for each of these four aspects.

It is well known how in the *Maṇḍukya Upaniṣad* the Praṇava, Om, is set forth in its four phases: *sthūlabhug vaiśvānara* (the waking state conscious of external objects), *praviviktabhuk-taijasa* (the dream state conscious of internal objects), *ānandabhuk-prājña* (deep sleep state conscious of vast blissful peace), and the *advaita* (transcendent consciousness, unthinkable and indescribable), the fourth. Upaniṣad Brahman equates the four phases of *upāya-nāman* with these four phases—*Vaiśvānara*, etc. He also explains here the nature of the three *guṇas*—*sattva*, *rajas*, and *tamas*—in these four states and refers briefly to the classification of the *guṇa*-complex and the nature and proportion of the admixture of these in each state, as worked out in the text called *Guṇatrayaviveka* ("Discernment of the Three Strands of Nature").

Rules for Name Reciters

Incidentally, Upaniṣad Brahman points out that the *adhikārins*, those fit to cultivate this form of *nāma*, are the whole humanity, irrespective of *varṇa* or *aśrāma*. *Nāma* is the universal redeemer from sin. In connection with the mention of sins which *nāma* is capable of destroying, the author refers to the ten sins likely to be committed by a *nāma*-reciter; these, referred to as *nāma-aparādha*'s, may be explained:

1. *San-nindā*—Reviling pious souls.

2. *Śrīśa-īśa bheda-dhiḥ*—Making a distinction between one Name and another (Śiva and Viṣṇu).

3, 4, 5. *Aśraddha śruti-śāstra-deśika-girām*—Lack of faith in scriptures, in sacred writings, and in the words of the teachers.

6. *Namni arthavadabhrāmaḥ*—Mistaking the greatness of the Name.

7, 8. *Nāma astīti niṣiddha niṣiddha-vṛitti-vihitai-yāgau*—Taking cover under the greatness of the Name and doing prohibited things and failing to do prescribed things.

9. *Karmāntaraiḥ sāmyam*—Taking the Name to be just on a par with other prescribed duties (helpful to mental purification).

10. *Asati vaibhavāntara-*, or *Asati nāma-vaibhava-kathā*— Discussing the glory of the sacred Name with the faithless, the wicked, and the indifferent.

The tenth *nāma*-offense is taken up separately as it involves some discussion; in the *Upeya-nāma-viveka*, it is listed as the second offense, and has not been set forth above. It is given as *asati vaibhavāntara-kathā*. In the version of this same verse quoted by Bodhendra in his *Nāmāmṛita-rasāyana*, a better reading is found: *asati nāma-vaibhava-kathā*. That this offense, whatever the reading of the verse here, means expatiating upon the glory of the Name before a wicked person or an unbeliever (*asat*) is clear from the description of these *nāma-aparādhas* in the *Padma Purāṇa*, quoted by Bodhendra; there this offense is set forth as trying to impart the Name to the faithless, to the indifferent, and the heedless.

Significance of Rāma's Name

The next section is devoted to the special importance and glory of the Name of Rāma. Although all Names are equal, Rāma's name has a special status as the *tāraka* or redeemer par excellence; and on this Upaniṣad Brahman quotes the *Rāmatāpinī-* and the *Rāma-rahasya Upaniṣads* (verses 26 ff.). The word "Rāma" really means *Brahman*: "By the name Rāma the sole undivided supreme reality is indicated."

This specialty of *Rāma-nāma* is sought to be brought out by a traditionally handed down explanation that RĀ-MA embodies the vital syllables of the eight-syllabled (*aṣṭākṣara*) Nārāyaṇa mantra and the five-syllabled (*pañcākṣara*) Śiva mantra. In the former, *om namo nārāyaṇāya*, the fifth syllable *rā* is the life, for if we take out that syllable, the mantra would become *nāyanāya*, meaning "not for salvation." Similarly, if we take out the syllable *ma* from the *Śivapañcākṣari*, that mantra becomes *na śivāya*, "not for good." Thus, *RĀMA* stands for both the Nārāyaṇa-mantra and the Śiva-mantra of which it is the vital essence (verses 28 ff.).

When and how many times *Rāma-nāma* is to be recited is the next question dealt with, and the author quotes here his text titled *Rāmataraṅgacandrikā*. On this and the efficacy of *Rāma-nāma*, the author quotes *Śruti* and *Smṛiti*, the *Rāmottaratāpinī Upaniṣad* and the *Bhagavad Gītā*; on the requisite qualities of the devotees of God, the *Bhāgavata Purāṇa* is quoted, and on the need for faith in the Lord, the *Bhagavad Gītā* again.

Up to this point, Upaniṣad Brahman has dealt with the first stage of adoring *Rama-nāma*, contemplating Rāma as *Vaiśvānara* or *Vairāja*, in the *sthūlāmśa* (objectified portion) of the *nāma*. He now proceeds to explain how, after success in the first plane, the devotee proceeds to the next higher stage of *nāma* in the *sūkṣmāṃsa* (verses 58 ff.). In this phase, the *nāma* represents *Hiraṇyagarbha* consciousness; it comprehends the subtle *liṅga-sarīra* (the subtle body accompanying the soul in its transmigrations enduring from one life to the next). The aspirant reaches then the third rung of the ladder when he concentrates on the further subtle aspect, *bījāṃsa* of the *nāma* (verses 63 ff.). In this phase, the *nāma-cit* that is adored shines just in the form of the one seed, the cause of everything, *bījamātra*. The last realm is then reached where it is the one impartite consciousness, *pratyag-brahmaikya*, the ultimate meaning of the Name, the *nāmārtha*. In this connection, the very word RĀ-MA is given the esoteric explanation that its two syllables stand respectively for the two words of the *mahāvākya*, Tat (That, the transcendent) and *tvam* (thou, the individual soul) (verse 68). By their primary and secondary meanings (*vācya* and *lakṣya*), the syllable *rā* signifies respectively the God-consciousness (primary) and pure Existence Consciousness and Bliss (secondary); similarly, the syllable *ma* means the consciousness in the form of the embodied being (*jīva*, primary) and the consciousness of the inner soul (*pratyak*, secondary) (verse 69). It is the identification of the two in their secondary meanings that gives the unity of *Tat* and *tvam*. All this is based on the statement in the *Rāmarahasya Upaniṣad* (XII.14). With this understanding, one should contemplate *nāman* in its fourth, transcendent aspect, *turīyāṁśa* (verses 73 ff.). The sovereign glory of *Rāma-nāma* must be cherished in *abheda-bhāvanā*, in a non-dualistic contemplation, and this should be done till one firmly establishes oneself as the substratum and onlooker of everything.[4]

According to the stage of spiritual evolution one reached, one may

[4] See verse 77 and following, and the commentary thereon.

even go straight to the final target and in one's desire for immediate release, *sadyo-mukti*, start cultivating the *upeyanāma* of the final phase.[5]

Traditional Precedents of Teachings About the Name

Some ideas available in the earlier writings may now be considered for the purpose of tracing possible connections between them and the special ideas expounded in the *Upeyanāmaviveka* by Upaniṣad Brahman. The *nāma*-reciters invoke as their Vedic authority the passage found in *Ṛig Veda*, I.156.3: (*āsya jānanto nāma cid viviktana . . .*): "Him have you satisfied, singers, as well as ye know, primeval germ of Order from his birth. Ye, knowing even his name, have told it forth; may we, Viṣṇu, enjoy the grace of the Mighty One."[6] There are indeed some hymns in the *Ṛig Veda* referring to *nāma* (e.g. *Ṛig Veda* 1.164.46: "To what is one the poets give many a name.") but there is no indication of any special stress laid on the superiority of *nāma* recital.

The *mīmāṁsā* philosophy of ritual developed the doctrine that when deities were invoked in sacrifices and other rites, it was the name of the deity, i.e. the word, *śabda*, which mattered and there was no other form of the deities behind those names (Jaimini IX.1.4.6-10). In this emphasis in *mīmāṁsā* on the Name, we may see an early forerunner of our present theme of *nāma-māhātmya*, praise of the name, but the point of view from which the emphasis is laid by Jaimini is different, as it is a corollary there of the primary importance of *karman*, efficacious ritual acts.

It would be more legitimate for us to look to the concept of *praṇava*, the syllable OM, and the ideas associated with its cultivation as a practice of chanting, for a precursor of the views of the later *Nāmasiddhāntins.* The *Maṇḍukya Upaniṣad*, from Śaṅkara's commentary on which our author makes a quotation in the present work, may be especially mentioned in this connection. Although Śaṅkara says more than once, in strict accordance with his school of thought, that Oṃkāra is the only means of knowing the *ātman*,[7] he states in the same context that OM which is the *abhidhāna* (name, appellation, title) of *Brahman* is identical with *Brahman*, its

[5] See verse 83.

[6] Translated by Ralph T.H. Griffiths, *Hymns of the Rig Veda* (Delhi: Motilal Banarsidass, 1986 reprint), p. 104. [Editor's note: I have given another translation of this passage earlier in this book.]

[7] *katham punar oṃkāranirṇaya ātmatattva-pratipatty-upāyatvaṃ pratipadyata iti*—introductory *bhāṣya.*

abhidheya (*abhidhānābhidheyayor ekatve*, etc.), an observation of which Upaniṣad Brahman takes hold.

In his commentary on *Kaṭha Upaniṣad* (I.2.16), Śaṅkara calls OM the symbol (*pratīka*) of *Brahman*. In his *Brahmā Sūtra* commentary (I.3.10) he states clearly that the *praṇava* is the means of attaining *Brahman* and the *śruti* texts speaking of it as being everything are to be taken only in a laudatory sense.[8]

Śaṅkara's *Bhagavad Gītā Bhāṣya*, VIII.13, commenting on the words of the *Bhagavad Gītā*, *om iti ekākṣaram brahma*, gives expression to the same standard advaitic tenet of *praṇava* being the *abhidhāna* or name of *Brahman*.[9] In the comments on the first name, Viśva, in the *Viṣṇu sahasranāma* commentary ascribed to him, Śaṅkara equates Viśva with OM and quoting several Upaniṣadic texts, as also the *Mandukyakārikās*, observes again in the following words the non-difference of *Brahman* and *Oṃkāra*, for essentially the Name and its meaning are not different.[10]

The *Viṣṇu sahasranāma* commentary by Śaṅkara, particularly its introductory portion, occupies an important place among the authoritative texts of the school of *Nāmasiddhānta*.

Maṇḍana, the elder contemporary of Śaṅkara, and a subscriber to the theory of *sphoṭa* (vibration), salutes the Supreme Being as *akṣara* in the opening verse of his *Brahmasiddhi* and, while explaining this in his gloss, says that the Supreme is so called because it is of the form of *Śabda*, i.e. *praṇava*; although the suffix *-kāra* is added to OM (*Oṃ-kāra*), it does not mean that it implies something else which is its meaning (*abhidheya*); as *-kāra* occurs with letters in expressions like *a-kāra* and refers to those letters themselves, *Oṃkāra* refers to *śabda*, primal sound, or *praṇava* being *Brahman* itself. Maṇḍana does not countenance the view that the *śruti* texts speaking of *praṇava* refer to *pratīkopāsanā*, worship of the abstract *Brahman* in a symbol or support (*ālambana*) for contemplation, *praṇava* being the Name or *abhidhāna* of *Brahman*. Quoting profusely from the *Upaniṣads* on OM and from the Ṛig Vedic *sūktas* relating to *Vāk*, Maṇḍana

[8] Editor's note: This paragraph has been incorporated into the text from the footnotes of the original. *Yadapi* "*Oṃkāra evedam sarvam*" *iti, tadapi brahmpratipattisādhanatvat stutyartham draṣṭavyam.*

[9] *brahmaṇo abhidhānabhūtam oṃkāram vyāharan uccārayan tadarthabhūtam mām īśvaram*, etc. Madhusūdana Sarasvatī clarifies further the correct advaitic stand that Om is the *vācaka* or symbol (*pratīka*) of *Brahman* (*brahmavacākatvāt pratimāvad brahmapratīkatvād vā*).

[10] *vācyavācakayor atyantabhedābhāvād viśvam ity oṃkāra eva brahmety arthaḥ.*

argues that the whole manifest universe is merged in *Vāk*, and as OM is the truth of all *Vāk*, *vāk-śakti* itself is *citi* or Knowledge. Therefore the *akṣara* is itself the *Brahman.*

In the *Brahmā sūtras* (I.3.10-12, *akṣaradhikaraṇa*), the question is discussed whether *akṣara* as it occurs in some Upanisadic texts refers to *vāk*, *sphoṭa*, and OM or to the imperishable *Brahman*; as *prasāsana* associated with *akṣara* could only be possible in the case of a sentient entity, *Vāk*, it is contended, is ruled out; but introducing the third *sūtra* of the *adhikaraṇa*, Appayya Dīkṣita says, in the *Nyāyarakṣamani*, that according to *śabdādvaitins*, *sphoṭa* is endowed with *caitanya*, sound has consciousness; and on this view, *Brahman* and *sphoṭa* (*akṣara*) are not different.

Maṇḍana's ideas form a more complete articulation of the *śabda* philosophy of Bhartṛihari, which has been repeatedly stated in the first book of his *Vākyapadīya.* But it has not been clearly shown as to how it leads to *mokṣa.* Bhartṛihari no doubt refers to it as the indestructible *Brahman* without beginning and end (*Vākyapadīya*, I.1), the inner light, the great *ṛiṣabha* with which one attains oneness, *sāyujya* (*Vākyapadīya*, I.I.30 especially).[11]

In his own commentary on this, Bhartṛihari waxes eloquent and describes this inner *śabda* as *ātman* (Self), as *mahān vṛiṣabha* (great might), as *prabodha* (knowledge), and as *sarveśvara*, Lord of all. In the *āntaraślokas* in *Vākyapadīya*, I.142, he identifies this inner light with the subtle imperishable sound, *sūkṣmā vāk.*[12] It is the immortal end of the entirety of Being.[13]

In the complex of thought referred to collectively as Kashmir Śaivism as it crystallized with all its facets in the hands of Abhinavagupta, the stage beyond *paśyanti* the fourth, *para vāk*, was identified as the *hṛidaya* or heart of the Lord and with His *vimarśa* aspect, and the Lord was referred to as *vācya* (to be spoken) and His reflective *citi* as *vācaka* (speaking).[14]

All these ideas, as they came over to the post-Śaṅkara advaitins, were integrated in the framework of Advaita proper. The *Śabda Brahman* was

[11] *api prayakturātmānam śabdamantaravasthitam prāhurmahāntamṛisabham yena sāyujyamiṣyate.*

[12] *svarūpajyotirevāntaḥ sūkṣmā vāganapāyinī.*

[13] *puruṣe ṣoḍasakale tāmāhuramṛitam kalām.*

[14] See *Paryantapanlapañciśikā* of Abhinavagupta, edited by V. Raghavan, *Annals of Oriental Research*, Univ. of Madras, vol. 8, 1950.

accepted as the penultimate step to *para Brahman* and the formulation of this adjustment is seen in clear terms in some of the minor *Upaniṣads* which mention two *Brahmans*, the *Śabda Brahman* and the *Para Brahman*, the former being a step to attain the latter.[15]

Whether as *praṇava* or as *nāda*, the *Śabda Brahman* was considered to be the final door or the supreme means of *Brahman*-realization or as the philosophy of music would say, the easier path through delectation to the final Beatitude.

In the *Yoga sūtras* of Patañjali, *praṇava*, the mantra Om, is the Name of Īśvara and the support of contemplation.

In the path of *bhakti*, in the *Purāṇas*, the contemplation of God through the repetition of a mantra embodying the holy Name, and through the repetition of the divine Name, was emphasized. The *Bhāgavata Purāṇa* made emphatic declarations on it, particularly in the Ajāmila and Prahlāda episodes and the statements in this *Purāṇa* became the basic texts on the doctrine of the efficacy of *kīrtana*, one of the nine kinds of *bhakti*. The entire further growth of the schools of devotion, laying increased emphasis on the Lord's Name and its recital and singing, stemmed from this, nourishing the twin movements of devotion and song. While the *Bhāgavata Purāṇa* extols the Name as most efficacious, it does not exalt it beyond its status as the Name of the Lord and as an instrument of invoking Him or establishing His thought in one's mind. "The articulation of a name of Lord Viṣṇu is the only thorough atonement for the sins of all classes of sinners . . . for thereby the Lord's own mind is directed towards the utterer."[16]

Three of the minor *Upaniṣads* are particularly related to the school of thought we are considering, the *Kalisaṃtaraṇa*, the *Rāmatāpini*, and the *Rāmarahasya Upaniṣads*. The *Rāmatāpini* is especially relevant as it is intimately related to our text which deals with devotion to Rāma and the potency of His Name. In fact, our text follows the *Rāmatāpini* in the identification of *praṇava* and Rāma and the elaboration of the four states, wakefulness, dream, deep sleep, and "the fourth," which the *Rāmatāpini* also gives by making the *Maṇḍukya* part of itself.

The explanation in our text as to how the *Rāma-nāma* is the Name or mantra par excellence, being made up of the vital syllables of the mantras of

[15] *dve brahmaṇī veditavye śabdabrahma param ca yet/śabdabrahmaṇi niṣṇātah param brahmādhigacchati* (*Maitrāyaṇī* VI.22). See also *Tripurātāpanī*, v. 17; *Brahmabindu*, 17.

[16] See especially VI.2.10 in *Ajāmilopākhyāna*: *nāmavyāharaṇam viṣṇoryata-ṣṭadviṣayā matiḥ*.

Nārāyaṇa and Śiva, is also found in some manuscripts of the *Rāmarahasya Upaniṣad.*

But in none of these *Upaniṣads* devoted to *nāma* or Rāma is there the mention of the idea of the Name itself being the ultimate thing or of the idea of the two phases of the Name as means and end, *upāya* and *upeya,* as stated in our text.

Bhakti, in the literature on it according to the different schools, has been spoken of in two forms: the means and the end, the *sādhana* and the *sādhya* or *para,* the former also called *gauṇa* and the latter *mukhya.* In the former aspect, through different further means, *bhakti* grows towards stabilizing itself; also, in this stage, it is practiced not for its own sake, but for some desired objective like relief from suffering and expectation of gain (compare the *Bhagavad Gītā,* VII.16-19, where the Lord speaks of four kinds of persons who worship Him including the *ārtha* and *arthārthin*). In the latter form, love of God has become complete and constant, and an end in itself with nothing extraneous to seek. Also, like *bhakti,* the Lord Himself has been spoken of as the way and the goal, *upāya* and *upeya.*

In the great development of the doctrines of the path of *bhakti* in the Caitanya school, Rūpa (c. 1495-1550) the great and prolific writer of the school, his brother Sanātana and nephew Jīva, put forth some ideas on *nāma* to which attention may be drawn here. Rūpa and Jīva said that there is no difference between the Name and the Lord, the two being identical (*nāmanāminor abhedaḥ*). In his *Bhagavatsaṃdarbha,* Jīva observed that the Name itself was the essence of the Lord (*bhagavatsvarūpam eva nāma*). Just like the *avatāras* of the Lord, this *nāman* is a kind of *varṇa-avatāra* (a subtle verbal embodiment or outward appearance of the divine on earth).[17]

In his work entitled *Nāmāṣṭaka,* Rūpa says (verse 6) that *nāman* has two forms, the *vācaka* and the *vācya,* the latter being the Lord Himself: Sanātana, in his *Bṛihadbhāgavatāmṛita* describes the two phases of *nāma-kīrtana* as *sādhana* and *phala,* practice and result. Earlier, Gopāla Bhaṭṭa had declared the identity of *nāman* and *nāmin* in his *Haribhaktivilāsa.*

The Kāverī Delta *Nāmasiddhānta* Renewal

In the fresh upsurge of the movement of *nāma*-recital in the region of the Kāverī delta, at the end of the seventeenth and beginning of the eighteenth centuries, several works on *nāman* were written by Bodhendra, Śrīdhara Veṅkaṭeśa Āyyāvāl and others. Āyyāvāl wrote a poem of sixty verses on

[17] *avatārāntaravat parameśvarasyo varṇarūpeṇa avatāro 'yam.*

the efficacy of *nāma* called *Ākhyāsaṣṭi*, but in none of these writings where the role of the Name of the Lord is exalted even above the Lord Himself, by reason of special emphasis, is there any description of the two phases of the Name or the *nāma* as *upāya* and *upeya.*

We have noted how Upaniṣad Brahman is given to adding new orientations and classifications in the existent body of thought in the school. The *Upeya-nāma-viveka*, his text on the Lord's Name, is an example of this characteristic of Upaniṣad Brahman. Apart from the advaitic background with which devotion cultivated through the recital of the Lord's Name is synthesized by holding the highest form of the latter as the contemplation of oneself as Rāma with the *bhāvanā* "*rāmo 'ham,*" and the pressing into service of the doctrine of OM, the *praṇava* with which the Lord's Name is integrated, Upaniṣad Brahman introduces also the idea of the Name functioning at two levels, as means and as end. As we have seen, although not directly, the trend of several old ideas on *nāma*, on OM, on *Śabda Brahman*, on *bhakti*, and on the efficacy of the Lord's Name inspired Upaniṣad Brahman to the formation of the leading idea of the present text, the *nāman* as *upāya* and *upeya.* It is in the nature of things that what is, at the earlier stages of endeavor, the means becomes in the end the very substance of the thing or the very character of its being. Śaṅkara says in his commentary on the *Bhagavad Gītā* when dealing with the characteristics of the *sthitaprajña* (II.55), and the *Bhāgavata Purāṇa* emphasizes, in its own eloquent manner, how even in the supreme state of self-realization, liberated souls for ever love God, serving Him and singing of Him, without any purpose (*ahaituka*), involuntarily—the most natural form of their free activity in that state. It is in this state and in this form that *bhakti* and the recital or contemplation (*kīrtana, anusaṃdhāna* or *bhāvanā*) of the Lord's Name is the end, *upeya.* The Name itself which is identified with *Brahman* and one's own self, in this state, is endowed with consciousness, as the *śabda* is for the *Śabda-Brahmā-vādins;* Upaniṣad Brahman thus refers to *nāma* as *nāma-cit*, name-consciousness.

15.

Tyāgarāja: The Singer-Saint[1]

In several respects, the genius of Karṇāṭaka or South Indian classical music may be said to touch its high water-mark in Tyāgarāja. The infinite play of imagination and originality is evident in him more than in other composers. In fashioning a variety of expressive forms in well-known melodies or in newly invented melodies, in the perfecting of the form of composition called *kṛiti*, and enriching it with inventive elements, in the poetry and philosophy of the text of the songs, in all these, he stands out as the foremost tone-poet and as the single complete example of the genius of Karṇāṭaka music at its best and highest.

It is no wonder that in the last half a century and more, his songs have come to dominate the concerts of Karṇāṭaka music. Even among the three great composers—the celebrated "trinity"—himself, Muttusvāmī Dīkṣitar, and Śyāma Śāstri whose compositions threw into the background the earlier works, Tyāgarāja enjoys a special popularity with musicians and lovers of music alike. His name, sometimes mentioned only as "Āyyāvāl" or "Svāmīgal," evokes a special sense of veneration among the votaries, active as well as passive, of the art. His anniversary is an annual festival wherever, in India or now in foreign countries too, there are South Indians.

Tyāgarāja appeared in a period which was thronged with giants in the arts, performers, theorists, composers, makers of dance-music, dance-drama, and authors of compositions of grammatical and scientific value (*lakṣanagītas, thayas, varṇas.* Girirājakavi, perhaps his maternal grandfather, was a poet and composer. His guru was one of the great masters of the time, Śoṇṭhi Veṅkaṭarāmanayya, son of Śoṇṭhi Subbayya. With all the roads for the artists leading at that time to Tāñjāvūr, Karṇāṭaka music was getting enriched from all sides and shaping itself through a ferment of theory and the formulation of its grammar and crystallization of the forms of its creative expression. To have appeared amidst this throng of talent and to have outshone the others with his creations is indeed the greatest testimony to his genius.

Tyāgarāja was born in 1767 at Tiruvārūr in Tāñjāvūr district of Tamil

[1] This essay first appeared in *Composers*, Cultural Leaders of India Series, edited by V. Raghavan (New Delhi: Publications Division, Government of India, 1979), pp. 20-39. I have omitted some passages because of considerations of space.

Nadu. Tiruvārūr is not only a renowned place in the religious history from the times of the *nāyanār* saints but was also the religious headquarters, in a manner of speaking, for the Mahratta rulers of Tāñjāvūr. Tiruvārūr was also famous for the arts of music and dance centering round the great temple of Tyāgarāja, the dancing Śiva deity at this place. Scholars and artists attached to the Telugu and Mahrātta courts of Tāñjāvūr were living at Tiruvārūr. A leading Telugu writer and composer among them was Girirājakavi and it is to his daughter that Tyāgarāja was born. It was after the presiding deity at Tiruvārūr that the child was named Tyāgarāja.

Tyāgarāja's family, on the side of his father, Rāma Brahmam, was living in Tiruvaiyāru or Pañcanada, a sacred place on the Kāverī river, about 11 kilometers from Tāñjāvūr, the seat of the ruling Mahratta dynasty. Tyāgarāja came of a Telugu Vaidika Muriginādu family named Kākarla, and his ancestors must have come from the Telugu area and settled here during the Nāyak rule of Tāñjāvūr. The name Tiruvaiyāru or Pañcanada refers to "five rivers" which flow through and near this place, a center of pilgrimage and festivals. Of the holy and beautiful Kāverī river flowing here, Tyāgarāja draws a fine picture in two of his songs, *Muripiemu* and *Sarivedalina*. Tyāgarāja loved the Chola country as he says in the first of the two songs referred to above: "The Chola-sima, most beautiful land in this world."

Tyāgarāja's Life

Details of Tyāgarāja's life are known only from tradition, some of which could be verified from references in his songs, e.g., the names of his family and father which he mentions. Tyāgarāja is said to have married twice, the first wife having died early without any issue. To the second wife was born a daughter named Sītālakṣmī, and a son named Tyāgarāja was born to her. When this grandson died issueless, the main line of Tyāgarāja ended.

Tradition speaks of an elder brother of Tyāgarāja named Japyeśa. To glorify Tyāgarāja and provide background for some songs of the composer, Japyeśa is made into a villain, who ill-treated Tyāgarāja, disapproved of Tyāgarāja's devotional activities, pressed him to seek royal patronage, threw into the Kāverī river the Rāma image worshipped by him, partitioned the ancestral house and so on.

There must be some basis for these stories to grow; actually in two of his songs, Tyāgarāja speaks of his elder brother: in the piece *Anyāyamu seyakurā*, he prays to God to free him from the troubles given by his elder brother and in *Nādupai* he refers to accusations against himself as being responsible for the partition of the ancestral house to enable him to celebrate his festivals for Rāma. In two other pieces (*Nāyeḍa vañcana* and *Eṭula gāpāḍutuvō*), Tyāgarāja mentions confrontations with his relatives (*dāyāḍis*).

Tyāgarāja had to face many detractors even outside his family. The single largest group of his songs—which are high-strung on the emotional side—represents what he sang in anguish of this hostile atmosphere in which he had to live. In the song *Prārabdhamiṭṭuṇḍagā*, he bemoans his fate: "Those whom I help turn against me; those whom I treat charitably level baseless charges against me." The detractors around him reviled his devotional activities as well as his music compositions. In a number of songs, he prays to Rāma to protect him from these revilers; in *Sarivārilōna*, he asks Rāma: "Have I not been sufficiently ridiculed among my compeers? . . . Is it fair on your part to be passive while seeing me agonize in the midst of these wild prattlers?" All these trials, like fire, made the gold of his faith in Rāma glow brighter and drew from him more and more masterpieces of moving music.

Tyāgarāja had vowed to lead the life of voluntary poverty. According to the tradition of the *bhāgavatas*, he adopted for his livelihood *unñchavṛitti*, going out every day singing the Lord's songs and receiving handfuls of rice from householders who might feel like giving. He sang of the Lord alone and avoided *nara-stuti*, the praising of mere man for obtaining rewards, which was prohibited according to the practice of the devotees of the Lord.

Tyāgarāja and Devotion to the Name

In the practice of devotion, Tyāgarāja followed the tradition of reciting Rāma's saving name, *tāraka nāma*, for the prescribed number of times. Rāma-worship came down in his family as mentioned by him in several songs and was strengthened by contacts with the active promoters of that path at that time like Upaniṣad Brahmendra of Kañci who was a friend of Tyāgarāja's father and the invitation from whom is preserved in the Tyāgarāja-manuscripts handed down in the Walājapet School of Tyāgarāja's pupils. Tyāgarāja himself mentions one Rāmakrishnānanda, a *sannyāsin* of his times, as his guru. Tyāgarāja is said to have successfully completed the repetition of *Rāma-nāma* 960 million times as prescribed, and succeeded in gaining the vision of Rāma.

Tyāgarāja's songs embody many doctrinal ideas of this school of reciting the divine Name (*Nāmasiddhānta*) and of the larger path of devotion, *bhakti-mārga*, songs which appear to have been specially composed for use in religious-musical discourses in *bhajanas*, *kīrtanas*, or *harikathās*. Not only on the efficacy of the Lord's Name but also on how best to recite it,

Tyāgarāja speaks in his songs. In the well-known song in *Pūrṇacandrika, Telisi Rāma*, Tyāgarāja emphasizes that the recitation of Rāma's Name is no mechanical muttering but should be based on a full realization of the significance that Rāma is the Supreme Being; and in another equally well-known song, *Rāma niyeda prema*, he stresses that the uttering of *Rāma-nāma* should be accompanied by real love for Rāma.

The *iṣṭa-devatā* or favorite form of God whom Tyāgarāja sought through the Name and whose glory he celebrated most in his songs is Rāma. He repeatedly declared that Rāma was his favorite deity (*Iṣṭadaivamu nive*—in a very appealing song—*Śyāma sundarāṅga*); "Rāma alone is my God" (*Rāma eva daivatam . . . me*); "Who is there to equal you, O Rāma" (*Rāma nī samanam evaru*); "Rāma alone is God" (*Vāḍera Daivamu*); and so on. This Rāma is not only the *avatāra* endowed with infinite excellences sung of by Vālmīki. Tyāgarāja has gone over, in his songs, the whole epic and the episodes and exploits of Rāma described there; but behind all this there is the faith that Rāma is the Supreme God beyond the Trinity (see his song *Manasā śrī Rāmachandruni*), indeed the *para Brahman* itself. In his well-known song *Telisi Rāma*, Tyāgarāja declares that the word "Rāma" is a name of *para Brahman*, recalling the well known elucidation "*Rāma padena asau param Brahmā abhidhiyate.*" As a minstrel of Rāma, by the quality and quantity of his songs on Rāma, Tyāgarāja takes his place in the galaxy of the great Rama-poets of India, who followed in the wake of Vālmīki. Tyāgarāja came of a *smārta* family of advaitin tradition and according to the universalistic outlook of this tradition, he sang of other deities too, Śiva, Devī, and others. In his song *Itara daivamula* he says that his mind is passionately in love with Rāma without harboring any prejudice towards other deities and faiths. He believed in a *bhakti* which had its consummation in the undifferentiated union with Godhead (*So'ham*, "I am Him"), as he says in his song *Intakanna*.

In a large number of songs Tyāgarāja expatiates on the character of true devotion and of a true devotee, on the futility of observing mere rites and rituals and other formalities and accessories like baths in sacred waters, long *pūjās*, etc., on the necessity for ethical and moral qualities rather than for conformity to mere orthodox habits, etc. These songs, in which Tyāgarāja is eloquent, follow the line of the exhortations of all the earlier saint-singers. In the song *Dhyāname*, for example, he points out that the best bath in Gaṅgā is the contemplation of the Lord. He refers in *Naḍaci naḍaci* and *Balamu kulamu* to pretenders who bathe, fast, close their eyes, and roll the rosary. The picture of a true devotee is given in the song *Bhaktuni cāritramu*:

> O Mind! Listen to the conduct of a devotee of Śri Rāma! The devotee who, without attachment to sense-pleasures, seeks Him, becomes a *jīvanmukta* and enjoys supreme bliss. Such a devotee should not boast of his having done *japa* and *tapas*; he should not behave or speak like a hypocrite; should not be weak, fickle-minded, and lost in attachments; should not regard material prosperity as real; should never make distinction between Śiva and Mādhava; should make no profession out of his qualifications; should not allow the sway of *rajas* (passion) and *tamas* (ignorance and inertia); should not desist from yogic practice and should never forget Śrī Rāma.

Similarly real *pūjā* is that which is done, not with a lot of external accessories but with a complete inner dedication, an internal worship, a *bhavapūjā*. He sings in *Paripālaya*:

> My body is your favorite abode (*pūjā-gṛiha*); my steadfast mind, your golden throne (cf. also his *Manasu nilpa*); my meditation of your beautiful feet is the Gaṅgā-water; my attachment to you is your beautiful dress; my praise of your glory, your sandal-fragrance; my remembrance and recital of your Name, the full-blown lotus for you; the fruits of all my past misdeeds is the incense to be burnt before you; my devotion to your feet is the all-day lamp to you; the very fruit of this kind of superior worship that I do is the food-offering to you; the lasting bliss that I derive is the pan (*tambula*) for you; my seeing you (*darśana*) is the waving of light before you.

Mere scholarship is of no use he says in *Kṣīṇamai*, and faith in astrology leads one nowhere he says in *Graha-balamémi*. Real *bhakti* alone saves and nothing else can be a substitute for it. Genuine devotion is the great royal road (*Cakkani rājamārga*). In many of these songs in which he exposes the prevailing shams and hypocrisies and emphasizes the essential things as against the accessories, Tyāgarāja's literary gifts, imagination, ability to develop an idea, and stinging similes and gift for wit and satire come out prominently.

Songs on the Sacredness of Music

Tyāgarāja is also remarkable, and singularly so, for a good number of songs in which he has expatiated on *nādopāsana*, on the art of music as an aid to devotion and contemplation, on God being the embodiment of *nāda*, subtle sacred vibration, and the absorption in the joy of melody as itself constituting spiritual liberation, *mokṣa*. In the exhortations in his songs, he holds up this high spiritual ideal for the musicians and condemns music devoid of devotion. For example, *Saṅgītajñanamu, Nādatanum, Gītārthamu, Nādopāsanace, Nādalōluḍai, Mokṣamugaladā*, and *Svara-rāga* are songs on these topics. In *Nādatanum*, he describes Śiva as the embodiment of *Nāda* (sacred sound), as constituting the essence of *Sāmaveda* and as delighting in the seven *svaras* (musical notes) born of His own five faces. In *Nādasudhārasambilanu*, he similarly portrays Rāma as the ambrosial *rasa*, the "essential juice" of *nāda* itself taken human form. "Devotion associated with the nectar of *svara* and *rāga* is verily paradise and salvation," he declares in his well-known song *Svara-rāgasudhārasa*. The burden of another well-known song, in *Dhanyāsi rāga*, is "Knowledge of music without *bhakti* will not lead to salvation." A third well-known piece, *Mokṣamugaladā*, shows the idea that Realization and Release (*sakṣatkara* and *mokṣa*) are not possible for those who are devoid of knowledge of music coupled with true devotion to the Lord; and the seven notes of music are manifested out of the *nāda* of the mystic syllable OM. "The joy of music is itself the bliss of *Brahman* that *Vedānta* speaks of," declares Tyāgarāja in three songs: "O Mind! drink and delight in the immortal elixir of melody and attain the fruit of *yāga* (Vedic sacrificial rituals), *yoga*, *tyāga* (renunciation of worldly rewards), and *bhoga* (enjoyment of worldly pleasures); those who understand that *Nāda*, *Oṃkāra*, and *svara* (musical notes) are nothing but Śiva are verily *jīvan-muktas*, those who have realized liberation here itself" (*Rāgasudhārasa*). "O Mind! He who delights in *nāda* attains the bliss of *Brahman*" (*Nādaloluḍai*). "The body that does not float on the ocean of the ineffable bliss of *Brahman* called music is a burden to the earth" (*Ānandasāgara*).

Tyāgarāja and Traditions of the Name

Mention of Vālmīki having been a hunter, of Rāma's Name being imparted by Śiva to all persons dying in Varanāsi, of Rāma's greatness being told by Śiva to Pārvatī, of the Name Rāma meaning Supreme *Brahman*, of Hānuman under the Parijata tree reading *Purāṇa*, these and several other details of this kind show that the whole literature of the Rāma tradition from the *Rāma tāpinī Upaniṣad* to different *Purāṇa* and *Samhita* texts and the different *Rāmāyaṇas* in Sanskrit, as well as the version of Tulasidās whom he mentions and salutes, were quite familiar to Tyāgarāja. Similarly he must have read the *Bhāgavata Purāṇa*, the Bible of the *bhakti-mārga*.

A manuscript of the Telugu *Bhāgavata* of Poṭana is among the Tyāgarāja manuscripts preserved by the Walājapet school. Upaniṣad Brahmendra's writings on the Lord's Name and its recitation, the idea that the Name "Rāma" is the vital essence of the five-lettered Śiva-mantra and the eight-syllabled Nārāyaṇa-mantra—mentioned in his song *Evarani*—is explained in detail by Upaniṣad Brahmendra in his *Upeyanāmaviveka.* Composers who came before Tyāgarāja who sang on Rāma and doctrines of *bhakti* and *nāma* and on music as a *sādhana*—Annamācārya, Purandaradāsa, Rāmadās—were also part of the heritage reflected in Tyāgarāja's songs.[2] Rāmadās of Bhadrācalam with his Rāma-devotion and suffering stood in a special relation to Tyāgarāja and is mentioned by name by Tyāgarāja in his *kīrtanas.*

Festival Songs

As already observed, Tyāgarāja belonged to the *Bhajana-sampradāya*, the

[2] There are three complete songs of Annamācārya singing the glory of the Lord's name, *Sakalasaṁgrahamu*, *Tatigoniyemaraka*, and *Japiyiñcare sarvajanula yi nāmamu*, the last one of *Rāma-nāma* itself. These may be compared with the several *kṛitis* of Tyāgarāja on *nāma.* In the first Annamācārya describes *Hari-nāma* as the essence of all *Vedas*, *Śāstras*, and *Purāṇas* and as the king of all mantras, *mantra-rāja.* In the second one in *Dhanyāsi rāga*, Annamācārya has a precious idea which Tyāgarāja also has in a song of his. In the first *caraṇa* (lyrical "foot" or quatrain) of this piece, Annamācārya says that the Lord's name is to the devotee what the *maṅgala-sūtra* is to a Pativrata, a good wife who has taken marriage vows. (*Kappi pativrataku maṅgalasūtramuvale.*) Pressing before Rāma that although there are several Gods, Rāma was his *iṣṭa-devatā*, Tyāgarāja compares the former to different kinds of ornaments that a woman wears and Rāma to her *maṅgala-sùtra* wedding necklace. The song *Śrī Rāma padama* of Tyāgarāja, in which Ahalyā figures prominently, may be considered an offspring of Annamācārya's *saṅkīrtana* on the Lord's feet in *Mukhari rāga*, which begins *Brahmā gadikina padamu* where Ahalyā's purification occurs as one of several wonders. Not only does Annamācārya frequently speak of Rāma in his songs, although they are mainly addressed to Lord Veṅkaṭeśara, he has also songs on Rāma specifically, on *Rāma-nāma*, on Sītā, Añjaneya etc. in all of which the leading ideas of Rāma *bhakti*, such as the belief in Śiva imparting *Rāma-nāma*, which are met with at every step in Tyāgarāja, are seen also in Annamācārya; in these songs, Annamācārya too, like Tyāgarāja later, used the entire Rāma-milieu as found in the different *Rāmāyaṇas* in addition to that of Valmīki. (The text of this footnote is taken from V. Raghavan's article entitled "Tyāgarāja and Annamācārya," in the *Souvenir* of the Forty-first Conference of the Music Academy, Madras, 1967. Pages unnumbered.)

codified devotional song program tradition, which was at its height in the Kāverī delta at that time. In the *bhajas* conducted by groups at homes or in special halls, *bhajana maṭhas*, they celebrated special festivals, the marriage of Rāma and Sītā or Krishna and Rukminī and held congregational singing of devotional songs, for all of which a pattern, *paddhati*, had evolved, starting with the announcement of the Lord's arrival (*Heccharikagā*), his taking the seat in the court hall (*Kolu*), the marriage which includes Gaurī *Kalyānam* or the actual marriage, *Nalaṅgu* or the divine couple in play, *Ārati* or waving of light, *Lali* or enjoying the swing; laying the Lord to bed (*Pavvalimpu*) and the waking Him up next morning (*Suprabhatam* song). For use in the *pūjā* of the Deity, as part of such celebrations, there were songs for the offering of the different *upacāras* to the Deity. A set of songs was composed by Tyāgarāja for use in such congregations and festivals. These songs, called *Utsava-sampradāya-kīrtanas* numbering about twenty-seven, are simpler in setting but rich in ideas and literary quality. Of the same type and for similar congregational singing by devotees, Tyāgarāja composed many other songs, about seventy-eight in number, which go by the name *Divya-nāma-saṅkīrtanas.* Many songs from these two groups figure now in concerts where musicians render them in the closing part of their performances.

Tyāgarāja's Contributions

Tyāgarāja's chief contribution to Karṇāṭaka music is the perfection of the composition form called *kṛiti* or *kīrtana* which was evolving at this time out of the older *prabandha* and the immediate predecessor *pada* and which comprised in itself all the aspects of music and displaced earlier and more ponderous media of rendering or preserving the *rāgas* in unbound or bound forms. In one of his *kṛitis,* he describes what a *kṛiti* should be like in form and content. In this song, *Sogasugā,* he says that the *kṛiti* should be couched in words conveying the true spirit of the *Upaniṣads,* should have correctness of the musical notes of the *rāgas* in which they are set, should be marked by beauties of alliterations and successive increases and decreases of notes or syllables, should be conducive to the cultivation of true devotion and dispassion, and as literary expression they should possess grace and simplicity and embody all the nine *rasas* or aesthetic moods. He had distinguished contemporaries specializing in the same line—Muttusvāmī Dīkṣitar and Śyāma Śāstri, but he excelled them by the all-round excellence of his creations.

The most remarkable feature of Tyāgarāja's compositions is the "variations" or *saṅgatis* which they embody in the very opening of the *pallavi.* These *saṅgatis* synthesize, one could say, the bound and unbound forms by providing for improvisation within the framework of a fixed tune and setting. This Tyāgarāja took no doubt from *pallavi*-singing on the one hand and the improvisations in dance-music where variations are done for *abhinaya* and the bringing out of different phases of the basic feeling. By grafting it on to his *kṛitis*, Tyāgarāja gave scope for the singer to bring out not only the total phases of the *rāga* of the song but also the emotional phases of the meaning of the prominent idea of the text of the song as given in the *pallavi.* Some well-known and oft-sung masterpieces of his, which open with this cascade of *saṅgatis* may be recalled: *Sakkani rāja mārga, Rāma nī samana,* O *Raṅgasayi, Nā jīvadhara.* But the *saṅgatis* form a part of all his songs, so much so that they have come to stay as part of Karṇāṭaka music itself and even the *kṛitis* of other masters like Dīkṣitar which belong to a different style and aesthetics are rendered by musicians in the same *saṅgati*-ized style. Although Tyāgarāja has some songs in the slow tempo, the medium one is his chief characteristic tempo. The medium tempo (*madhyama*) is also an adjunct of this *saṅgati*-style and that tempo has also become the prevailing one for Karṇāṭaka singing and even Dīkṣitar's music which is in the *vainika* style in slow tempo, with *gamakas* as its life, is also spurred up to the middle and fast tempo. In fact, all *kṛiti*-composition of the post-Tyāgarāja composers, like Pattanam Subrahmanya Iyer, is after Tyāgarāja's model. Thus, as is the case of Kalidāsa, we may say of Tyāgarāja too: "All that was before him was thrown into the background; all that came after has been on his model."

In keeping with his advaitin tradition and following several of his predecessors who illumined, in his part of the country, the three paths of advaitic *jñāna*, *bhakti*, and music—Nārāyaṇa Tīrtha, Sadāśiva Brahmendra, his elder contemporary Upaniṣad Brahmendra, and his own teacher Rāmakrishnānanda, Tyāgarāja took to *sannyāsa* vows towards the end of his life. In two of his songs (*Giripai* and *Paritāpamu*), he refers to Rāma's promise to him to bestow *mokṣa* on him. His *sannyāsa* is certainly one of the elements that added to the halo of his personality and is responsible for the annual observance of the day of his *samādhi.* Tyāgarāja attained *samādhi* on January 6, 1847 (*Puṣya bahula pañcami*). At his *samādhi* in Tiruvaiyāru where a shrine has been built by his devotees, his anniversary is a sacred day for all musicians who make their pilgrimage every year to this place and pay their homage to the master by singing his songs there. In fact, there are several ardent followers of his, who observe his day, wherever they are, every month on this fifth day of the dark fortnight (*Bahula pañcami*) on which he passed away, assemble and sing his songs before his portrait.

The Enduring Quality of His Work

Through his direct disciples, three schools, traditions, or styles of rendering his *kṛitis* became established, the Umayālpuram school which is the best and most widely represented, the Tillaisthānam school, and the Walājapet school. The last-mentioned played a part on the eve and the turn of the present century in bringing to light Tyāgarāja's compositions and leading to their increasing vogue in the concerts. But for the emergence of Tyāgarāja, and along with him, of his two contemporaries, Muttusvāmī Dīkṣitar and Śyāma Śāstri, Karnāṭaka musical heritage might not have been consolidated in the recent past and handed down to us. Taking their stand on the tradition, these men of genius saw into the future, and therefore, although two centuries have rolled by since Tyāgarāja appeared he continues to be, to this day, the mainstay of Karṇāṭaka music. The *Dūra-deśa*, distant parts of the country, where, according to his own song (*Daśarathi*), his music had been made famous, is today a continuously expanding world.

> How can I ever repay you, O Rāma,
> You have made me known in far-off lands!

16.

Mahātma Gandhi: *Bhajans*, Prayer, and the Name[1]

One of the most popular expressions of Gandhiji's religious activity was his prayer meetings, recitations of hymns, *bhajans*, *Rāmdhun*, recitation of *Rāma-nāma*. This one thing of all, put him in tune with the saints, *sadhus*, and *bhaktas* ranging from Valmiki to the latest singer of *Rāma-kīrtanas*. In his article "Nothing without Grace" Gandhi said that God's grace could be obtained by repeating the divine name all the twenty-four hours of the day and by realizing that God resides within us. Along with *Rāma-nāma*, he mentioned also the *dvadasākṣara* "twelve syllable" mantra as being equally efficacious but it was *Rāma-nāma* that was his favorite.

In agreement with all devout Hindus, Gandhi believed in carrying mantras which one should repeat. He said "The mantra becomes one's staff of life." Quoting the great medical authority Charaka, he believed that the recitation of God's name was an aid to cure oneself of illness. He called *Rāma-nāma* "a sovereign remedy" and "an unfailing panacea of all ills." "Repetition of *Rāma-nāma*," he said, "has been a second nature with me with growing knowledge and advancing years." He was well-versed in the tradition and literature of the doctrine of recitation of God's name, for he says in one place, "But more potent than Rāma is the Name"—which has reference to a tenet of this school of *nāma*-reciters that God had two real forms, the sound-form or Name, and his appearance (*rūpa*), and that of these two, the former is superior. In fact, we can compare some of his expositions on this subject to those of a traditional expounder of the greatness of the divine Name—*Nāma-mahātmya*—like Tyāgarāja. How the recitation of the Name should come from the heart, how Rāma means the Supreme Godhead and so on, —Gandhi's teachings on these topics can be compared to similar statements found in Tyāgarāja's songs.[2]

He repeated the name Rāma, but held that this, as also the thousand Names in the *Viṣṇu sahasranāma* hymn do not exhaust the names of God.

[1] Though he was not from the Kāverī delta region, Mohandas K. Gandhi was a well known Hindu of our times to whom the Name was very important. First published in *Swarājya* journal. [Editor's note: I have not been able to trace the issue number or date.]

[2] See for example songs like "*Rāmaniyeda permarahitulaku nāma-ruci telusuna*," "*Telisi Rāma cintanato Nāmamu Rāma yani parabrahmamunaku peru*," and so on.

"You may give Him as many names as you like, provided it is one God without a second whose Name you are invoking. That also means that He is Nameless too."[3] Many asked him "Who is the Rām of the *Rāmdhun*?" and he had no hesitation in saying, "I have accepted all the names and forms attributed to God, as symbols connoting one formless omnipresent Rāma." Gandhi had evidently in his mind what all devotees of Rāma had in mind, what the *Rāma pūrva tāpinī Upaniṣad* had said: "This name of Rāma delights the world, and for that reason shall really continue to be treasured up in the memory of the world for ever and ever. This (Rāma), the *Paramātman* (Supreme Being) is known by the name of Rāma [meaning "that which delights"], for the reason that yogins delight in this infinite existence, in this eternal bliss of the character of the *Ātman* of sentience."[4]

To the question could non-Hindus join in *Rāmdhun*, Gandhi gave an answer which he said was not his own but was that of Tulasidās himself. He replied, "My Rāma, the Rama, of our prayers, is not the historical Rāma the son of Daśaratha and King of Āyodhya. He is the eternal, the unborn, the one without a second."[5]

[3] *Harijan*, Dec. 21, 1936.

[4] *Rāmānte Yogino'nante nityanande chidātmani iti Rām-padena asau param Brahmā abhidhiyate* (1.6). Translation from *Vaiṣṇopaniṣads* (Adyar, Madras: Theosophical Publishing House, 1953), p. 381.

[5] *Harijan*, April 28, 1946.

Part IV

CONCLUDING ESSAY

17.

V. Raghavan's Autobiographical Reflections[1]

Family Background and Connections with Musicians

Mention may be made of my maternal grandfather Śrī A. Nārāyaṇaswāmī Iyer, the first Tamil Vakīl (advocate) at Tiruvārūr. He came of a stock of Vaidikas steeped in Sanskrit from the village of Nannargudi; his cousin (Ammanji) Raju Ganapathin was a contemporary and friend of Mm. Raju Śāstrigal and was well versed in *mantra-śāṣtra*, and had *siddhi* (accomplishment) in *bala-mantra* (devoted to Tripurasundarī). Nārāyaṇaswāmī was a *yajusha* Ganapathin and he was put in charge of the Veda Paṭhaśala at Vedāranyam; and although young, he was able to manage also the economic affairs of the Trusts and Endowments of the Yazhpanam merchants made in the Vedāranyam very well. The English Collector who saw his capacity called him and asked him to pass some tests in the Civil and Criminal Procedure Codes which he said should be of very little strain to one who mastered so much of the *Vedas*. Young Nārāyaṇaswāmī accordingly passed and became the first Vakīl at Tiruvārūr and was known for continuing his orthodox activities along with his work as a Vakīl. Whenever Mm. Raju Śāstrigal came to Tiruvārūr for Tyāgarāja *darśanam* (to see a holy person or image and be blessed)[2] he stayed with this maternal grandfather of ours.

Near Tiruvarūr is a village called Kootampadi where some of Appayya Dīkshita's descendants had settled. The Kootampadi people had a house in Tiruvārūr a few houses to the west of our maternal grandfather's; but Mm. Raju Śāstrigal preferred to stay with our grandfather. The contacts had continued and at one stage, as my mother's sister had told me, there had been serious talk of my mother being given in marriage to Yajñaswāmī Śāstrigal.

Nārāyaṇaswāmī Iyer's second son, N. Mahādeva Iyer, my mother's younger brother, who passed away in 1967, was a very well-known lawyer in the whole of Tāñjāvūr District for a number of years, and retired as Government Pleader at Tiruvārūr; he was devoted to a number of religious

[1] Written in 1968. This narrative is taken from a photocopy of a typed manuscript obtained from V. Raghavan's daughter, Nandini Ramani.

[2] See his *Tyāgarāja Śaṭakam*, edited by V. Raghavan.

activities, himself being a Subrahmaṇya *upāsaka* (devotee). He was very good in Sanskrit, particularly on the literary and aesthetic side, and was a pioneer in organizing musical activities in Tiruvārūr. He was a great personal friend of Pushpavanam who was very much under his influence and stayed with him in his house often.

Mahādeva Iyer looked after the medical treatment of Pushpavanam during his last days at Tanjore. Mahādeva Iyer discovered also Chidambaram Śrīraṅgāchāriār, father of Embar Vijayaraghavachariar and had arranged in our own house at Tiruvārūr several series of Harikathās (musical discourses) on the *Rāmāyaṇa* epic, the *Bhāgavatha Purāṇa*, the lives of the Nāyanmārs (South Indian Śaivite saints), etc. Along with him Jagannātha Kavi stayed in our house at Tiruvārūr more continuously. Jagannātha Kavi was a young Telugu poet who composed admirably both in Telugu and Sanskrit songs and verses for Śrīraṅgāchāriār for his Harikathās. There was also a gifted Tamil composer of Mayuram, Tyāgarāja Deśikar (an *odhuvar*, a South Indian man who sings Tamil devotional hymns and songs in temples dedicated to Shiva, Ganesha, and Murugan). The compositions in Tamil, Telugu, and Sanskrit of these two composers may still be heard in many of the performances of Embar Vijayaraghavachariar. I can recall the days and the occasions when these composers wrote some of these pieces and the lively atmosphere of their being given the contexts of their producing the compositions and reading them out and their being rendered in music and enjoyed. Along with Harikathā Kalakṣepams, there were also in those days Vedaparāyana *ghoṣthis* (recital of Vedic prayers) going on in our house during the annual festival at the Tyāgarāja temple. A memorable and complete series of *Bhāgavata Purāṇa* expositions by a renowned pandit Raṅgasamudram Veṅkaṭarama Śāstrigal which filled the gaps when there were no Harikathās. Then there were music series connected with Rādhā Kalyāṇa Utsavam which was an annual feature in which all top musicians of those days with a number of accompanists staged the older-type of long drawn kutcheries. There was hardly a stalwart of the music world of those days who had not come and sung there and stayed at our house.

During this time there was also staying in our house for a number of years Papanāsam Śivan as a young bachelor, singing his songs and doing *bhajanas*. It was towards the end of his stay with us at Tiruvārūr that he was married. It was in continuation of this association, that I began to take interest in him afterwards in Madras, in the forties. It was I who brought him into the motion pictures, first for the Sītā Kalyāṇa produced at Kolhapur for which I wrote scenario and dialogue and from which his new life as a cinema composer started.

Mahārājapuram as a youngster had his debut at the *Gṛihapraveśam* (a ritual and celebration after a wedding, in which the bride enters her husband's home, and festivities are held) of my uncle's house, which became a well-known rendezvous and port of call for musicians. His legal help was freely available for musicians and dancers. It was a litigation that brought Bharatam Nallūr Nārāyaṇaswāmī Iyer to our uncle and the association continued over years. When these were all coming from outside, there were the native local masters of Nāgaswāra, notably Tiruvārūr Swāmīnāthan and his brother Kittuchami, the former being the father-in-law of the late Flute Swaminathan Pillai of Tirupambaram. As I have narrated in the Preface to my Patel Lectures, along with the above, must be mentioned, the *bhajanas* carried on in the month of Mārgasirsha for which traditional *bhajana* experts used to come from neighboring villages and I fell in line with them and became engrossed in *Giri-pradakṣinam* (circumambulating the holy mountain) and *bhajana* recitals.

On my father's side my grandfather Śrīnivasa Iyer was a powerful figure well-known for his capacity in dealing with men and things. A tall, strong man, he owned 15 *vaḷis* (a measurement of land) at Pavitramanikkam on the border of Tiruvārūr and was a Karnam (village accountant and record-keeper) of that village. My father's elder brother Rāmaswāmī Iyer was a Magistrate with Civil and Criminal duties known for his strictness and integrity, and he had left a lasting impression in our family. I myself was given the *śarman* (blessing) after his *śarman*, at the time of my *upanāyanam* (initiation). . . . My mother and my mother's sister were interested in devotional literature and there was the practice in the family of getting by heart a large number of *stotras* (verses), *Ārya Dvisati* (*Lālita Stave Ratna*) of Durvāsas and the *stotras* of Śrīdhara Veṅkaṭeṣa Āyyāvāl being two of their favorites; I still cherish the copy of the collected *stotras* of Āyyāvāl in *grantha* script (an old form of written Tamil) used by my aunt. They, along with the other *stotras*, I got by heart when I was quite a young boy. During my boyhood I got by heart quite a large number of *stotras* long and short.

Sanskrit Background

Both my parents passed away while I was seven. My father's sister, who was devoted to traditional learning and in the old world way, and was a capable manager of domestic affairs, took charge of our family; she put me and my young sister and my maternal uncle's son under a Sanskrit *pandit* (scholar), Sengalipuram Appaswāmī Śāstrigal, pupil of Mahāmahopadhyāya Kodavasal Narsimhāchāriar. With this *pandit* I learned Sanskrit in the traditional style in addition to the Sanskrit as second language in the school where we had a very competent *pandit* in Nārāyaṇa Vejapeyar also. I must mention also an interesting person who created a lot of enthusiasm in my young mind, an old lady named Sundari Patti of Chai, who had mastered Sanskrit and could converse in Sanskrit with *pandits.* She was a friend of my mother's sister and often checked up our progress in Sanskrit and I learnt some Sanskrit compositions from her, notably a very good Rāmāyaṇa *odam* (boat song) in Sanskrit which is still unpublished and was probably composed by one of her ancestors. There was also another lady distantly related to us, Kutti Āmmāl alias Lakshyanandam who had taken to *Vedānta* philosophy and read Sanskrit *advaita* (monism) works with well-known *pandits.* I have mentioned these two ladies in my account of Woman Sanskritists which I wrote in Tamil long ago in *Kalaimaṅgal.*

In the school Sanskrit was only my second language and my optional subjects were Chemistry and Botany. When I came for an admission in Presidency College, Madras, I wanted to pursue Botany, in which I had done special work even while in the fifth and sixth Form; even at that time I had compiled a glossary of plants, trees, creepers etc. in Sanskrit literature with their Tamil name and Sanskrit name and Botanical and common English names.

Owing to the communal politics of the Justice Party at that time which had seriously affected College-admissions, I could not get a seat in Botany and I had to take a new group in which I was the sole student—Ancient History (Greek and Roman), Logic and Sanskrit in all the three of which I got Distinction in the Intermediate Examinations. Of course my Sanskrit grounding was already very good and I remember that the very first set of Sanskrit verses which I composed are dated during the years of my Intermediate course in Presidency College.

In addition to the practice of writing out *stotras* and getting them by heart, there was also the practice of keeping diaries and notebooks in which all good and quotable verses interesting from one point of view or other, heard or read, were written out and also learnt by heart if possible.

My maternal uncle Mahadeva Iyer had his own private *subhashita* (gems of wisdom) notebooks. This he had imbibed from Tiruviśanallūr Raghava Śāstrigal who, as stated elsewhere, was related to us; he was the Indian industrialist Rājarāma Śāstri's elder brother and father of R. Ramachandran (of Gemini). Raghava Śāstrigal (one of Dhanam's sons-in-law) was perhaps as much a savant of Sanskrit as of music and was the brother's son of Tiruviśanallūr Rāmachandra Śāstrigal. I had picked up the habit of keeping my own *subhāshita* notebook and getting by heart best verses from my early days; this steadily grew with the development of my own studies. When I happened to live in Triplicane during my Sanskrit Honors course especially, not a day passed without my spending at least three hours with

Raghava Śāstrigal, reciting Sanskrit verses of special beauty and taking down from him verses which I did not know. In fact I possess two or three books written in the hand of Raghava Śāstrigal containing select verses from all over Sanskrit literature, which he left with me before he died. It was Raghava Śāstrigal who had taught Kumārasambhava to Sirkali Sundrachariar, a family friend, my uncle and aunt having lived sometime in Egmore along with Sundrachariar's sister, who had married in Dewan Bahadur T. Rangachariar's family.

The contacts with Sundrachariar which began in Triplicane and in the Sanskrit Academy were a renewal of old ties. Outside of my academic studies one of the most effective influences which widened my study and appreciation of Sanskrit classics, was that of Sundrachariar. It is through his inspiration that I took to the reading and mastering of the *Bhāgavata Purāṇa* and *Mahābhārata* epic systematically, getting by heart several portions of the *Bhāgavata* especially. It is on coming to know of this that my Prof. Kuppuswāmī Śāstrigal asked me to speak in those days on the Gītā Day; and I spoke on the *Bhāgavata* and *Gītā* at V.P. Hall when Śrī K. Chandrasekharan was the Secretary, and again on the greater *Gītā* at the Ranade Hall. The late Padmanabha Śāstrigal who was my teacher in Vyākaraṇa in the Presidency College called me and fondly expressed his joy at my mastery of the *Bhāgavata* when I was so young. Falling in the line of the earlier formative forces in the field of *bhakti* and *bhajana*, the *Śrīmad Bhāgavata Purāṇa* has been the mainstay and force in all my later writings reaching up to *The Spiritual Heritage of Tyāgarāja.*

In addition to the musical background derived from early life at Tiruvārūr, academic interest in music and dance and in the Sanskrit texts thereon started with a fresh zest when I had to deal, during my Ph.D. work, with *Matsya Śāstra* with Abhinavagupta's commentary and several allied works. During this time I was in close associations with the late Śrī K.V. Ramachandran with whom we had all lived at Luz Corner for some years. K.V. Ramachandran and I had jointly pursued work on behalf of music, dance, and dance-drama and we two were the first to go to some of the Tanjore villages and to bring to light the traditional *nātakas* (dance performance styles) of the Bhāgavatas at Merattur, Soolamangalam, etc.

Although engrossed in academic research and scientific study, edition of texts and scrutiny of manuscripts and the pursuit of logic and philosophy, there had been a persistent urge almost from the very beginning towards original literary activity which started expressing itself through Sanskrit verses, prose, plays, skits, essays, *stotras*, etc. in Tamil and English. However, considering the domestic circumstances, a career was not possible without a permanent employment in this country, although one of my twins in this line of activity, Manjeri S. Iswaran, classmate from Intermediate, thought otherwise. The latter discovered rather late in his life that I was right and one required a permanent position both financially and otherwise to be able to pursue writing activity. If I had been otherwise placed in private life, I wonder whether I would have become at all a research scholar or a University man, and whether I would not have gone away to the field of freelance writings or of journalism. I had actively cultivated the associations of the leading writers in all the languages of India and had been fairly intimate with several of them occupying front ranks in their own languages.

In the young days of consuming energy and overflowing enthusiasm, when one was bursting with ideas, I had written out for several friends film scenarios of *stotras* from epics, *purāṇas*, and Sanskrit classics, of course without any business knowledge or inclination to make money out of them.

Other Acquaintances and Formative Influences

Nārāyaṇaswāmī Iyer, my maternal grandfather, had a younger brother named A. Śrīnivāsa Iyer who married the sister of Tiruviśanallur Rajaram Śāstrigal (Indian industrialist) and died prematurely. He was a brilliant person and had been selected for Provincial Civil Service along with N. Gopalaswāmī Iyengar, R. Śrīnivāsa Iyer (later Accountant General), and others of that time. He was also a man of striking qualities which endeared him to all. It happened that in George Town, Madras my elder maternal uncle, who had been also selected for such Service was living with my mother's sister who had become widowed when quite young. At that time, they were living together with B. Rajam Iyer, author of *Kamalāmbāl Charitram* and *Rambles in Vedānta.* Rajam Iyer took a fancy for A. Śrīnivāsa Iyer and it has been handed down in our family that Rajam Iyer had Śrinīvāsa Iyer in mind when he drew some of the pictures in *Kamalāmbāl Charitram,* his unfinished story in English entitled "True Greatness of Vasudeva Śāstrigal" included in the *Rambles.* There is also an episode in the *Kamalāmbāl Charitram* of a bogus *sadhu* deceiving a person. This, we have been told, was an account of an actual incident which happened at Tiruvottriyur for my elder maternal uncle V. Subramania Iyer with all of whom Rajam Iyer was living.

One of the formative influences during the two years of my Intermediate Study (when I was living with my eldest brother next to Mylapore Club) was my frequent visits to the Rāmakrishna Maṭh where some of the Swāmījīs took to me, and I spent hours with them whenever I went there. Even while in the S.S.L.C. I had read Vivekananda's Lectures and the interest grew, as time passed, in the Vivekananda Rāmakrishna lectures and movement. Later association developed further through the *Vedānta Keśari* journal and Rāmakrishna Mission International Centers, all of which were visited by me in Europe, U.S., and South East Asia. There is hardly a leading Swāmījī in the Rāmakrishna Missions from California to Singapore with whom I have not come into contact.

Mention may also be made of the early development of interest in Tagore. In S.S.L.C. I stood first in English among those who passed from the Government High School, Tiruvārūr. Among the books I received as a present was Tagore's *Gora*. During my two years of Intermediate study, I had read a great deal of Tagore literature and I even now preserve my notebook of those days in which I had in my own way imitated *Gītañjali*, *The Gardener*, etc. All these lead up to the threshold of the Sanskrit Honors which I took in the teeth of domestic opposition, my brothers pressing me to take up History or Economics. After obtaining distinction in Sanskrit and with all the earlier interest in Sanskrit, I had come to know by reports about Prof. Kuppuswami Śāstrigal. N. Gopala Iyer of Mannargudi, who was an advocate in Tāñjāvūr, who as younger brother had married my maternal uncle's daughter, had been a hotel-mate of Kuppuswami Śāstrigal and he introduced me to Professor. Professor used to take snuff in those days and Gopala Iyer and he were snuff-chums and they were together messing in the same hotel in the Kucheri Road at just the place where the Matthala Narayanan Street takes off.

Studiousness and academic distinction in my generation in the family were first seen in the case of my eldest brother V. Balasundaram, who came out with a brilliant record in school and college, particularly in mathematics. He was a pet of Mr. Littlehall, who wanted him to go up for further studies in mathematics. He unfortunately chose the career of an Advocate in the Metropolis for which he was temperamentally not suited, despite his talents. Balasundaram had also a keen literary flair and was given to wide reading in English literature and was particularly good in Shakespeare.

Another interesting personality in my family may be mentioned—my father's sister's husband Vaidyanātha Śāstrigal of Erukkur on the Kolli dam. A Sāmavedin (a family of *brahmans* traditionally associated with the *Sāma Veda*) like us, and a Mirasdar (landlord), he took a fancy for starting a business, and having thereby lost his estate, he fell upon his Vedic learning and training. He learned also *mantras* to cure severe reptile bites and skin eruptions from a Muslim and his house became a most crowded center for people who came for his cures.

It was during the several public activities in Madras in the field of

Sanskrit and Indian Culture that I became intimately associated with late S. Satyamurthi, the political leader of whose oratory, like many other youngsters of the time, I had been a regular listener and admirer. This also proved a sort of renewal of older family ties and his father-in-law (father of his second wife) was a classmate and kinsman of my father. When Satyamurthi was living in Triplicane my contacts with him were very frequent.

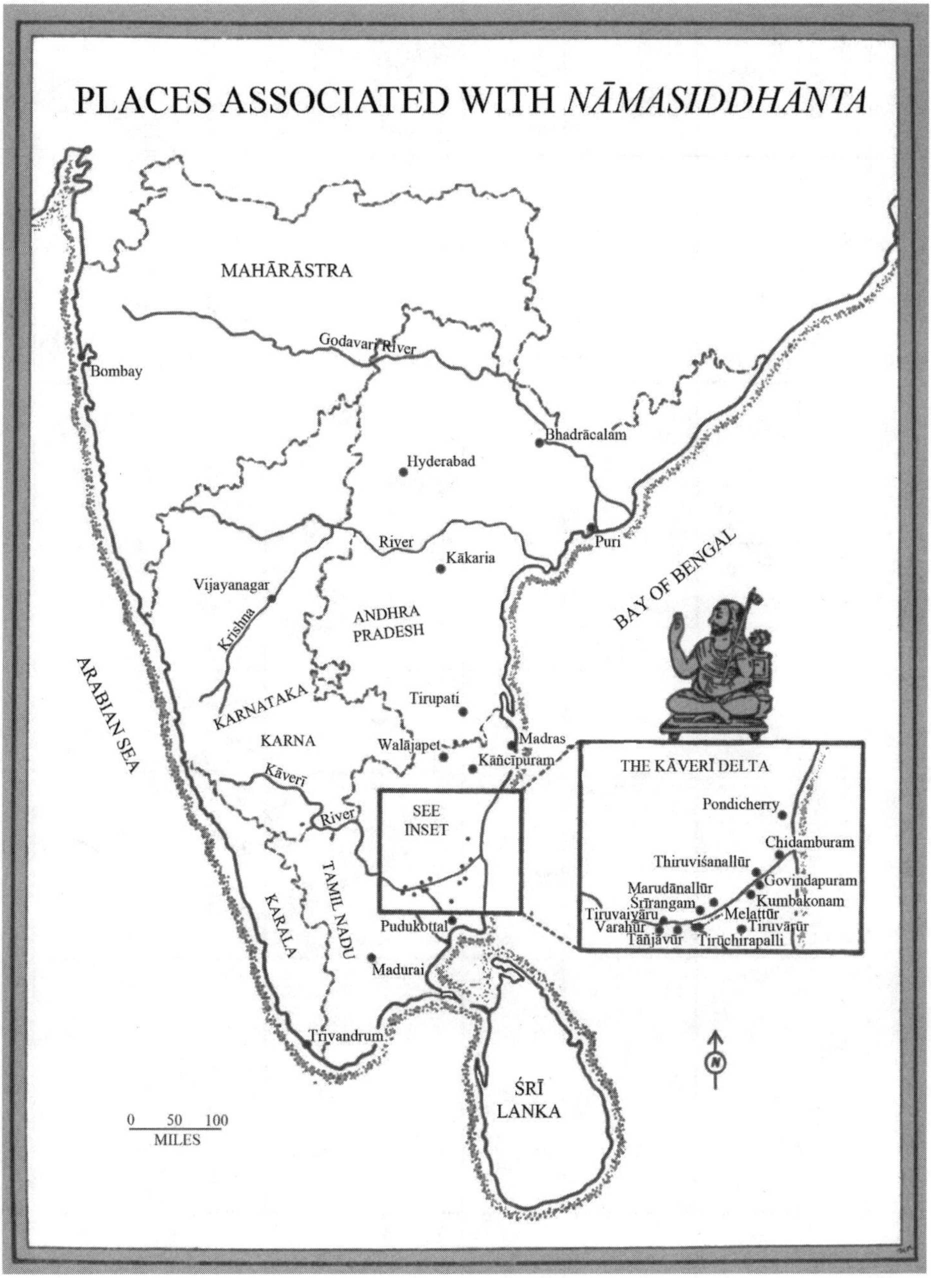

PLACES ASSOCIATED WITH NĀMASIDDHĀNTA
MAHĀRĀSTRA
Godavari River
Bombay
Bhadrācalam
Hyderabad
River
Kākaria
Puri
Vijayanagar
Krishna
ANDHRA PRADESH
BAY OF BENGAL
ARABIAN SEA
KARNATAKA
Tirupati
KARNA
Walājapet
Madras
Kāñcīpuram
Kāverī
River
SEE INSET
TAMIL NADU
KARALA
Pudukottai
Madurai
Trivandrum
ŚRĪ LANKA
0 50 100
MILES
THE KĀVERĪ DELTA
Pondicherry
Chidamburam
Thiruviśanallūr
Govindapuram
Marudānallūr
Śrīrangam
Kumbakonam
Tiruvaiyāru
Melattūr
Varahūr
Tiruvārūr
Tāñjāvūr
Tirūchirapalli

Kāverī Delta Saints of the Name

1. Name	**Bhagavannāma Bodhendra**	**Śrīdhara Veṅkaṭeṣa Ārya—Āyyāvāl**	**Śivarāmakrishnan Sadāśiva Brahmendra**	**Govinda Śastri Nārāyaṇa Tīrtha**	**Veṅkaṭarama Sadgurusvāmī**
2. Birth/ Death	b. early 17th century d. 1692, Kāñcī	b. 17th century d. Mysore	b. early 18th century d. in Tiruviśanallūr	b. 17th century d. 1745 (or 1735?)	b. 1776 Tiruviśanallūr d. 1817
3. Varna-Aśrama	Telugu *Brahmin* unmarried	Telugu *Smārta Brahmin*, married	Telugu *Brahmin;* married; Āyyāvāl's disciple; became *Sannyāsin*	Telugu *Brahmin;* married; became *Sannyāsin*	Telugu *Brahmin;* married
4. Village Association	to Govindapuram returned to Kāñcī	Tiruviśanallūr		Guru: "Go South" Went, guided to Varahūr	moved to Marudānallūr
5. Relation to King	*Sannyāsin* accepted no King's patronage	Accepted patronage from King Śāhajī who gifted Tiruviśanallūr to *Brahmins*	Gave king his book; blessed children	No association with king	Initiated Śarabhojī to *Rāma-mantra;* offered King's realm. Received help to build Bodhendra's *samādhi*
6. Works	Scholar; wrote treatises on Name, *Nāma Amṛita Rasāyanam Bhajana* program	Poet: *Ākhyā Ṣaṣṭi Dāya Śatakam, Bhagavannāma Bhūṣaṇam*	*Advaita bhakti* songs Sanskrit verses *Ātmavidyavilīsa*	Wrote Sanskrit play with songs: *Krishna Līlā Taraṅginī* and Sanskrit treatises	Founded math, codified bhajans, including Tirupathi tradition and languages Bhāgavatadharma 6 Rules

7. Typical Miracles	Vowed to drown in Ganges; became *Sannyāsin*	Revived cobra bitten *Brahmin*; brought down rain with song; converted bandits	Paralyzed threshers. Muslim ruler cut off his arm—unconcerned, it healed. "Died" in Nerur, Manamadurai, Varanāsi	Stomach ache relief: Tāñjāvūr temple dream: two boars led to village	Speechless as child; guru whispers mantra he said "Rāma," spoke
8. River in His life	*Brahmin*'s wife reconverted at river through *Rāma-nāma.* Buried himself in riverbed at *samādhi.* Met Āyyāvāl at Rāmeśvaram	At river saw frog under cobra, took *Sannyāsa* vow. Gave food to starving untouchable; Ganges rose in his well to purify him.	Buried in river by flood; one or four months later he came to.	River threatened voice; Took *Sannyāsa.* "Bathe in Divine name confluence: Rāma= Ganges; Krishna= Yamunā; Govinda= Sarasvatī river"	Bodhendra's *samādhi* washed away by river. He heard sand echoing name of Rāma, located.
9. Mantra	Repeated Rāma's name 108,000 times a day. Taught oneness of Śiva and Viṣṇu in Hariharādvaita Bhuṣanam	Repeated Śiva mantra, visualized as Goddess. Taught *Rāmayāna*; wrote praise of Krishna	Unspecified *mantra.* Songs in praise of Śiva, Rāma, Krishna	Devoted to Krishna. Aescetic told him of vision, 120 million repetition of name	Daily says *Rāma-mantra* 108,000 times; believed saying name insufficient. *Bhakti* song also
10. Avatār Position and Miscellaneous	59th Kāñcī Jagadguru, Arādhana celebrated Govindapuram September, October	Incarnation of Śiva. Annual *utsava* Tiruviśanallūr Karthigain	Called Avadhūta Jīvanmukta, great *siddha.* Roamed naked, homeless. *Jīva Samādhi* at Nerūr. May birthday *arādhana*	Incarnation of Jayadeva. Yearly *arādhana* at Tirupanthuruthi, Masi	Incarnation of Rāma: Āyyāvāl and Bodhendra in one. Died after 14 years *uñchavṛitti* (gleaning)

Bibliography

Primary Sources: *Nāmasiddhānta* Texts:

Nārāyaṇa Tīrtha. *Krishnalīlātaraṅgiṇī*. Madras: Vavilla, 1967. (Sanskrit text in Telugu script.) For a more recent edition in Devanāgarī script, with English translation, see *Śrī Krishnalīlātaraṅgiṇī*, trans. B. Natarājan. Madras: Mudgala Trust, volume I, 1988; volume 2, 1990.

Sadāśiva Brahmendra. *Śivamanasikapūjā Kīrtanani Ātmavidyāvilāsa*, trans. (into English and Tamil) V. Narayanan. Madras: Śrī Kamakoṭi Kośaṣṭhānena Prakāśitam, 1951.

Sadgurusvāmī. *Bhajana Ratnākara*, ed. K. Pancapagesa Iyer. Madras: author, 1972.

———. *Bhakti-samdeha-dhvanta-bhaskara*, ed. A.B.S. Rāmasvāmī. Rev, ed. New Delhi: Delhi *Bhajana* Samaj, 1958.

Śrīdhara Veṅkaṭeśa Āyyāvāl. *Sāhendravilāsa*, ed. V. Raghavan. Tiruchi: Tanjore Saraswati Mahal Library, 1952.

———. *Ākhyāṣaṣṭiḥ śatakam*, ed. V. Raghavan. Kumbakoṇam and Madras: Kāmakoti Kośaṣṭhanam, 1944. No. 15 contains introduction, No. 25 contains text.

Śrī Bodhendra Sarasvatī. *Bhagavan-nāmāmṛita rasodayam; Nāma rasayanam; Nāma suryodayam; Nāma taraṅgam; Harihara bhedadikaram; Harihara advaita bhūṣanam; Mūrthabrahma vivekam; Bhagavan nāmāmṛita.* Manuscripts at Saraswati Mahal Library, Tāñjāvūr.

———. *Harihara advaita bhuṣanam*, ed. T. Chandrasekharam. Madras: Government Press, 1954.

Upaniṣad Brahman. *Upeya-nāma-viveka*, ed. V. Raghavan. Madras: Adyar Library, 1967.

The Vaiṣṇavopaniṣads (*Rāma-tapinīyupaniṣad, Rāmarahasyopaniṣad, Kalisamtaranopaniṣad*, etc.) Adyar: Theosophical Society, 1923.

Viṣṇusahasranāma with the bhāṣya of Śaṅkarācārya, tr. (into English) R. Ananthakrishna Sastry. Madras: Adyar Library, 1980.

Lakṣmīdhara. *Bhagavannāma Kaumudi.* Kāśi: Prakāśaṣṭhānam Acyutagranthamālā Kāryālayaḥ, 1907.

Rāma-Tapanīya-Upaniṣad (also the *Rāma Upaniṣad* with the commentary of Nārāyaṇa, ed. by Vindhyeśvari Prasāda Śarman; also the *Hanumaduktarāma Upaniṣad*). Banaras: Benares Printing Press, 1879.

Selected Secondary Bibliographic Sources:

Harvey P. Alper, ed. *Understanding Mantras.* Albany: State University of New York, 1989. (See especially p. 359 "The Significance of Names" and p. 327 and following, "A Working Bibliography for the Study of Mantras.")

———. "Regression Towards the Real." *Parabola* 8, no. 3: pp. 72-81.

F.R. Allchin. "The Place of Tulsi Dās in North Indian Devotional Faith." *Journal of the Royal Asiatic Society*, 1966, pts. 3 and 4, pp. 128-129 especially.

Sinnappah Arasaratnam. *Merchants, Companies, and Commerce on the Coromandel Coast, 1650-1740.* Delhi: Oxford University Press, 1986.

Guy L. Beck. *Sonic Theology: Hinduism and Sacred Sound.* Columbia: University of South Carolina Press, 1993.

Joachim Ernst Berendt. *Nāda Brahma: The World is Sound.* Rochester: Destiny Books, 1987.

Agehananda Bharati. *The Tantric Tradition.* London: Rider and Co., 1965.

Usha R. Bhise. "The Importance of *Naman* in the Ṛgveda." All-India Oriental Conference Summary of Papers, 25:2-3.

Madeleine Biardeau. *Sphota siddhi (La Demonstration du Sphota) par Mandana Misra, introduction, et commentaire par Madeleine Biardeau, texte etabli par N.R. Bhatt avec la collaboration de T. Ramanujam.* Pondichery: Publications de l'institut francais d'indologie, 1958.

John Blofeld. *Mantras: Sacred Words of Power.* London: Allen and Unwin, 1977.

A.K. Coomaraswamy. "Spiritual Authority and Temporal Power." *American Oriental Society Journal.* New Haven: AOS, 1942.

Harold Coward. *Sphota Theory of Language.* Delhi: Motilal Banarsidass, 1980.

——— & Krishna Sivaraman, eds. *Revelation in Indian Thought.* Emeryville, Calif.: Dharma Publishing, 1977.

Francis X. D'Sa. *Śabdapramanyam in Sabara and Kumarila: Towards a Study of the Mimamsa Experience of Language.* Wien: De Nobili Research Library, 1980.

Alain Danielou. *Hindu Polytheism.* New York: Bollingen, 1964, especially pp. 334-349: "The Thought-Forms or Mantras."

Raghav Chaitanya Das. *The Divine Name.* Bombay, Author, 1954.

Shashi Bhusan Das Gupta. "The Role of Mantra in Indian Religion." *Bulletin of the Ramakrishna Mission Institute of Culture*, Vol. VII, no. 3, March 1956, pp. 49-57.

———. "Some Later Yogic Schools." *Cultural Heritage of India*, Vol. 4.

Calcutta: The Ramakrishna Mission, 1956, pp. 291-299.
R. De Smet. "Nāma Japa in Christianity." *Mountain Path.* Tiruvannamalai, Ramanashram, April 1981, pp. 91-93.
Louis Dumont. *Religion/Politics and History in India: Collected Papers in Indian Sociology.* Paris: Mouton, 1970 (1st ed. 1962).
Eknath Easwaran. *The Mantram Handbook.* London: Routledge and Kegan J. Paul, 1978.
Franklin Edgerton. *Mīmāṁsā Nyāya Prakāśa or Āpadevī: A Treatise on the Mīmāṁsā System by Apadeva, Translated into English, With an Introduction, Transliterated Sanskrit Text, and Glossarial Index.* New Haven: Yale University Press, 1929.
Maryla Falk. *Nāma-rūpa and Dharma-rūpa.* Calcutta: University of Calcutta, 1943.
Richard G. Fox, ed. *Realm and Region in Indian History* (includes "The Segmentary State in South Indian History" by Burton Stein). Durham, NC: Duke University, 1977.
M.K. Gandhi. *Rāmanāma,* ed. Bharatan Kumarappa. Ahmedabad: Navajīvan, 1949.
L. Gardet. "Un Probleme de mystique comparee: la mention dun Nom divin. . . ." *Revue Thomiste,* 1952, pp. 642-679; 1953, pp. 197-216.
Nadiedja Gorodetzky. *The Prayer of Jesus.* Oxford: Blackfriars, 1942.
Jan Gonda. "The Indian Mantra." *Oriens* 16, 1963. pp. 244-297. (Also included in Jan Gonda's *Selected Studies.* Leiden: EJ. Brill, 1975.)
———. *Medieval Religious Literature.* Wiesbaden: Otto Harrassowitz, 1977, especially pp. 267-270.
———. *Notes on the Names and the Name of God in Ancient India.* Amsterdam: North Holland Pub., 1970. Verhandelingen . . . series number 4, deel 75.
———. *Vision of the Vedic Poets.* The Hague: Mouton and Co., 1963. Republished in New Delhi: Munshiram Manoharlal, 1984.
Kathleen Gough. *Rural Society in Southeast India.* Cambridge: Cambridge University Press, 1981.
Lama Govinda. *Foundations of Tibetan Mysticism, According to the Esoteric Teachings of the Great Mantra.* London: Rider and Co., 1959, 1967.
John Stratton Hawley & Mark Juergensmeyer. *Songs of the Saints of India.* New York: Oxford University Press, 1988.
J.C. Heesterman. *The Inner Conflict of Tradition: Essays in Indian Ritual, Kingship, and Society.* Chicago: University of Chicago Press, 1985.
Heinrich Heiler. *Erscheinungsformen und Wesen der Religion.* Stuttgart: W. Kohlhammer Verlag, 1961, pp. 276, 341 ff.
Norvin J. Hein. "Caitanya's Ecstasies and the Theology of the Name." In

Hinduism: New Essays in the History of Religion, ed. Bardwell L. Smith. Leiden: E.J. Brill, 1976, pp. 19-32.

Arthur Maurice Hocart. *Kings and Councillors.* Chicago, 1970 (1st ed. 1936).

———. *Kingship.* Oxford: Oxford University Press, 1927.

K.R. Srīnivāsa Iyengar, ed. *Guru Nānak: A Homage.* New Delhi: Sahitya Akademi, 1973.

Toshihiko Izutsu. *Language and Magic.* Tokyo: Keio Institute of Philological Studies, 1956.

Mohanlal Bhagawandas Jhavery. *Comparative and Critical Study of Mantraśāstra, with Special Treatment of Jain Mantravada.* Ahmedabad: Sarabhai Manilal Nawab, 1944.

E. Kadloubovsky and G.E.H. Palmer. *Writings from the Philokalia on Prayer of the Heart.* London: Faber and Faber, 1951.

R. Krishnamurthy. *Saints of the Cauvery Delta.* New Delhi: Concept Publishing Co., 1979.

T.S. Kuppuswamy Śāstri. "Rāmabhadra-Dīkshita and the Southern Poets" (including Āyyāvāl). *The Indian Antiquary*, July 1904, p. 187.

Richard Lannoy. *The Speaking Tree.* London: Oxford University Press, 1975.

David Ludden. *A Peasant History of South India.* Princeton: Princeton University Press, 1985.

T.M.P. Mahadevan, ed. *A Seminar on Saints.* Madras: Ganesh and Co., 1960.

Louis Massignon. *Essai sur les origines de lexique technique de la mystique musulmane.* Paris: P. Geunther, 1922.

J.L. Mehta, *Religion and Philosophy.* New Delhi: Indian Council for Philosophical Research, 1990.

A.L. Mudaliar, ed. *Bibliography of the Books, Papers, and other Contributions of Dr. V. Raghavan.* Ahmedabad: New Order Book Co., 1968.

B. Natarajan. *Śrī Krishna Leela Taraṅginī by Nārāyaṇa Tirtha.* Vol. I, Translation and Notes in English. Madras: Mudgala Trust, 1988.

Andre Padoux. "Contributions a l'etude du mantraśāṣtra: I, La selection des mantra (mantroddhara)." *Bulletin de l'École francaise d'extreme-orient* (Hanoi), 67:pp. 59-102.

———. "Some Suggestions on Research into Mantra." *Indologica Taurinensia* (*Turin*) 6: pp. 235-239.

T. S. Parthasarathy. *Music Composers of India.* Madras: C.P. Rāmaswāmi Aiyar Foundation, 1982.

V. S. Pathak. *Smārta Religious Tradition.* Meerut: Kusumañjali Prakashan, 1987.

Hanuman Prasad Poddar. *The Divine Name and its Practice.* Gorakhpur: Gorakhpur Press, n.d.

Swami Pratyagatmananda. *Japasutram: The Science of Creative Sound.* Madras: Ganesh and Co., 1971.

Krishna Premi. *Gospel of Mahātma Sree Sree Krishna Premi*, trans. Śrī Natesa Prabhu. Paranur: Premika Grandha Prakasa Sabha, 1983.

V. Raghavan. "Bhāgavata Purāṇa." *Vedānta Keśari*, Oct. 1965.

———. *The Great Integrators.* New Delhi: Publications Division, Ministry of Information and Broadcasting, Govt. of India, 1966, 1969, 1976, 1979.

———. *The Indian Heritage.* Bangalore: Indian Institute of World Culture, 1956.

———. "Nārāyaṇa Tīrtha." Madras: Śrī Nārāyaṇa Tīrtha Festival Celebration Committee, Tirupunturutti, n.d.

———. "Sadāśiva Brahmendra." *Service* II, ii, April 1952, pp. 84-85, 88.

———. "Śrī Sadāśiva Brahmendra's Ātmā-Vidyāvilāsa." *Vedānta Keśari*, XXXVII, viii, Dec. 1950, pp. 301-304.

———. "The Tattvasaṁgraha Rāmāyaṇa of Rāmabrahmānanda." *Annals of Oriental Research*, Vol. X, pt. 1, Madras: University of Madras, 1945.

———. "Upanishad Brahman: His Life and Works." *Journal of the Music Academy of Madras*, Vol. XXVII, 1956.

———. "Vak Devata." *Dilip*, May-June, 1975.

———, ed. *Composers* (Cultural Leaders of India Series). New Delhi: Publications Division, Ministry of Information and Broadcasting, Govt. of India, 1979.

———, ed. *Devotional Poets and Mystics.* Vols. I and II. New Delhi: Publications Division, Ministry of Information and Broadcasting, Govt. of India, 1978, 1981.

——— & C. Ramanujachari. *The Spiritual Heritage of Tyāgarāja.* Madras: Rāmakrishna Maṭh, 1966.

Rāmakrishnayya. *Telugu Literature Outside Telugu Country.* Telugu Series, no. 9. Madras: University of Madras, n.d.

R. D. Ranade. *Mysticism in India: The Poet-Saints of Mahārashtra.* Albany: State University of New York, 1983 (reprint).

J. F. Richards, ed. *Kingship and Authority in South Asia.* Madison: South Asia Studies, University of Wisconsin Madison, Publication Series, #3, 1978. (Articles by Heesterman, Burton Stein, Ronald Inden.)

Nilakanta Śāstri. *A History of South India.* Madras: Oxford University Press, 1976, 1981.

Robert P. Scharlemann, ed. *Naming God.* New York: Paragon House, 1985.

Frithjof Schuon. *Language of the Self*, trans. M. Pallis and M. Matheson. Madras: Ganesh and Co., 1959.

———. *The Transcendent Unity of Religions.* New York: Harper and Row, 1975.

S. Seetha. *Tanjore as a Seat of Music.* Madras: University of Madras, 1981.

B.A. Selatore. *Social and Political Life in the Vijāyanagar Empire.* Madras: B.G. Paul, 1934 (especially Vol. II).

Bhadrashila Sharma. *Mantrasiddhi ka upaya.* Prayag: Kalyan Mandir, 1969.

T.R. Sharma. *Studies in the Sectarian Upaniṣads.* Varanasi and Delhi: Indological Book House, 1972, pp. 27, 111, 120.

James Silverberg, ed. *Social Mobility in the Caste System in India: An Interdisciplinary Symposium.* Berlin: De Gruyter Mouton, 1968.

Milton Singer, ed. *Krishna: Myths, Rites, and Attitudes.* Chicago: University of Chicago, 1966 (especially pp. 90-172).

C.K Śrīnivāsan. *Marāṭha Rule in the Carnatic.* Annamalai: Annamalai University, 1944.

J. Frits Staal, ed. *Agni: The Vedic Ritual of the Fire Altar.* 2 volumes. Berkeley: Asian Humanities Press, 1983.

———. "Ritual, Mantras and the Origin of Language." *Amṛitadhara: Professor R.N. Dandekar Felicitation Volume.* Poona, 1984, pp. 403-25.

Burton Stein. *Peasant State and Society in Medieval South India.* Oxford: Oxford University Press, 1980.

K.R. Subramanyam. *The Marāṭha Rājas of Tanjore.* Madras, 1928 (Delhi: AES reprint 1988).

D .T. Suzuki. *Mysticism: Christian and Buddhist, the Eastern and Western Way.* New York: Collier, 1962, pp. 123-157.

Stanley J. Tambiah. "The Magical Power of Words." In *Culture, Thought, and Social Action: An Anthropological Perspective.* Cambridge: Harvard University Press, 1985.

Kailash Vajpeyi. *The Science of Mantras: A Manual for Happiness and Prosperity.* New Delhi: Arnold Heineman, 1979.

Swami Vivekananda. "On Mantra and Mantra-Chaitanya." In *Complete Works*, Vol. 7. Calcutta: Mayavati Memorial Edition, 1962, pp. 407 ff.

Vandana-Mataji. *Nāma Japa: Prayer of the Name in the Hindu and Christian Traditions.* Bombay: Bharatiya Vidya Bhavan, 1984.

Charlotte Vaudeville. "The Cult of the Divine Name in the Haripath of Dñyāndev." *Wiener Zeitschrift fur die Kunde Sud- Und Ostasiens*, 12-13, 1968-69. Leiden: E.J. Brill, p. 395 ff.

Archimandrite Kallistos Ware. *The Power of the Name: The Jesus Prayer in Orthodox Spirituality.* Oxford: Fairacres Publishers, 1977.

Alex Wayman. "The Significance of Mantras, from the Veda Down to Buddhist Tantric Practice." In *Buddhist Insight: Essays by Alex Wayman*, ed. G. Elder. Delhi: Motilal Banarsidass, 1984.

Albrecht Friedrich Weber. "Vāc und Logos." *Indische Studien*, Vol., 9, Berlin 1965, pp. 473-80.

Sir John Woodroffe. *The Garland of Letters.* Madras: Ganesh and Co., 1969, pp. 305-313, "Mantra Sādhana."

Index of People and Places

Index of Technical Terms and Texts

For a glossary of all key foreign words used in books published by World Wisdom, including metaphysical terms in English, consult: www.DictionaryofSpiritualTerms.org.
This on-line Dictionary of Spiritual Terms provides extensive definitions, examples, and related terms in other languages.

Biographical Notes

V. RAGHAVAN (1908-1979) was a Sanskrit scholar, cultural theorist, and musicologist. Professor Raghavan chaired the Department of Sanskrit at the University of Madras from 1950 to 1969. During that time he built up the department and expanded its reputation for excellence. He was a member of the Sanskrit Commission, Government of India, and during his tenure at the university he brought out five volumes of the New Catalogus Catalogorum, a catalog of all known Sanskrit works. For this scholarly achievement he was awarded Padmabhushan in the year 1962, an honor awarded by the government of India to the most distinguished scholars and writers. The author of over 120 books and 1,200 articles in journals and periodicals, Raghavan was a great custodian of traditional Indian culture for much of the twentieth century. He served as secretary of the Music Academy, Madras, from 1944 until his death in 1979. Renowned for the books he wrote on Karnataka music and on aesthetics in Sanskrit literature, in 1963 he edited and translated Bhoja's masterpiece *Śṛṅgāra-prakāśa*, an extensive work about traditional Indian poetics and dramaturgy. For this translation and the accompanying commentary, Raghavan was presented with the Sahitya Akademi Award for Sanskrit in 1966. His work included finding works which were lost, or forgotten. For example, he discovered and edited the ancient Sanskrit drama, *Udatta Raghavam* by Mayuraja. He founded a cultural organization, *Samskrita Ranga* in 1958 to promote Sanskrit theater. He was known both for his command of primary texts and for making them accessible through his articles and commentaries. Raghavan was active in cultural preservation in South India, including the reconstructing of classical Indian dance, Bharata Natyam.

WILLIAM J. JACKSON is Professor Emeritus at Indiana University-Purdue University Indianapolis (IUPUI), where he taught courses in Comparative Religion in the Department of Religious Studies for 25 years. He served as the first Lake Scholar at the Lake Family Institute on Faith and Giving, Philanthropic Studies Center, IUPUI, from 2005 to 2008, and published *The Wisdom of Generosity: A Reader in American Philanthropy* (2008). He has published several books about South Indian religious culture, including *Tyagaraja—Life and Lyrics*, *Songs of Three Great South Indian Saints*, and *Vijayanagara Visions* (all published by Oxford University Press). He is also the author of a book entitled *Heaven's Fractal Net: Retrieving Lost Visions in the Humanities* (2008), about the symbolic meanings of fractal-like geometrical patterns found in the world's cultures. He lives in Indianapolis, IN.

M. NARASIMHACHARY was born in Arthamur, Andhra Pradesh, India, and earned his Ph.D. in Sanskrit from the University of Madras, under the guidance of Dr. V. Raghavan. He was Assistant Professor of Sanskrit and Research Director at Vivekananda College, Madras, and then Reader in Sanskrit at the University of Madras, Chennai. He later founded and chaired the Department of Vaishnavism at the University of Madras. He has been a Visiting Professor at the Universiti Malaya, Kuala Lumpur, and at Mercyhurst College, Erie, Pennsylvania, and a Visiting Academic at the Centre for Hindu Studies, Oxford University, UK. He is presently the retired Head of the Department of Vaishnavism at the University of Madras, and is a Visiting Fellow at the School of Indological Studies at Mahatma Gandhi Institute, Moka, Mauritius, where he teaches Hindu Theology, Indian Philosophy, and Sanskrit Grammar. His publications include *Handbook of Hindu Gods, Goddesses and Saints* (co-authored with H. Daniel Smith) and *Spiritual Heritage of Sri Annamacharya*, Vols. I and II (co-authored with M.S. Ramesh).

Other Titles on Hinduism by World Wisdom

A Christian Pilgrim in India:
The Spiritual Journey of Swami Abhishiktananda (*Henri Le Saux*),
by Harry Oldmeadow, 2008

The Essential Sri Anandamayi Ma:
Life and Teachings of a 20th Century Indian Saint,
by Alexander Lipski and Sri Anandamayi Ma, 2007

The Essential Swami Ramdas: Commemorative Edition,
compiled by Susunaga Weeraperuma, 2005

The Essential Vedanta: A New Source Book of Advaita Vedanta,
edited by Eliot Deutsch and Rohit Dalvi, 2004

A Guide to Hindu Spirituality,
by Arvind Sharma, 2006

Introduction to Hindu Dharma,
by the 68th Jagadguru of Kanchi, edited by Michael Oren Fitzgerald, 2008

Lamp of Non-Dual Knowledge & Cream of Liberation:
Two Jewels of Indian Wisdom,
translated by Swami Sri Ramanananda Saraswathi, 2003

The Original Gospel of Ramakrishna,
by Mahendra Nath Gupta, 2011

Paths to Transcendence: According to Shankara, Ibn Arabi & Meister Eckhart,
by Reza Shah-Kazemi, 2006

Timeless in Time: Sri Ramana Maharshi,
by A.R. Natarajan, 2006

Tripura Rahasya: The Secret of the Supreme Goddess,
translated by Swami Sri Ramanananda Saraswathi, 2002

Unveiling the Garden of Love:
Mystical Symbolism in Layla Majnun & Gitagovinda,
by Lalita Sinha, 2009

The Wisdom of Coomaraswamy: Reflections on Indian Art, Life, and Religion
edited by S. Durai Raja Singam & Joseph A. Fitzgerald, 2011